GOLF
is MY
LIFE

Glorifying God Through the Game

JON DECKER

ISBN 978-1-63525-343-6 (Paperback)
ISBN 978-1-63525-345-0 (Hard Cover)
ISBN 978-1-63525-344-3 (Digital)

Christian Faith Publishing, Inc.
296 Chestnut Street
Meadville, PA 16335
www.christianfaithpublishing.com

Biblical scriptures were taken from the following: The New Revised Standard Version (NRSV), King James Version (KJV), New International Version (NIV) and the American Standard Version (ASV).

Printed in the United States of America

This book is for the struggling golfers of the world. I pray the stories help to grow the game that I love and help to lead a lost soul to my personal Lord and Savior Jesus Christ.

ACKNOWLEDGMENTS

The following people have shaped my life in so many positive ways. I am sure there are many of you that I will miss, and to you, I say, "I am sorry." I thank God for blessing me with each one of you. All of you, in some way, have contributed to this book. I love you all!

Pastor Mike Bowie, thank you for giving me the confidence to begin this writing journey and for taking your personal time to write the foreword for this book. No one leads a service like you.

Pete McDaniel, God chose you to lead me in this writing journey. I thank God, and I thank you for all your help. No words can express my gratitude; you have been a true blessing. I love you brother.

Glenn Wilcox Sr., thank you for spending an afternoon listening to my vision for this book. Your referral led me to Christian Faith Publishing. I will always be grateful and always remember our prayer together.

My family: Sam Decker, father; Ann Marie Woffindin, mother; Michael Decker and Brett Decker, brothers; and Shelby Decker, sister. Other family members include Nikki Decker, Lois Loyd, Sam Woffindin, Claudette Decker, Terilynn Decker, Beth Eckstein, Annie Eckstein, Xanthe Tabor, Will and Allison Eckstein, Elizabeth Sossamon, Rick and Judy Quinn, Cliff and Alice Decker, Tom and Liz Glockzin, Tom and Rachel Decker, Betty Holloway, Devin Kennedy and Nick and Mary Manutes.

Grandparents (deceased) Cliff and Uda Decker and Leroy and Ora Lee Sossamon.

Great grandmother (deceased) Dee Dee.

I would like to thank the following people for their time and contributions to the book with their amazing personal forewords: Helen Alfredsson, Bill Burrows, Bobby Cremins, Brad Daugherty, Luke Fisher, Kenny Ford, Fred Griffin, Kraig Kann, Brad Johnson, Cory Luke, Pete McDaniel, Phil Rodgers, Bob Sowards and Bill Stines.

I would like to thank Wally Armstrong for his contributions as well.

My early golf instructors Byron Bailey, Jessie Haddock, and Les Stradely.

Caddies Chevis Earl and Tommy "Coon" Landers.

Members of the Black Mountain United Methodist Church, Black Mountain, North Carolina, and the Stonybrook United Methodist Church, Gahanna, Ohio.

Pastors Nikki Baker, Jeff Cranston, Ben Lilly, Mike MacDonald, Bob Thomas and Al Ward.

I have so many personal friends who have affected my life. The following men have always been there for me, and I consider you brothers: John Chapman, Jeff Davis, Jim Davis, Sean Gilsenan, Chris Jackson, Fred Lewis, Mike Nadeau, Bob Parker, Scott (Skillet) Studenc, Rich Thurston and Dean Waters.

Coaches Bruce Arrowood, Bill Burrows and Ralph Singleton.

To the thousands of students from the Grand Cypress Academy of Golf, I say thank you. I learned so much from you over my twenty-year career. To the staff from GC, you are simply the best! Cam Abascal, Carl Alexander, Jason Bell, Gabe Bergin, Martin Carroll, Rick Cefaloni, T.J. Cosgrove, Curtis Cowan, Mark Cox, Eric Eshleman, Ed Fernandes, Bruce Geroux, Fred Griffin, Joey Hidock, Tammy Hildebrandt, Bob Honohan, Gus Holbrook, Lee Houtteman, David Kochi, Doug Lowen, Dr. Ralph Mann, Todd Meena, John Menichini, Kevin McKinney, John O'Leary, John Page, John Pinel , Brenda Pfeifer, Kyle Phelps, Will Roberts, Phil Rodgers,

Dave Seeman, Adrian Stills, Bernie Tanner, Sean Taylor, Blake Terry, and Harry Zimmerman.

I cannot possibly thank all my classmates, teammates, or fraternity brothers but wanted to say "thank you and I love you" to the following:

Classmates, basketball and golf teammates of Charles D. Owen High School—Go, Warhorses!

Classmates of East Carolina University —Go, Pirates! Arrgghh!

Brothers of Phi Kappa Tau Fraternity, ECU

To the "gang" of the Black Mountain Golf Course (The Rock). Through you, I learned to be street-smart on the golf course and learned the lessons of playing the game: Byron Bailey, David Ballard, Jerry Ballard, Carl Bartlett, Tom Blizard, Doc Brake, Bromo, Jack Campbell, JT Davis, Jimmy Earl, Bruce Edwards, Gary Edwards, Rebo Edwards, Fats, Bill Fussell, Jim Gaddy, Bud Hainey, Bud Harper, Richard Hudson, Harry Hyder, Tommy Landers, Kevin Logan, Paul Martin, Mark Marett, Mike Marett, Jimmy Maxwell, Tim Maxwell, John Michaels, Sonny Melton, J.R. Penley, Ralph Singleton, Daron Slone, Swinn, Roland Slone, Larry Tuttle, Scott Tuttle, Ted Tipton, Bubby Tyson, Chris Waters and Wilburn Waters.

I would like to thank the wonderful membership of the New Albany Country Club, New Albany, Ohio. Thank you for supporting me, our teaching programs and our amazing staff: Justin Armour, Timmy Brown, Michael Cagganello, Dalton Coker, Briton Gerber, Tom Green, Ryan Hosack, Paul Hollenbaugh, Corbin Holliday, Chad Evans, Dee Kossoff, Ryan McCafferty, Steve McVey, Scott Miller, Sarah Morton, Tony Shill, Kelsey Snedaker, Larry Taylor, Kate Williams and Mike Wesley.

I would like to thank 104.7 The River for your Christian music as well as Pirate Radio 1250 and 930 for your support of East Carolina University and this book. Specifically Troy Dreyfus and

Jonathan Ellerbe as well as UBE, Greenville, NC (Don Edwards and Chad Thompson).

I would like to thank the following news organizations and people: *Asheville Citizen Times* (Bob Berghaus), the *Black Mountain News* (Paul Clark and Fred McCormick), *the Morganton News Herald and the Raleigh News &Observer* (Scott Sharpe).

I would like to thank the following people for their contributions: Ed Gately, Mike Hayes, Erica Meabon and Jane Peters.

Finally, I would like to thank the more than 28,000 men and women of the PGA of America who support and grow the game of golf. I admire your hard work and efforts in growing the game we all love to play. I would specifically like to recognize the North Florida Section and the Southern Ohio Section.

FOREWORD

Pastor Mike Bowie

Why are dreams important? They are a vital way to connect our subconscious needs and conscious actions. Following a dream often takes courage. But when we do it, especially when divinely led, we are able not only to change our lives but also to impact others.

A dream is defined as thoughts or images we have while we're sleeping, a vision or mind-set, or even simply a strong goal or wish. Dreams ignite hope, purpose and passion. Think of the impact one small dream can have: Dr. Martin Luther King, Jr.'s dream, which he voiced in the 1960s, changed the American landscape to this day. English politician William Wilberforce never wavered from his dream to abolish the slave trade throughout the British Empire. In Genesis, the dreams of Jacob's son, Joseph, initially caused him to be sold into slavery and imprisoned but later helped him save many lives during a famine, including the family members who had persecuted him!

On August 1, 2012, while I was serving as lead pastor at Stonybrook United Methodist Church in Gahanna, Ohio, one of our members, Jon Decker came into my office and shared two dreams he had, one spiritual and one personal. When he was a high school sophomore, Jon experienced a divine dream in which he was caught in a battle between good and evil. In the midst of this battle, Jon heard the audible voice of God declaring, "I am who I am. I am the Alpha and Omega, the beginning and the end." At that moment, Jon knew it was God's voice and assumed that he was facing death. But Jesus responded, "It's not your time." I still recall the goose bumps I felt listening to the story that summer day. When Jon finished, I absolutely believed him. I told him that I believed he was still here because God wanted him to share his dream with others.

Jon also told me that his childhood dream was to be a professional golfer, but ultimately, God led him to become a golf instructor. For some people, not being able to reach their goal of the PGA Tour would have been the end of their dream. But Jon realized that by *teaching* the game of golf instead of *playing* it for a living, he could have a far more positive effect on the lives of others, not just the privileged or the elite. Why? Because the rules and principles of golf apply to everyday life and should be available to everyone, no matter their age, color, sex or socio-economic level.

Golf looks simple, but in reality, it is extremely difficult and takes a lifetime to master. Sometimes you can't see the flagstick from the tee box. Sometimes you have to divert your shot to avoid a hazard. Some days hitting a trap is inevitable, so you have to build skill with diverse tools to manage these obstacles and challenges. You also have to play by the rules and accept the penalties for infractions. And most important, some days you're in the zone, and some days the zone has you.

Today, Jon's passion for Jesus Christ has inspired him to fulfill a new dream: To use the game of golf to help everyone win at the game of life. God has given all of us a dream and a purpose. The book that you are about to read illustrates one man's decision to pursue and live his God-given dream and, through it, to influence many and help change the world.

Embrace life.

Dr. Michael L. Bowie Jr.
Senior Pastor at St. Luke "Community"
United Methodist Church
Dallas, Texas

Our first golf lesson. I gave Pastor Mike a dozen golf balls and said, "These are your 12 disciples but they do not walk on water."

My Story

"I can do all things through Christ who strengthens me" (Philippians 4:13).

"Blessed assurance, Jesus is mine! Oh, what a foretaste of glory divine! Heir of salvation, purchase of God, Born of His Spirit, washed in His blood. This is my story, this is my song, Praising my Savior all the day long; this is my story, this is my song, Praising my Savior all the day long." ("Blessed Assurance," Francis J. Crosby 1873).

These simple yet powerful words from the gospel hymn "Blessed Assurance" would often play like a metronome in my mind as a teenager after worship service on a Sunday afternoon. The melody to this iconic song would put me in a hypnotic trance while creating a rhythm that lasted throughout the day as I meandered my way to the golf course, chasing my ball and my dreams. As an adult, I grew to love these words; as a child, I simply loved the song's refrain. Words often form beautiful pictures in one's mind, and from this canvas comes a song, a poem or even a novel. The story for my life, which inspired this book, did not form in my mind during adolescence. It formed as I developed my trade, under the searing Florida sun, as an exuberant college graduate trying to make his way until Friday's payday.

God brought passion into my life at an early age when I saw my very first golf club. This passion turned to love and gave birth to a dream. Fueled by this dream, I worked diligently to one day be a PGA Tour player. However, God's plan for my life did not include professional golf as a participant. God's desire was for me to be the less-heralded supporting cast. Led by the hand of God to a path not foreseen in my childhood dreams, I became a teaching professional, teaching the game that I love.

I was raised in the United Methodist Church, went to Sunday school, Bible camp and rarely missed a Sunday worship service as an adolescent. I come from a loving family and have been truly blessed in every way. Yet something was missing in my life. I remember asking myself as a child, "In the Bible, God was everywhere, and Jesus walked the earth. He healed the sick and performed miracles. Why have I never seen him or heard from him?" I asked the same questions that many of God's children ask and tried to comprehend what I was learning. I finally took a leap of faith and simply believed what I was told.

During my sophomore year of high school, my life would be forever changed. One cold, winter night I was severely ill and had a life-altering, supernatural experience that appeared to me in the early morning hours. I had a powerful dream, a vision where I heard the voice of God, felt the presence of the Holy Spirit, and stood face to face with my Lord and Savior Jesus Christ. In one dream, I experienced the Trinity. I heard the Father, saw the Son, and felt the Holy Spirit. It was a true miracle, just like I had learned on Sunday mornings. I was healed immediately! God gave me a gift, which I selfishly tucked away into the back of my mind and cowardly asked myself, "What am I to do with this dream? Who will believe me? Why did this happen to me?"

During my formative years, I was an above-average student but was never a reader or writer. After college graduation, God's masterful plan for my life unfolded moving me south to Florida where I found my calling. Standing on the lesson tee at the Grand Cypress Academy of Golf in Orlando, I would watch and empathize with my students as they struggled to grasp the game. I began to notice how teaching golf and learning the game of life were synonymous, and I began to experience something that was new and exciting. Stories started slowly forming in my mind, stories of my life, my triumphs and failures as a player, man and teacher. It was as if God was planting seeds in my mind.

In time the seeds began to grow, and my mind began to be consumed with my stories. After ten years of teaching, I knew God wanted me to write a book. However, like so many people, I put that adventure on my bucket list. I believed I wasn't ready to share my stories with the world. In the spring of 2013, during a six-month hiatus in Hilton Head, South Carolina, I began to tell my story. My thoughts were now words that would sometimes reveal my insecurities as a new writer. I forged on, sharing my stories with family and friends. I have never felt more vulnerable in my life. To my pleasant surprise, the feedback was positive, boosting my confidence to finish the task God had placed on my heart. As time passed, I realized the thoughts that flowed from my fingers onto my computer screen were not from me. They were from God. Through the Holy Spirit, my stories began to flow like a river in unpredictable directions. On Christmas Day 2014, I awoke in the early morning with the missing piece for the completion of my final chapter. It was wrapped in my mind with shiny paper and a bow like a present under the tree. After several hours of writing, my task was finished (or so I thought). Fittingly, my grand adventure had been completed on the day we celebrate the birth of Jesus Christ. I rejoiced in the realization that after almost two years of writing, my story was now on paper for the world to see. However, during the editing process, I was asked by editor Pete McDaniel to rewrite the final chapter. I finished the rewrite on January 12, 2016—my forty-ninth birthday.

I invite you to share my story—a journey fraught with disappointments, frustrations and triumphs as I strove to be the best golf instructor, man and Christian as possible. Along the way, through my eyes, you will meet the likes of Tiger Woods, Paul Azinger, Seve Ballesteros, Payne Stewart, Arnold Palmer, Bill Murray, Gale Sayers, Brad Johnson, Brad Daugherty, Bobby Cremins and Roy Williams. My experiences around these well-known men are a key ingredient to the recipe of this book, but my stories are much more than that. Throughout this book, there are several *forewords* titled "As Seen Through My Eyes" that provide a personal entry into the chapter.

My story is reinforced through God's living Word—the Bible. The Word of God is a critical ingredient to the structure and flow of this book. Through the power of the Holy Spirit, I learned to turn my writing over to the Lord and trust His direction. The stories from this book are meant to glorify God and His son Jesus Christ. My hope is that this book will lead a lost soul to find Christ or strengthen a Christian's faith. Regardless of your beliefs, I pray this book allows you to look at your own life and reflect on how God has written your unique and personal story, wrapped it in the blood of His son Jesus Christ, and delicately placed it under the tree waiting to be opened when He says it is time.

Through this writing journey, I have learned many lessons, but one stands out in my mind. I am really not an author; I am a messenger. The messages from my stories have been with me for years and highlight life-changing events from childhood to adulthood. Some of these stories and their messages instantaneously formed in my mind. All of my stories are true and made me realize how God imprinted in my mind a life experience, often for decades, to be shared to the world as a book. Sharing my stories was difficult at first because they were intimate and personal, and I often felt insecurity and fear. In time, I realized my fear was not from God but from the enemy. Through the support of my family, church, and friends, I moved forward and did not allow the enemy to thwart my progress.

These stories are no longer mine. In reality, they never really were—only in my mind for a time as I taught a lesson, played in a mini-tour event or took an evening shower. My stories were meant to be shared with the world! Enjoy the melody and harmony of the message and listen to them in your heart and mind while enjoying a round of golf or spending time with a loved one. "This is my story, this is my song, Praising my Savior all the day long. "This is my story, this is my song. Praising my Savior all the day long!"

As Seen Through My Eyes

Helen Alfredsson, Ladies Professional
Golf Association (LPGA)

When I think of Augusta National, I think of the history of golf and one of the first true American sports heroes, Bobby Jones. Jones, a man known to have a huge heart, loved the game of golf and built one of the most famous golf courses in the world, because of his passion for the game. Every April, golf fans around the world treat "Masters Week" as the holy grail of the sport. Even those not familiar with the game recognize the significance of the green jacket. People love history, and no other sports venue relishes its heroes like Augusta National, where past winners tee it up with top amateurs. In addition, during the Wednesday Par 3 Contest, children serve as caddies.

During the late 1990s, I was invited to play Augusta National by former LPGA Commissioner Charlie Mechem and Vice Chairman of Augusta National Golf Club Joe Ford. I knew the history of this famous venue, and I knew the rules and decorum of this famous club. Golf and life are so similar; they are parallels to each other. In a society of get-rich-quick schemes and instant gratification, time stands still in Augusta, Georgia. I will always remember my day walking through Amen Corner and seeing a perspective from inside the ropes that men and women, boys and girls only dream about.

While training for the LPGA at the Grand Cypress Academy of Golf, I had the pleasure of meeting Jon Decker. In fact, I was invited to his home for his fortieth birthday celebration. When I think of Jon as a teaching professional, one word comes to mind: *passion*. Although I have not worked with Jon personally as a student, I have watched him first hand in action. Jon brings energy and enthusiasm to all his students and possesses the one quality that all great teachers have: care for their student. His personality, creativity, and sound teaching fundamentals bring comfort to his students, allowing them the best opportunity to learn the game.

I am proud of Jon's effort in his writing journey. His life story shows his passion for the game of golf, as well as his faith. Through this book, I know Jon will help grow the game of golf and enlighten each reader to their individual purpose and path. I hope you enjoy Jon's story as much as I have enjoyed getting to know him over the years.

CHAPTER 1

Augusta

"In the beginning when God created the heav-
ens and the earth, the earth was a formless
void and darkness covered the face of the deep,
while a wind from God swept over the face of
the waters. Then God said, "Let there be light,"
and there was light. And God saw that the light
was good; and God separated the light from the
darkness." (Genesis 1:1–4)

These words from the Bible mark the beginning of time. They also mark the first known miracle God produced. In the first four verses of the most-read book in the world lies the essence of what all beings need for life—a beginning. Each year of life, we celebrate our beginning with a cake, some candles, and perhaps a few presents. We mark each year as one of growth—a way of looking in the rearview mirror to where we began our journey and the road we've traveled to arrive in our current state. We mark that day, for our lifetime, as our day of birth.

Many people assume that this birthday or birthplace is random and in the grand scheme of things, really doesn't matter. I don't agree. I believe, as it says in the Bible, that God knows us before we are born. He also knows our triumphs and failures before they're recorded or reported. I believe that God knows the second we are to be born, the place where we are to be born and the instant that we will leave this Earth. I also believe that with each birth comes a story, the story of a life—a biographical footprint in the sands of time, unique to each individual. We write a book of stories, a compilation of conversations with family members around the dinner table and memories from our childhood, even those special moments of parenthood. Sometimes those stories flow through fingers and a word processor, compiling the various chapters of one's journey. For the birthplace of my life, God led my young parents to a place where neither of them had ever lived, to a destination where neither of them knew a single soul, to a small town rich in history. The great Bobby Jones built his pastoral masterpiece in this place, and every April the golf world shifts its focus squarely on an emerald former nursery that meanders amid mighty Georgia pines to witness the game's greatest players compete for the most coveted piece of fabric in all of sports—the *green jacket* awarded the Masters champion. The Masters is the only "major" tournament in professional golf played at the same venue; a golf paradise traversed by every great player from Jones to Hogan to Palmer to Nicklaus to Woods. It is the calling card for a city where time seems to stand still. This is the same place God chose for my life to begin; the place they call Augusta.

On January 12, 1967, I was born at Fort Gordon Army Base in Augusta, Georgia. To golf fans, Augusta is world renowned, but for my parents, Augusta was anything but. Fort Gordon was the base and temporary home where the army had stationed my father, a training ground for a newlywed couple. My father, Sammy Decker, had just graduated from Wake Forest University. He was twenty-one years old, who, as a college football player, played alongside the legendary Brian Piccolo and quarterback John Machovic. In 2000, his high school inducted him into the Valdese (North Carolina) Hall of Fame. Dad grew up in a very humble environment. Golf was not part of his life as a child. However, he would grow to love the game after taking it in physical education class his senior year at Wake.

1963 Sammy Decker, sophomore year Wake Forest University

1962 Ann Marie Sossamon receiving the
Governor's Award, Raleigh N.C.

My mother, Ann Marie, was twenty and a junior at Wake Forest. As a senior in high school, she was named Athlete of the Year in Western North Carolina. Mom had serious skills. In fact, she scored 45 points in a game against Franklin High. That same year, she was voted Miss Youth Fitness for the state of North Carolina. Like many young women, she had to make a difficult choice to temporarily drop out of college to raise her new son. My brothers (Michael and Brett) and I were very proud to watch her induction into the Swain County Hall of Fame in 2004. We were even more proud when she received her degree in psychology from the University of North Carolina at Asheville and a nursing degree from Asheville Buncombe Technical College. Her commitment to higher education and determination to finish the course had a lasting impact on my brothers and me. My parents were married twenty-seven years until their divorce. Although their marriage failed, they did not fail as parents. They raised me, nurtured me, disciplined me, instilled in me Christian fundamentals of the Methodist Church, supported me, attended all my games, and provided for us. More importantly, they loved me and told me as much on a daily basis. In retrospect, they provided the foundation of who I was at the time and who I would eventually become. Like builders, they utilized the best materials to construct lives sound in mind, body and spirit.

A month after my fathers graduation in June of 1966, my parents were married. The simple fact that my parents were two great athletes was not going to put food on the table; plus there was a baby on the way. Dad volunteered for the Army after completing ROTC, eliciting vocal criticism from friends who thought he was crazy with the Vietnam War escalating. Several months later, he received his orders to go to Augusta for Advanced Signal School. My parents packed up the '67 Ford Falcon with their life possessions and made the move south to Augusta. Their lives would now be in Georgia, and their son would be born in an army base, delivered by doctors and nurses they had never met.

After settling into Augusta and their new apartment, my father decided to see this golf course named Augusta National. He had now caught the golfing bug and wanted to see the grounds where his hero Arnold (Arnie) Palmer had won his four green jackets. He and my pregnant mother drove up to the gate to the famed course, assuming that visitors were allowed to take a look around. As the car approached the gate, Dad drove right through the entrance, intent on a quick visit to the pro shop and maybe a souvenir. "I drove through that gate like I owned the place," he would say later. Suddenly, he heard a barrage of whistles and applied the brakes, the Falcon screeching to a halt. Dad stuck his head out the window.

"I just want to go to the pro shop," he explained.

"Back that thing outta here buddy," replied the guard. Suddenly, several guards jumped out of the bushes in front of the car.

"I just want to go to the pro shop," Dad insisted.

"Back that thing outta here buddy," yelled the guard. Dad acquiesced reluctantly. He has told that story many times among friends and family. It is woven into the fabric of a father-son relationship and their love of golf.

Augusta National has a very distinguished, select membership. I was excited to hear the news of the club's acceptance of African Americans and women in recent years. But in 1966, I will go on record as being the first fetus to get kicked out of this prestigious club!

Augusta is my alpha, my beginning. God chose this spot for me to begin my life. He chose two young athletes to be my parents. He also chose the game of golf to be my passion and my career. I watched my first PGA Tour event in person in 1980 when Uncle Louis Eckstein scored three practice round tickets to the Masters. On the drive to Augusta, Uncle Louie gave a dissertation on the history of the Masters, carefully explaining that the Masters was not a regular PGA Tournament. The Masters was a major. "Who is your favorite player?" he asked Michael and me.

"Jack Nicklaus!" we shouted in tandem.

"What about Arnold Palmer?" he asked.

Michael and I looked at each other and said, "Who?" I often think about that conversation, especially when I ask a junior golfer, "Do you know who Payne Stewart is? Do you know who Jack Nicklaus is?" More often than not, they have a similar response as my brother and me. Dad was drawn to Augusta National because of Arnie, and my brother and I were drawn to Augusta National because of the *Golden Bear*. Tiger has been the main attraction at the Masters for nearly two decades now. Soon it might be Rory McIlroy or one of the game's other young guns. Only God knows. At the time, though, uncle and nephews were there to see Arnie and Jack, respectively.

We finally arrived in Augusta, parked our car, and entered the grounds of Augusta National. My pulse rate quickened with every step as we made our way toward this jewel I had only seen on TV. Upon entering one of the gates for patrons, the enormity of the great expanse opened up like pictures in a fairy-tale book. I felt like a character in a Disney movie, although I tried to conceal my enthusiasm. To this day, I consider that initial sight the most beautiful golf course I've ever seen. It sure was the greenest grass I had ever seen, too. The grounds were immaculate. Young grounds keepers in white coveralls stood by with small pitchforks picking up the tiniest litter as soon as it hit the ground. I felt the crush of patrons in fancy, colorful clothing; a canvas of springtime among genteel socialites. Surprisingly, I believe commoners blended in, too. I remember when we arrived for the Tuesday practice round, Uncle Louie took us straight to the 10th hole, a long, downhill, dogleg left, par-4 named *Camellia*. Immediately, my uncle recognized one of the players in the fairway, Bill Kratzert. Uncle Louie had taught economics at the University of Georgia and Bill had been one of his students. I was amazed when Bill came over to Uncle Louie and said hello as they shook hands.

Kratzert would be the first PGA Tour player I would meet up close and personal. I experienced many firsts that day. If I had a bucket list on that special day, I would have checked off several must-dos. I got to see Augusta National and my idol, Jack Nicklaus. And I got an autograph.

Augusta represents other firsts for me, including my first day on this Earth, my first experience with a major tournament, and the first time I walked 18 holes on one of the most famous golf courses in the world. Uncle Louie was the first person to expose me to professional golf, an experience that shaped my life forever.

Looking back on my life, I can see where God has brought me, led me, and nurtured me along the way, often without me knowing it. I believe God has a plan for each one of us. My plan was to start in Augusta. We would live there four months before moving to Germany, where Dad was deployed. My friends were wrong to criticize my father for volunteering for the army. The army moved us to Germany, not Vietnam. Nineteen months later, Michael was born in Landstuhl. The security guards were doing their job when they stopped my parents from driving through the gates. Their negative experience didn't alter my perception of that golfing paradise. My dream of one day playing Augusta National lives on.

Augusta will always hold a special place in my heart. As a teacher of the game, I dream about one of my students playing in the Masters and of me walking the course alongside my student among the patrons and the azaleas. We all have a beginning and a story detailing the first day of our life. Mine is centered on a small southern town that hosts the grandest spectacle in golf. I am so thankful that God chose Augusta as my birthplace. Time measures us all. We all have a beginning, and we will all have an end. I don't believe in coincidence. I do, however, believe in fate. My parents have lived for nearly seventy years, yet only four months were in Augusta. I have lived nearly fifty years and of those years, only two months in Augusta. God carefully chose this place to be my beginning.

Every April around Easter, my mind, heart and soul focus on the Masters. The roar of the crowd wafting through the pines and thundering along Washington Road evokes grown men and women to shout for joy. My birth a few miles away from that cathedral caused far less commotion, but just like Rae's Creek courses through fabled Amen Corner, the city itself is in my blood. I thank God for my alpha, a place they call Augusta.

CHAPTER 2

The Closet Door

For Jon and Michael, mischief was always around the corner

*"Then the high priest took action; he and all
who were with him being filled with jealousy,
arrested the Apostles and put them in the public prison. But during the night an angel of the
Lord opened the prison doors. Brought them
out, and said, "Go stand in the temple and tell
the people the whole message about this life."
When they heard this, they entered the temple
at daybreak and went on with their teaching."*
(Acts 5:17–21)

There are moments in one's life where opportunity knocks, when a
pathway is forged and a door suddenly opens. These moments often
are not recognized until days, months or even years have passed. Such
is the case for my introduction to the game of golf, a moment in time
that is very recognizable with hindsight but not so evident during
adolescence. The first golf experience of my life was not in a private
lesson, nor was it held under the guidance of a parent or coach. If
anything, it was chaotic, disorganized and unsupervised. Fortunately
for my siblings and I, no one was injured during this childhood experience. As a six-year-old boy with two younger brothers, I didn't have
to go far to encounter some sort of mischief. Looking back it seemed
to lurk around every corner. I will always remember my initial golf
experience and the feelings of discovery in that moment in time,
the moment when I first walked down the hallway and opened the
closet door.

It was 1973, US troops were withdrawing from Vietnam, the
Watergate hearings were underway and a curious youngster was
about to make a discovery that would alter his life forever. Our family had returned from Germany and moved to Bryson City, North

Carolina, where my father's military service was now complete. With three young boys, my father began his search of a new career and started working for my grandfather, Leroy Sossamon, selling used cars at my grandfather's Ford dealership. Located at the dealership was an airport, Sossamon's Airfield. My grandfather loved to fly aircraft and would often take us up for a ride through the Smoky Mountains. We felt like navigators soaring through the air in that prop plane, the roar of its engines ringing in our ears. We were fearless and giddy, our hearts sinking into our stomachs as the plane ascended and rising into our throats as it descended to earth. The mountains were beautiful. In the distance, rooftops of homes dotted the landscape among the huge trees. I remember thinking, "If it isn't heaven, it is awfully close." Just down the street, our family resided in a duplex apartment. I have lived in many homes, countless apartments and a rowdy fraternity house. I've even slept on a few floors, but my earliest childhood memories occurred in that duplex apartment. My great-grandmother, Dee Dee, lived in an apartment above us. Although my young parents struggled to rear a family and pay the bills, we children were oblivious to the challenges facing them. Those early days of family life still hold a special place in my heart. One of the many advantages of having young parents was the opportunity to know my great-grandmother, who passed when I was thirteen, and all four of my grandparents, who were blessed with long lives.

Bryson City is a tiny rural town west of Asheville, the major metropolis in the western part of the state. It had a nine-hole golf course with sand greens, and my father was starting to play the game on a regular basis. He purchased a set of Tommy Armour Silver Scot Tourney clubs, an example of his budding dedication to playing the game well. Those clubs are now proudly displayed on the wall in the family room of his home. I had heard my father speak of this game called golf, but I didn't know what a golf club looked like, where the golf course was located, or the objective of the game. Dad kept his clubs in the hallway closet. I don't remember witnessing my father storing his clubs in the closet, but I do recall the first time I opened the hallway closet door. Who knew that a passion so strong that it consumed me was behind that door? It was a passion so fervent that it filled my heart with a longing surpassed only by that for a relationship with God Almighty.

Temptation started with Adam, Eve and an apple. In the Decker household, it was Jon, Michael and a set of brand new golf clubs. I opened the hallway closet door and was immediately drawn to the corner of the closet. Why I opened that  closet door is still a mystery, but I was immediately enchanted. The clubs called for my attention. I knew that disturbing Dad's slumbering set of golf clubs could get me punished. Yet, I couldn't resist the siren's song. I grabbed the entire set and boldly carried it into my bedroom. One at a time, I pulled the clubs out of the bag. My hands stroked the smooth, leather head covers. I marveled at how the numbers were etched into the metal, sole plates of the wooden clubs, and on the soles of the chrome-finished irons, glistening in the sunlight that filtered through my bedroom window. I opened the golf bag with wild excitement, reminiscent of an early Christmas morning. At that very moment, temptation had turned into a love affair. As I reached into the bag, I found my dad's brand-new Titleist golf balls. I remember the way I marveled at the countless dimples on a single golf ball as if hypnotized. I gazed at the writing on the ball, examining every detail and was mesmerized by the numbering. How was this ball made? Who wrote the numbers on the ball? These were the questions I asked myself. I stared at the ball for nearly an hour.

I had never seen a ball so white and clean, without blemish or stain. All of my baseballs started out nice and clean but before you could say strike, they were soiled.

Without a single thought about the consequences of getting caught, Michael and I took the clubs outside and began recklessly swinging. We were blinded by the possibilities, powerless to make a rational decision. Armed with nothing but ambition and all the strength our youthful bodies could muster, we swung those irons back and through. That was fun but not nearly as much fun as actually hitting a ball, I thought. So I reached in the bag, retrieved a ball, and placed it on the grass. I made a mighty swing, or so I thought, but missed the ball completely. Like many before me, my first swing at a golf ball resulted in a whiff! Before I knew it, a family golf clinic was taking place in the Decker front yard. Balls were flying everywhere. The sensation of making contact for the first time is etched into my memory. I was immediately hooked on that feeling. One at a time we reached into that bag; one at a time we hit the balls. For the first time in my life, I felt a true passion for something. The same passion my father had experienced for the game while taking golf in physical education class, the same passion I now share for teaching and the same passion other kids may have or share for music, the arts or dance. I was in love. I felt freedom, and I felt at that very moment true joy. Forty years later, the glow of love still burns brightly.

After several minutes of hitting balls all over the place, our supply of Titleists inexplicably ran out. "Surely there would be more balls in the bag," I thought. But there weren't any to be found. Suddenly, I heard a car coming down the street. I knew the sound of that car. A lump the size of a golf ball formed in my throat. My mouth was bone dry. Fear gripped me tighter than a tour pro facing a three-foot, downhill slider with the Masters on the line. My hand was caught in the largest cookie jar in Bryson City, and there was a reckoning nearing the driveway. There was also no place to hide and no talking myself out of this one. The look on Dad's face said it all—"You boys are in trouble!" My father was a stern disciplinarian and not afraid to punish his boys. He believed in tough love. He was also blessed with the spirit of forgiveness, especially when it came to his mischievous sons. Still, I must admit I was surprised and relieved when he simply asked us to go find all the balls. He wasn't angry, nor did he mete out any punishment. He still laughs at the fact that as children, we could hit the balls in the trees and bushes but spend no time looking for them. Dad seemed excited that his boys were now *hooked* on the game of golf. In our naïve minds, there was an endless supply of balls in the bag. Conceptually, golf is simple. Each ball represents an opportunity. Reach in the bag, swing the club, and make the most of that one opportunity.

On that summer day in 1973, I opened a door and took a chance at an opportunity. Consequently, I fell in love with the game of golf. That enduring love led me into teaching the game. I am so blessed to love my career. My grandmother, Uda Decker, once told me, "Jon, find a career that you enjoy and you will be good at it. Once you become great at it, the money will come." From time to time, I think about the advice my grandmother gave me. I think about my struggles as a golfer and my career as a PGA golf instructor. All those early struggles with the game of golf, combined with glorious moments of triumph and a wonderful career as a teaching professional can all be traced back to that closet door.

Uda Decker

I am fortunate to have had the opportunity to open that closet door. Many children will never hold a club in their hands. Their closet door may lead to gangs or even prison. I believe that all public schools in the United States should require kids to take a physical education class with an emphasis on golf. Golf is truly the game of a lifetime. It can be an asset in business, social affairs and a way to spend quality time with your family and friends. It breeds competition, forces discipline, and teaches rules and etiquette. Perhaps the most complex asset the game offers is also the simplest. Golf is the only game played that mirrors life. In golf, you should help others, be polite, know the rules, work hard, prepare and know your history. In baseball, you steal a base. In football, you tackle and defend. In basketball, you try to block a shot. Name another sport where you actually try to help your opponents by repairing a ball mark, raking a bunker, replacing a divot so the next person has a clean lie or moving your shadow so it doesn't cover the hole. The examples that golf sets are the same examples we strive for as Americans and as Christians. Many of the rules and disciplines of golf, parallel the values of God's Word, the Bible.

The Bible is symbolic in nature. The story of the apostles' cell door opening by the hand of the angel in many ways is symbolic of my path in life to become a teaching professional. The Bible's stories have a way of replicating every situation we as human beings face in our daily lives. God is the same today as He was when He created the heavens and the earth. Why should man's sins, shortcomings and difficulties be any different? They are the same sins, shortcomings and difficulties, from the Bible, only with different people involved. In essence, we humans can learn valuable life lessons from the many parables and stories of the Bible. The Pharisees despised the Christian movement, the popularity of Jesus and the disciples. The Pharisee Gamaliel stated, *"I tell you, keep away from these men and let them alone; because if this plan or this undertaking is of human origin, it will fail, but if it is of God, you will not be able to overthrow them" (Acts 5:38–39).*

The angel from heaven opened a cell door that meant so much more than simply freedom for the disciples. The act of opening this doorway was a critical opportunity for God's Word to be spread, for the development of Christianity and the formation of the Church as we know it today. My closet door allowed me to have an experience that was much more than finding my father's golf clubs. My closet door was my opportunity to experience a game that would shape my life forever. The disciples were set free to become teachers. God gave me a passion for golf so that I could become a teaching professional. The disciples were instructed to travel the world spreading the word of Jesus Christ. Through the game of golf, the church and through the guidance of God in my life, I was inspired to write this book. The apostles gave their lives to spread Christianity. I have been reborn through a new commitment to Jesus Christ in my life, to write a book to glorify God's Word. Whether one writes a book, sings a song, helps a neighbor, gives to the needy or does a good deed, the Christian message must be spread. It is the responsibility of all Christians to do their individual part to spread God's Word. *"Go into all the world and proclaim the gospel to the whole creation. Whoever believes and is baptized will be saved, but whoever does not believe will be condemned" (Mark 16:15–16)*

My opportunity to play this wonderful game was because fate had me open a closet door. As a PGA instructor, I hope to open these same doors for children of all races, religious backgrounds, plus every gender and social standing. Through the promotion of this great game, I hope all children get an opportunity to *whiff* the ball, then see it fly through the air on their next swing. I hope that all parents can spend one day walking with their children on the golf course and that those same children will someday pay it forward. I hope people of all ages try golf at least once in their lifetime, whether in a private lesson, clinic or a PGA-sponsored Golf Get Ready Class. The door is in front of you. Take the opportunity, step forward, and relish in the joy of spending time with friends or loved ones, enjoying the outdoors and watching that golf ball fly through the air for the very first time. I guarantee it will be well worth it.

CHAPTER 3

Protecting the Field

Standing in my front yard on Airport Road, Bryson
City, N.C. Number 3 is still my lucky number.

"And you shall love the lord your God with all your heart, and with all your soul, and with all your mind, and with all your strength. The second is this, 'you shall love your neighbor as yourself.' There is no other commandment greater than these" (Mark 12:30–31)

It was an Indian summer afternoon in September as I rode the school bus home. The foliage had just begun to change its wardrobe from a brilliant green to a hint of yellow, orange and red. Even as a third-grader, I loved that time of year if for no other reason than football practice was in full swing. My competitive juices flowed like a mountain stream during football season. On this day, I could hardly wait to get home and get into my football gear. The Swain County School District was so small that children of all ages and grades rode on the same bus. This meant that much older kids in middle school and high school were riding along with the younger students. I learned very quickly that the older kids ruled the roost. Like children of all generations, I heard name-calling and witnessed kids being picked on. My saving grace was a group of high school girls who took me under their wings and protected me from the bullies. Many other children did not receive the same grace as I, which led to some very difficult life lessons, lessons I learned not from the bullies riding the school bus but from my father. This day would not be routine for it still reverberates in my mind all these years later. On this day, I learned the importance of protecting the field—an all-important concept in golf that speaks to integrity, honesty and respect for the game. I also learned how to apply this concept to life.

Our neighbors across the street had a son about my age named Nathan. He had a learning disability, and the older kids would often laugh at him. He was such a nice kid. Every day he would give the school bus driver a hug and kiss when he got on and off the bus. One particular day the kids were laughing at Nathan. It infuriated me but I didn't know what to do about it. All I could do was to sit quietly and look down at the floor as the cruel behavior continued. One day while Nathan was getting off the school bus, he hugged the bus driver and said something humorous, prompting me to laugh. I wasn't laughing at Nathan, just laughing at his funny remark. I noticed that Nathan looked in my direction during the laughter and then quietly got off the bus. My stop was next. I went inside and changed into my football uniform and went off to practice with my mother. After practice, my father was standing by the car. From the expression on his face, it was clear he was agitated about something. Dad asked me to get into the car and told me that Nathan's mother had called him at work. Nathan was crying after getting off the school bus because the kids on the bus were making fun of him. Nathan's mother mentioned that I was one of the kids laughing. My father sternly asked, "Jon, were you laughing at Nathan today?"

I replied, "Yes, Dad, but not at him. He made a funny remark and I couldn't help but laugh." Thankfully, Dad believed me and I averted any punishment, at least in the form of a whipping. Instead, my punishment would be an apology to Nathan and his mother. As the sun set over the Smoky Mountains, Dad drove me to Nathan's house. As he sat in the car with the lights on, I walked toward the sidewalk thinking to myself, "Why should I apologize? I've done nothing wrong. I laughed only for a second." My father would later explain that children often joke and have fun but never at someone else's expense.

I still remember the clacking sound of my cleats on the concrete as I walked down the sidewalk and up to the front door. I was hungry, tired and nervous. Suddenly the porch light came on. I rang the doorbell while my father watched from the car. At that moment, I realized the magnitude of my mistake. The tears streaming down my face revealed my shame. When Nathan's mother opened the door she had tears in her eyes, too. Through a shaky voice I managed a sincere apology. It was a very short one but the tears showed that it was heartfelt. She gave me a hug and a kiss on the cheek and said, "It will be all right, Jon." In a single gesture, Nathan and his mother forgave me for my sin. I felt very small as I looked into her eyes. Frankly, I would have preferred at that moment to have had the whipping from my father. I will never, ever forget the look in her teary eyes. My father understood the frivolity of youth; that boys will be boys. But what Dad would not tolerate was the fact that his healthy, able-bodied son didn't stand up for someone less fortunate. Dad wanted his oldest son to learn the importance of protecting the field.

In the game of golf, it is the responsibility of each player to protect the field. In competition, each player is a rules official. So, knowing the rules of golf is paramount. If a player does not know the rules then how can he possibly protect the field? I make a point in every junior clinic to take the time to educate the junior golfers on the rules of golf. For example, the average golfer doesn't know the proper procedures for taking relief from a cart path or the five, yes, five options of a lateral water hazard. What if you find your golf ball in the middle of the trees and you have no shot? Do you know the three options for an unplayable lie? The rules of golf can be complicated. However, the rules of golf are designed to help players save strokes, not lose them.

Another often-neglected facet for the game of golf is etiquette. Etiquette is a fancy word for manners. Learning where to stand while a player is hitting, how to tend the flagstick while your competitor is putting and how to properly rake a bunker are some of the many manners a player should learn before ever going onto a golf course. In my opinion, learning the etiquette of golf is more important than learning the rules of golf for the novice player. Having your cell phone go off while your boss is hitting a shot would not only be embarrassing but could lead to a total tongue lashing. I was very fortunate that my father took the time to explain the etiquette of golf before I played my first round. He had no problem making me aware of when I stepped in his putting line, placed my bag too close to the green or had my shadow covering the hole while he was putting. To play the game of golf, one must be educated. My early education for golf came through my dad. For most people, it should come through a PGA golf professional. The key initiative of the PGA of America is to promote the game of golf. Learning the rules and etiquette is an integral part of the developmental stages of the game. I encourage everyone to take a rules seminar or class at least once. If you are learning the game through private lessons, have at least one of your lessons be on rules and etiquette.

In one of my many attempts to try and qualify for the U.S. Open Championship, I encountered a rules violation where I was disqualified after one hole of play. It happened at Disney's Palm Course. Before the round, I marked my Titleist golf balls with a Sharpie pen. The pen had black ink and I put a single dot over the *ei* of Titleist. I prefer to mark my ball the same way for every tournament. Marking your golf ball is a very important part of pre-tournament golf. As is customary with all tournaments, the rules official went over our order of play, gave us our scorecards, handed us our pin sheets and local rules sheet, told us the number of qualifying spots and asked us to identify our golf ball to our competitors. I stated, "I'm playing a Titleist 3, with a dot over the *ei*." One of my competitors was playing a Nike ball and the other one was playing a Titleist 3 as well. I remember thinking to myself, "Wow, he marks his ball very similar to the way I mark my ball." In the scorer's tent, 20 feet away, was a jar full of assorted-colored Sharpie pens. I saw the pens but thought to myself, "We won't have any problems identifying our balls today. I will change to a different numbered ball instead." The smarter course of action would have been to grab a red Sharpie and add another dot to distinguish my golf ball. My lack of attention to detail would prove my downfall.

Hole number 1 at the Palm is a par-5 that heads due east. Our time was 7:50 a.m. and the sun was directly in our eyes. The entire group had to assist each other in locating the flight of the balls after they were hit. I was last to tee off. My fellow competitor with the other Titleist ball teed off, looked up and asked, "Where did it go?"

I responded, "You're fine. It went down the right side of the fairway." I teed off and looked up and was immediately blinded by the sunlight. My fellow competitors agreed it had been a good shot on a similar line as the shot that preceded mine. One of the many things I love about the game of golf is the importance of etiquette. We all helped each other locate our drives, something you would never see in other sports. As the three of us walked down the fairway with our caddies, I looked at my caddie, Chevis Earl, and said, "It's going to be a good day." Because I was last to tee off, my competitors were ahead of me walking down the fairway. The Nike ball was on the left side of the fairway and the two Titleist golf balls had settled in the intermediate rough on the right side of the fairway. My playing partner got to his golf ball first, and I stood by my ball some 20 feet away. I remember looking down at the ball and noticing a clump of mud all over it. I was 250 yards away from the green and was going for the par-5 in two shots, which meant we had to wait for the green to clear.

The number one thing that all players should do after finding their drive is to identify their golf ball. Under the rules of golf, I could have marked my ball with a tee, picked the ball up (without cleaning it) and replaced it exactly in the same spot after confirming that I was playing the proper ball. Instead, I took a quick glance and was more concerned with the mud and how it would affect the ball's flight. Although my playing partner neglected to properly identify his golf ball as well, the mistake was mine. I can only control my actions on the course. Had I taken an extra few seconds to identify my own golf ball, the problem would never have occurred.

We both played our shots and finished out the first hole. Technically, we were both disqualified, once we teed off the second hole. However, we didn't realize the problem until I got to the second green. I hit my ball 15 feet from the pin while my partner's shot went over the green. I walked up, marked my ball and thought to myself, "That's not my golf ball." Why I didn't realize the mistake on the first hole is still a mystery. I called my partner over and said, "We've got a problem." I knew at that moment we were disqualified. Had we fixed the problem on the first hole we would not have been disqualified. Instead, we would have incurred a two-stroke penalty. I called a rules official over and turned us both in. My playing partner was not happy, but I knew the rules. I protected the field and learned another valuable life lesson in the process.

In my professional life, I use the United States Golf Association's *Rules of Golf* in teaching and playing the game of golf. In my personal life, I try my best to use the Bible to live. The *Rules of Golf* and the Bible are similar in many ways. Structure for performance, rules and decisions of play and rules of etiquette are all emphasized in the Bible and *Rules of Golf*. The USGA *Rules of Golf* have thirty-four rules with more than one hundred sections and subsections. There are an estimated five hundred laws in the Bible, including the Ten Commandments. As a struggling Christian, I now read scripture on a daily basis to better familiarize myself with the many laws and commandments; not necessarily to see where I have gone wrong but to bring comfort in knowing that my belief in Jesus Christ offers forgiveness—just as Nathan and his mother forgave me. As a PGA professional, I have also pledged to increase and further enhance my knowledge of the rules of golf. Every week the PGA Tour has a tournament and every week at the bottom of the field, I see players with the letters DQ by their name, which means disqualified. I have been playing golf most of my life, and I've seen DQ by my name only once. When I returned to the scorer's tent at the Palm Course, I notified the officials that I was disqualified. I waited to watch them put DQ beside my name. I wanted this very difficult lesson to be embedded in my brain. I never, ever wanted to see DQ beside my name again.

I wish I could say that I became close with Nathan, that the two of us are lifelong friends. As a third grader, I was trying to pave my way through life and more concerned with my grades, my football team and my friends than anything else. I had yet to play golf or learn any of its thirty-four rules. I attended the Methodist Church and Sunday school on a regular basis and was just starting to learn the Ten Commandments and some of the stories from the Bible. I did, however, learn a valuable lesson from Nathan. Whenever I'm teaching junior golfers and witness the occasional teasing or even some bullying, I think of Nathan and what he went through. I immediately nip it in the bud and often pull the child aside and explain that behavior will not be tolerated. Like my father many years ago, I have become adept at making the guilty party sense the shame of their actions. A handshake and an apology are requirements for total penance. *"In everything do unto others as you would have them do unto you" (Mathew 7:12).*

In the end, the Bible and the *Rules of Golf* are exactly the same. Both are designed to help you! I am so thankful that Nathan and his mother forgave me of my sin. Nathan loved everyone he came into contact with, including the school bus driver. The world would be a better place if we all lived by Nathan's example. The Word of God breathes life into the people of God. Live each day by these beautiful words. Remember to always live by Nathan's examples of kindness and love. We are charged to love and cherish our neighbors. In the game of golf and the game of life, remember to always protect the field.

As Seen Through My Eyes

Pete McDaniel, former Editor/Senior Writer *Golf Digest*

During a long career as a sportswriter, I've had the privilege of speaking around the world. One of my signature lines is "If I live to be 100, I'll never understand man's inhumanity to other men." Although lacking in originality, it accurately expresses a belief developed through experiences growing up in the South. I describe a most painful one in the introduction to my book, *Uneven Lies: The Heroic Story of African Americans in Golf.*

> *The pain from the blow to my back raced along my spine from neck to buttocks. The force from the blow knocked me into a briar patch. The handlebars pressed into my chest as I lay there in shock. I wheeled my head around just in time to get a good look at who and what had hit me. In the bed of the pickup truck, grinning, stood a freckle-faced, carrot-top teenager holding what appeared to be a slab of tire rubber. His companions—a driver and passenger—roared in laughter, oblivious to the oncoming traffic. Blood trickled down my face but my eyes remained dry. For*

*a long time, their twisted faces and guttural jocular-
ity would wake me from a sound sleep. Forgiveness
did not come easy for me, but neither did quitting.
A social climate hotter than Mama's chili would not
quash my determination to be part of a world whose
welcome mat had reservations.*

The incident occurred as I was riding my bike home after caddy-
ing at Biltmore Forest Country Club near Asheville, North Carolina.
There were certainly others less dramatic (being called the "N" word
or being ordered to the back of the Greyhound bus). Such were the
times in which I grew up. Talk about the racial divide; today's pales
in comparison.

In assisting Tiger Woods with the foreword to his father's semi-
nal book, *Training A Tiger*, I really wasn't all that surprised by Tiger's
tale that on his first day in kindergarten back in Southern California
classmates tied him to a tree and pelted him with fruit. Man's inhumanity to other men is not bound by age or geography.

My healing process included telling the stories of the brave men
and women who endured tremendous hardships and horrible discrimination as they attempted to exercise their rights as citizens of
this country, including the right to access the game of golf. That
they endured and succeeded, some to great degrees, inspired many
attempting the same.

In this chapter, Jon parallels the racial intolerance prevalent in
his youth to the task of playing the 17th hole at Black Mountain
Golf Course in Western North Carolina. It was a monstrous par-6 at
nearly 750 yards in length. Symbolically, it depicts the racial divide
we have faced in this country since little black girls and boys were
placed in the company of little white boys and girls.

My constant prayer is that this book will glorify God through a better understanding that we're all God's children in this thing together. And that even the longest hole can be successfully negotiated through God's enduring love.

CHAPTER 4

The World's Longest Hole

"Do not speak evil against one another, broth-
ers. The one who speaks against a brother or
judges his brother, speaks evil against the law
and judges the law. But if you judge the law,
you are not a doer of the law but a judge"
(James 4:11).

Shortly after learning the invaluable lesson about protecting the field,
I encountered another situation of life-altering significance. It, too,
was connected with formal education in elementary school. Later
that autumn, I sat in my third-grade classroom full of anticipation
as my teacher prepared to go over our afternoon assignments. We
had just returned from lunch and my favorite activity, recess. Like a
pack of playful puppies reluctantly coming in from the backyard, my
classmates and I were energized—our minds ready to soak up every
word of instruction. While Mrs. Potts was going over our assignments for the remainder of the day, suddenly the intercom came on
and the principal spoke in a very stern tone. "Would the following
people please come to my office," he said. As the principal announced
the names of the students, I sat patiently wondering what trouble

these fellow classmates were in and if they were going to get pad-dled. Suddenly I heard the unthinkable—the name, "Jon Decker," among the students ordered to make the long walk of doom to the principal's office. I was mortified as the rest of my classmates turned and looked directly at me. My heart began to race. It felt as though it would beat right out of my chest. I might have even broken into a cold sweat. I was that scared. I knew that I was in trouble but had no idea what I had done or why I was being called into the principal's office. Surely this was a mistake; there had to be an explanation. I had never before been called to the principal's office. I got out of my chair, bowed my head and made the walk of shame. "This wasn't fair. I've done nothing wrong," I thought to myself. I was about to not only discover my offense but the consequences of my transgression. I would also come face to face with one of mankind's most unfortu-nate triage of misbehaviors—hatred, racism and discrimination. It was the day I learned that the world is not always easy, kind or fair. The ultimate takeaway, however, came in the knowledge that man's inhumanity toward others is a senseless part of his journey as he con-tinues to tackle *the world's longest hole.*

During recess I had been on the playground enjoying the warm sunshine and fresh air of the Smoky Mountains. The Swain County School District was so small that all the grades—kindergar-ten through twelfth—were educated in the same building, used the same cafeteria and rode the same school buses. The demographics of Swain County during the 1970s were primarily whites with very few blacks. In fact, I was exposed to more Cherokee Indians than blacks during my early childhood. Several of the older students had yelled at one of the black children on the playground. They cavalierly used the N word as if it were part of their everyday vocabulary. I had never heard that word before and had no idea what it meant. I had never experienced that kind of hostility directed toward anyone. However, it proved contagious because before I knew it, I had chimed in with the N word. Our harassment chased the young black to run away. To this day, I have no idea why I yelled out that word, but I did. And because I had repeated what I heard, I was about to learn another very difficult lesson—not altogether different from the one Nathan had taught me. I was going to learn as a third grader that human beings are not born to discriminate. It is a learned behavior. I was simply repeating what I heard from the older boys, and I'm sure they were simply repeating what had been taught to them.

As I walked into the principal's office, I was trembling with fear. The principal asked me if I yelled the N word at the black child on the playground. I said, "Yes, I did." He asked if I knew what that word meant and I said, "No, I do not." I was given a stern warning what would happen if that word ever escaped from my mouth again. Thankfully I escaped corporal punishment and returned to my class-room. I was ready to go home, forget this day ever happened, and go to football practice. After school my mother drove me to prac-tice, but I didn't mention to her what had happened during recess and certainly not what happened afterward. As practice concluded, I saw my father in the distance standing by his car. I eagerly ran in his direction. As I got closer to the car, I noticed a man that I didn't recognize sitting in the passenger's seat. I ran faster to give my dad a hug and suddenly, I recognized the man sitting in the passenger's seat. It was my principal! I came to a screeching halt and thought to myself, "I'm in big trouble!" I slowly walked to the car, got into the backseat and the three of us proceeded home. Not a single word was exchanged—the deafening silence nearly causing me to have an anxiety attack. After a few minutes, Dad turned around to me and said, "Jon, your principal came in today after school to buy a car. I thought I would invite him home for dinner."

As the family sat around the dinner table, we said grace, served our food and began to eat. Normally my appetite was that of a typical boy's. I could eat my portion and more if allowed. On this evening, though, I had completely lost all appetite. The suspense was killing me. I had no idea what my parents knew, whether Dad was going to whip me or if I was getting expelled from school. I was on the verge of tears. After several agonizing minutes, my father broke the silence. "Jon," he said, "I heard you had to go to the principal's office today." I couldn't contain the tears. I have never cried like that in my entire life. I was speechless. Mom, sitting beside me, tried to console me, but it was impossible. I was humiliated and embarrassed as everyone stared at my crying face. Dad asked me why I had to go to the principal's office, but I couldn't answer—the words wouldn't come. Finally, Dad explained to me what the N word meant and that it was not to be used in our home and certainly not in public. I started crying again and choked out the following: "Dad, I didn't know that it was a bad word. I was just repeating what the older kids were saying."

To this very day, I cringe when I hear the N word whether it is used in jokes, in casual adult conversation, in movies or used by rap artists that many of today's youth idolize. It is time for our society to learn from our mistakes, grow and move on to eliminate these narrow-minded stereotypes. Unfortunately for my personal situation in the third grade, I never apologized to that classmate who was on the receiving end of the racial abuse. I have no idea what impact that day had on his life, and I'm sure he cried as much, if not more, than I did that very same evening. God has a way of allowing His children to reap what they once sowed, and the next year, I got a very small taste of what the black child on the playground must have felt. Life allowed me the opportunity to squeeze into the shoes of folks facing discrimination. It was a tight fit, and it hurt. You might ask with a degree of skepticism, "How is it possible that an American Christian boy with blonde hair, blue eyes, and a healthy body feel the effects of discrimination?" Well, it is possible. And the effects of that discrimination left a lasting impression.

During the summer of 1976, my brother, Michael, and I were going to experience summer camp for the first time, Camp Gwynne Valley. Weeks before leaving for camp, my parents informed us that our family was moving east from Bryson City to Black Mountain, another sleepy suburb of Asheville. My father had accepted a job with Merrill Lynch in Asheville. He was leaving his job selling cars in Bryson City to become a stockbroker. He was chasing his dream and seizing a wonderful opportunity. I remember crying in my room that night. What would happen to all my friends in Bryson City and how would I survive in a larger city? Black Mountain is actually a small town about fifteen miles east of Asheville, but in the mind of child, Asheville was comparable to New York City or Boston. I wondered how I would fit in and who my friends would be in my new hometown. The transition seemed so unfair.

Two weeks later, Mom picked up my brother and me from camp and drove our family to Black Mountain. Dad was still in New York finalizing his training with Merrill Lynch. There was a nervous energy in the car that day. My mother assured us that everything would be all right, but I felt uneasy and restless. At that very moment, God sent me a sign that comforted my heart. It was also a sign that only He could deliver, and one that assured me that everything was going to work out for our family. The *sign* was actually a billboard on the side of Highway 70 outside Black Mountain. The billboard simply read "Welcome to Black Mountain, North Carolina, Home of the World's Longest Hole." Black Mountain Golf Course was famous for having the world's longest hole. The 17th hole was a par-6. That's correct, a par-6! It measures 745 yards in length. In 1976, it was featured in the Guinness Book of World Records as being "The World's Longest Hole." Suddenly Black Mountain was cool! That single experience would be a defining moment in my life and my future career, leading me to new and exciting adventures. ***"You make*** *known to me the path of life; In your presence there is fullness of joy" (Psalm 16:11).*

Upon seeing that billboard, my mind immediately began to focus on golf. I had to play this monster hole, even though at that point in my life I had only hit a few golf balls for one day in the front yard of the duplex apartment in Bryson City. I had never actually played the game of golf, but that billboard refueled my desire to play the game. I couldn't wait for my father to return from New York. I knew we were now going to play golf together as a family. It was going to be great. After two months, the day finally arrived, and my father returned from his training. Our family was so excited to see him and to see if he brought any gifts for his three boys from the Big Apple. I look up to both my parents, but the relationship between a father and a son is priceless. In my mind, he was an army hero and football star. His return home from New York also meant that my time on the golf course was about to begin.

Soon after his return, Dad came home from work and told me the very sad news. "Jon," he said, "you can't play golf at the Black Mountain Golf Course."

"Why?" I asked.

"You're not old enough," he said. The words still haunt me. I couldn't believe my ears, but unfortunately, the news was true. Black Mountain was a public golf course, and because of liability reasons, all players had to be at least ten years old to play on the course. I had just experienced age discrimination. Sadness and rejection left me feeling empty inside. I was devastated. It would be months before my tenth birthday. Back then, months seemed more like years.

On Jan. 12, 1977, I turned ten. That birthday will always be the most memorable one of my life, because on that day my parents gave me my first set of junior golf clubs. I cuddled up with those clubs in my bed, bag and all, and felt a comfort with my new friend. I embraced them, marveling at their craftsmanship. I must have counted and recounted the new wooden tees I had received a dozen times. I was amazed at the whipping on the wooden head of the driver and three-wood. I organized my bag, clipped on my new towel, counted the clubs in the bag for the tenth time and prepared for my first round of golf. January 1977 will also go on record as being one of the worst winters in U.S. history. Snow blanketed the mountains of Western North Carolina, and each night, our family watched the nightly news and heard the same words, "No school for Buncombe County." Although the idea of not going to fourth-grade classes seemed appealing, the hard reality of not getting to play golf began to sink in. I remember putting golf balls into a glass jar in my bedroom, but still no golf on the course, as each day brought more and more snow. Black Mountain had no driving range or indoor facility, so the only use the golf course was getting was from the kids sledding down the hilly fairways. It is a winter I will never forget, and our school district missed more than three weeks of school in January alone. Golf would have to wait until spring arrived as time seemed to stand still.

The winter of 1977 taught me many lessons in life. I now know what it feels like to be told, "You can't play." I am not for one minute suggesting that the discrimination I felt was the same as the black child felt on the playground. My experience did, however, give me a brief perspective on what it felt like to have a dream crushed because others said, "No!" That experience, although difficult at the time, was necessary for me in my childhood and gave me great overall perspective. Today there are still country clubs in the U.S. that discriminate based on race, gender and religious beliefs. God has many plans for me in my lifetime, but judging others is not one of them. I accept the fact that there are clubs all around the world where membership is restrictive. I also acknowledge that many of my fellow PGA golf professionals work at facilities that restrict membership. That's their personal choice to which they're entitled. The policy to restrict membership is the decision of the club's members, not mine. As a Christian and teaching professional, I have made the personal choice for my career to never work for one of those restrictive facilities. I am proud of the fact that the facilities I have worked for in my career allow open memberships to everyone.

I was also exposed to one of the most important lessons of my life during the winter of 1977, something I struggle with on a daily basis. That struggle is patience. Often students make the comment to me, "Jon, you have the patience of Job." I do have patience with other people for I am a people person. I help struggling golfers and offer words of encouragement daily, but unfortunately, with God and His plans for me, I am not so patient. My Creator, my Lord, the One who knows all, the One who knows my ultimate path in life, whom I walk with daily is the One to whom I have the least amount of patience. God's time-table doesn't move fast enough, in my mind, for my life. The many months I had to wait on the sidelines to play the game of golf were the first time in my life I recall experiencing impatience. God used the game of golf to introduce patience into an adolescent's life. "Patience is bitter but its fruit is sweet" (Aristotle).

Great players know their strengths and weaknesses. Patience is one of my weaknesses, but because I have defined this as a weakness, I now grow stronger. I pray for guidance. I pray for my family. I pray for those in need, and I pray that God gives me the patience to let His plan evolve. When I finally got to play my first round of golf that spring, I shot 130. Years later, I would shoot 65 on that same course. Time, practice, and patience allowed me the opportunity to cut my score in half. I believe there is no better way to learn the virtue of patience than by playing the game of golf.

In retrospect, racism and impatience are man's twosome play-ing the World's Longest Hole. Symbolically, the journey is both long and difficult. Racism has been a part of our nation's history since its inception. Although our country has made strides in civil rights, the problem still exists. At age eight, I learned a difficult lesson about hatred and the power of negative words from a small black child on a playground in the mountains of North Carolina. Another year older but just as naïve, I learned how it felt to be told *no* simply because of one's age. In my life, God has used these experiences to help me learn the value of treating every human being as a child of God and that we are born to love not to hate. God sends us signs every day. He used a snowstorm to teach a virtue called patience to a nine-year-old boy and a billboard on the side of the highway to fuel my desire as a child for the game of golf. God's classroom of hard-learned lessons made 1977 unforgettable. In one year, I left my friends in Bryson City only to have God double my friendships in Black Mountain. I felt temporarily the sting of age discrimination only to gain a lifetime of joy playing the game of golf. I learned that this great game should be played by everyone, not just the select few. Like putting the ball into the cup on the World's Longest Hole, I look forward to the day when discrimination will be gone in society and the game of golf. I also pray the day will come when I can finally learn to channel my fear and anxieties of impatience. Ultimately, what I cherish most from 1977 is the initial feeling of standing on the tee box of the 17th hole with my father, ready to take on the World's Longest Hole! I finally putted the ball into the hole, ending a hole of both joy and frustration, and recording a score of 13. The World's Longest Hole was definitely worth the wait!

(L to R) 1. World's Longest Hole/Tee shot 2. Second Shot 3. Third shot

As Seen Through My Eyes

Bill Stines, Director of Golf, Scioto CC

Recently I was walking across a field near my hometown of Canton, North Carolina. During my stroll, I came across a broken down fence and beside the fence was a fence post with a box turtle sitting on the top of the post. Well, I knew one thing for sure: The turtle did not get there by itself. This site quickly reminded me about my own life. I began to recollect about all the people that had helped me along the way and had given me guidance to get me where I am today. As my mind recounted, I thought about my parents and my grandfather who always taught me that giving back is such an important part of life. When you give back, you get rewarded ten-fold in the end.

I was fortunate to play college golf at Wake Forest University from 1980–1984. In the summers, I worked as a Camp Counselor of Jesse Haddock Golf Camp, Wake Forest's Hall of Fame Golf Coach. In the summer of 1981, I met a young man from Black Mountain, North Carolina, named Jon Decker. He was a bit intimidated but was an extremely hard worker. The week quickly passed, and we did everything we could to encourage and move Jon along with his golf game. By the end of the week, Jon was making progress but wanted more. I remember him calling his parents begging them to stay another week. Well, to our surprise, he convinced them and Jon stayed another week. He worked extremely hard, harder than any other camper. By the week's end, Jon had made significant improvement. Jon returned home and began to improve rapidly. He went on to pursue a career in golf as a teacher and has become one of the best! His excellent work ethic, ambition and perseverance have made him a success. Jon has become one of the finest teachers in the game. In 2007, I was honored to be a reference for him and help him become the director of instruction at New Albany Country Club in New Albany, Ohio. Jon has done an outstanding job and truly come a long way from that hot day in Jesse Haddock Golf Camp back in 1981. It is truly a pleasure to see someone advance as far as Jon has in our profession and to become the outstanding Instructor he is today. He is a fabulous teacher and a better person. Enjoy his story!

CHAPTER 5

The Demon Deacons

"Jesus wept" (John 11:35).

I remember the first time I ever saw my father cry. I was a child watching television on a cold and blustery Saturday afternoon. In the mountains of North Carolina, there are very few sports or outside activities played during the winter months. My brothers and I were stuck inside for the day, so we turned on our television and flipped through our three channels (affiliates of ABC, NBC and CBS). I was disappointed that there were no games to be watched, only a movie and some news. I decided to turn the channel to the movie and became intrigued because it was about the Chicago Bears football team. I love football and was instantly captivated. The scene showed a man sitting in a cafeteria with the other players on the team. He was singing the Wake Forest University fight song, which immediately captured our attention because Dad had attended that prestigious university. On this memorable day, I would witness my father's heart break and feel the pain of a life lost to a man I would never know. I would also learn later that afternoon from my father more about the movie *Brian's Song* and Dad's history as a Demon Deacon.

Some of my favorite childhood memories are of my grandmother, mother and father telling me the stories of Dad's college football career at Wake Forest University. Often these stories were told before bedtime. There was the game Wake Forest played against Florida State and Fred Biletnikoff in Tallahassee. My father said the team was distracted by all the pretty cheerleaders and majorettes on the sidelines during warm-ups. There's the story of his first collegiate game against East Carolina University during the 1963 season. It was the opening game for East Carolina's new stadium, Ficklin Stadium (renamed Dowdy Ficklin Stadium some years later). East Carolina won the inaugural game for the stadium, 20–10. Dad sat out the game due to bruised ribs. As a proud 1990 East Carolina alumnus, I love to needle Dad about that loss. His response is always the same. "If I had been healthy, the outcome would have been different." Then there was the story of the Army game at West Point that my grandmother loved to tell. She was listening to the game on the radio and my father was returning a punt. He got hit from the side and tore his MCL in his right knee and all of his cartilage. His season came to a screeching halt on that play. She said the play-by-play announcer kept saying, "Sammy Decker is hurt! Sammy Decker is hurt!" I'm sure as a mother those words were difficult to hear. But there was one story I had not heard, not until that cold, blustery, winter day as a child in Bryson City. It was the story of Brian Piccolo.

I was totally enthralled with this movie, unable to look away from the TV screen except during commercial breaks. I was so excited to see a movie whose characters were talking about Wake Forest University. Suddenly, I heard the door close behind me and Dad entered the family room. I said, "Dad, there is a movie on television about a man from Wake Forest." My father said nothing and sat down in a chair behind me. Together we watched the movie. As the movie went on, the story line turned from the shared euphoria of competition and bonding of teammates to the sadness of a life-threatening disease. I was waiting for the football scenes, with players crashing into each other and the ball soaring through the air as a receiver ran underneath it. I thought that maybe they would show scenes from when my father played. I turned around to ask Dad a question and he was crying. It was the first time in my life I witnessed my father crying. Automatically, tears formed in my eyes, too. "Jon," said Dad, "I knew that man. His name is Brian Piccolo. I played football with him at Wake Forest." After the movie, my father pulled out playbooks, photo albums and a signed team football with Brian Piccolo's name on it. I will always remember the mixed emotions of that cold and blustery day.

As I grew older, my parents would take our family on most Saturdays to the Wake Forest football games. I remember going into the locker rooms hours before the games and watching the players getting their ankles taped. Doc Martin was the trainer for the team. I would sit and listen to Doc tell stories about Dad while meticulously wrapping the white adhesive just tightly enough to stabilize the ankle. Doc would later tell my father his knee injury was the worst he had ever seen in his twenty-two-year career at Wake Forest. As the kickers warmed up, my brothers and I would catch the footballs beside the nets at the field house. It was a special time in a boy's life. Till this day I love watching football, but my true passion for sports has always been golf. Although Wake Forest University is not known for winning National Championships in football, golf is a whole other story. Players like Curtis Strange, Scott Hoch, Gary Hallberg, Billy Andrade, Jay Haas, Lanny Watkins, Webb Simpson and Bill Haas, just to name a few, have played at Wake Forest. However, when you talk Wake Forest golf, you really only need to say one name— Arnold Palmer.

Coach Jesse Haddock was the driving force behind much of the Demon Deacons' early success in golf. Coach Haddock won three NCAA Division I national championships during his thirty-year career. In 1981, I got my first opportunity to meet this legendary coach. His presence and commitment left a lasting impression on me as a PGA teaching professional. I struggled as a young player during the late 1970s and early 1980s. Dad had limited experience playing golf and no experience teaching the game. I remember my struggles well—the frustration, the anger and the despair of not improving. Although I was a pretty fair athlete, golf did not come naturally to me. I know exactly how my new students feel. I have empathy for their pain and know that if they endure and withstand the urge to quit, they will improve. These struggles are the most difficult part of teaching the game of golf. I take every lesson as a challenge to always encourage, yet push my students to reach limits they thought were impossible. One of the reasons I do this is because of Coach Jesse Haddock. I only received a few tips from him, yet his influence resonates in my ability to motivate others.

When Dad first showed me the brochure for the Wake Forest golf camp, I was so excited I nearly did a back flip. I couldn't believe it. I was going to this prestigious camp for one week. I really had never had formal instruction and nor had I seen my swing on video. I was fourteen, tall and skinny. Like many of my peers, I was pretty much a know-it-all. My swing was unorthodox and I had a competitive temper. I relied on hard work, determination and my putting to get me around the golf course. Upon arriving at the camp, I looked around and watched the other camper's golf swings. All of a sudden, a large lump formed in my throat. Clearly I was out of my league swing-wise. Insecurity seemed to enclose me like a cheap suit.

Coach Haddock had a presence about him. A slender framed gentleman with eyes that seemed to penetrate straight through to your soul, he looked me in the eyes and applied a strong grip to my smallish hand. His warm smile immediately disarmed me and I forever felt comfortable around him. In a high-pitched voice that some of his former players would mimic during storytelling, he raved about my father and his football days at Wake Forest. The natural reaction of an offspring to praise for a parent's accomplishments in sport is intimidation. At least that's how I felt as Coach Haddock went on about Dad's athletic prowess. I immediately felt a pressure to be something I knew I wasn't—a star. The next day we began the camp on the driving range. I had only been to a driving range a couple of times. Former PGA Tour player Jim Simons, an ex-Demon Deacon, was also at the camp that day. He and Coach Haddock assisted each child with specific tips. I was so nervous, impatiently waiting for my turn to hit in front of these two icons. I could hear Coach Haddock and Jim praising the other students. All of them were talented and displayed great technique. Finally, it came time for me to hit my shot. I took a mighty swing and hit a great shot. Boy was I relieved! Not a word of praise or encouragement. It was apparent to me at that very moment that my homemade swing relied on two things—hand-eye coordination and effort; certainly not technique. However, I had hit a great shot by my standards. I'm sure Coach Haddock and Jim thought, "How are we going to fix this mess?" The first thing they said to me was, "Well, you got away with it, but you need to work on it." The list of swing changes began right then and there.

During the camp, our counselors filmed our golf swings. One of the counselors was Bill Stines. Bill was from Western North Carolina and played at Wake Forest. He took me under his wing that week because our fathers were close friends. Bill became the head pro at Scioto Country Club in Columbus, Ohio. That night, all the kids watched the video of their golf swings as a group. Mine was the last swing that was shown. I will never forget the horror of watching my swing. It was the first time I had ever seen my swing on video and very similar to the first time I heard my voice on a tape recorder. "That's not me," I thought to myself. I wasn't a graceful athlete, just a skinny fourteen-year-old kid with a strange set up and a swing with twelve loops in it. I felt sick to my stomach and frankly wanted to cry. Teenage insecurities can seem so dramatic, but at that time, they were so real. So real that as an adult, I can still feel them. So real that it fueled my desire to improve my swing technique.

During the week I struggled and as we came to the last few days. I wasn't getting any better. I returned to my room each night and cried, feeling like a complete failure. I wanted to be a great player. My dreams were to be on the PGA Tour. I called my parents that night from the pay phone. "I am not getting any better," I said. "I need more time. May I please stay another week?" There was dead silence. Wake Forest golf camp was very expensive. It included all day instruction, golf, three meals a day plus our accommodations. I knew this would be a financial strain on my parents, I knew it was a stretch, but I asked anyway. After begging and pleading, my parents both agreed, "Yes, you can stay Jon." I will always be grateful for my parent's generosity.

The next week we worked out in some of the summer's most oppressive heat. Each day was in the high 90s with elevated humidity. I didn't care. I was determined to get better. One afternoon while on the driving range, the counselors yelled, "Water break!" All the kids ran from the range to the shelter to grab a cold drink; all the kids but me. I refused to leave the range and continued hitting balls. That's when I learned a valuable lesson: The greatest gift a teacher can give a student is the gift of time. Jesse Haddock walked out of the shelter, came over, and started teaching me. We were the only two people on the entire driving range. He spent twenty minutes with me, while the other kids sat in the shade, drank their water and complained about the heat. I remember the lessons learned that day when I see a kid struggling with golf. The extra time can make all the difference. The next night the phone rang in the dormitory where we were staying. One of the other campers yelled, "Hey Jon, the phone's for you."

It was Coach Haddock. "Jon," he said, "I admire your work ethic. One day you will be a great player because you're a hard worker. You're athletic and you come from great genes." That day Coach Haddock gave me the self-confidence that a skinny teenager needed at a time when he needed it the most. Coach Haddock taught me that encouragement is the root of being a great teacher. After all, when you "root" for someone, you show encouragement! Because of Jesse Haddock, I try my best to bring encouragement to every lesson I teach.

The summer of 1982 brought the dedication for the new sports dormitory at Wake Forest University—the Brain Piccolo/Arnold Palmer Sports Dormitories. My father proudly packed our entire family, plus my grandparents into our Ford van as we made the two-hour drive to Winston-Salem, North Carolina. As our van pulled up to the dedication ceremony site, my father screamed, "There's Arnold Palmer!" Mom, startled by Dad's reaction to seeing his hero, had a fairly loud reaction herself. "Sam," she yelled, "what in the world are you doing?" I looked to my right and there they were, Arnold Palmer and Coach Haddock walking side by side down the sidewalk. Dad slammed on the brakes, put the van in park, jumped out of the seat, ran around and slid open the van door and our entire family piled out of that vehicle like children running down the steps on Christmas morning. I honestly believe Arnold Palmer, for one brief moment, thought he was being kidnapped by a band of terrorists. The traffic behind our van came to a screeching halt as Mr. Palmer graciously shook our entire family's hands, smiling and giving me a wink in the process. It was his way of letting me know that Dad's enthusiasm was humorous to him. All the while my faced turned several shades of red. His giant mitt felt like a vice-grip as he shook my hand. As I shook Mr. Palmer's hand, Coach Haddock complimented me on my hard work during the camp. His words warmed my insides like hot cocoa on a cold, winter's day. It was a dream come true for a kid from a small town in North Carolina. That afternoon, my father also introduced me to former Wake Forest point guard and longtime CBS basketball analyst Billy Packer. I also got to see my former counselor Bill Stines. It was a magical afternoon.

During the next few years, my game began to blossom. In the spring of 1985, I became the first player in the history of Charles D. Owen High School to win the Western North Carolina Sectional Championship. I won it in dramatic fashion—a single-hole playoff against Eric Morgan—and for the third straight year, our team qualified for the State Championship in Chapel Hill, North Carolina. After sectionals, I received a letter of congratulations from Coach Haddock. Coach Haddock took the time to congratulate me on being tournament medalist. I felt a sense of accomplishment that day because I knew that Coach Haddock helped me achieve my goals.

WAKE FOREST
UNIVERSITY

Jesse I. Haddock
  Golf Coach

May 30, 1985

Mr. Jon Decker
461 Chapel Road
Black Mountain, NC 28711

Dear Jon:

    Congratulations on your play in the Western
Sectional Tournament. I received a clipping through the
mail that appeared in the Asheville Times, Thursday, May
16.

    Best wishes to you and your family.

           Sincerely,

           JESSE I. HADDOCK
           Golf Coach

JIH:jcd

In a two-year span, these Demon Deacons impacted my golfing career and laid a foundation for me as a teacher. The movie *Brian's Song* caused Dad to emote in a way I'd never seen before from him. My parents taught me that crying is a sign of strength not weakness because it shows that you are not afraid to show or share your emotions. After all, the shortest verse in the Bible is "Jesus wept." If Jesus can cry comforting others in their time of need, we human beings should be able to show the same emotion without fear of appearing weak to others. During the movie *Brian's Song*, Brain Piccolo and Gale Sayers become friends until Brian's unexpected death at the age of twenty-six to cancer. Years later, while working at Grand Cypress, I had the privilege of meeting Mr. Sayers following his lesson. He had taken the lesson with my friend and former coworker Gus Holbrook. We had a great conversation while Mr. Sayers was hitting golf balls. I said to him, "My father played football with Brian Piccolo at Wake Forest." He stopped hitting balls and looked at me. The emotion on his face said it all. He mentioned what a great man Brian was. But, sometimes in life, you don't need to hear the words to get the message. I left Mr. Sayers alone to continue his practice.

The ceremonies for the Brian Piccolo/Arnold Palmer dormitories allowed me to meet Arnold Palmer for the first time. The movie *Brian's Song* gave me a perspective of Brian Piccolo as a man and the life he lived. Coach Jesse Haddock's inspiration gave me hope and confidence as a teenager when I needed it most. And Bill Stines took me under his wing as my camp counselor. In 2006, the New Albany Country Club was looking for a director of instruction for their teaching facility. The search committee contacted Bill at the Scioto CC. Bill recommended me for the job--a gesture for which I will always be grateful. His recommendation allowed me to spread my wings and further my career.

Although I never personally attended Wake Forest University, the influences of that wonderful institution taught me personal lessons for life; specifically that hard work, manners, etiquette, drive, ambition, preparation, and perseverance, along with knowledge and technique, are the cornerstones for success in golf or any other career path. I will forever be grateful to those Demon Deacons for their inspiration and support. In addition, those Demon Deacons taught me to lead by example and look a person in the eye when shaking their hand. By extension I've taught my students that time is a gift and to use it wisely. That is also a sign of generosity, an example of Christian behavior espoused in the Bible. I am eternally grateful for my parents' generosity in allowing me to stay an extra week at camp. They also sacrificed to pay for more time while Coach Haddock gave of his time unselfishly. *"If anyone forces you to go one mile, go with them two miles. Give to the one who asks you, and do not turn away from the one who wants to borrow from you" (Mathew 5:41–42).*

By watching *Brian's Song*, I learned the cleansing power of revealing one's emotions. Men in today's society would do well to purge themselves similarly and not yield to the stigma of men shedding tears. I learned that teenage insecurities, if harnessed properly, can provide desire and motivation. I am thankful to have had parents, coaches and mentors to help me during those difficult teenage years. I learned that hard work does pay off. One of society's ills is that many folks want to be paid immediately for any hard work. Instant gratification is the norm. I learned that sometimes in life the hard work you put in now is paid down the road with a much greater reward. My golf game improved in the short term while at Wake Forest's camp, but my real reward was years later when Bill gave me the referral. It was attestation to my past hard work while attending the camp and also of my work ethic while at Grand Cypress. This hard work paved the way for the advancement in my career. To my parents, the movie *Brian's Song*, Jesse Haddock, Arnold Palmer, and Bill Stines I say, "Thank you and go, Deacs!"

Coach Bobby Cremins, retired NCAA basketball coach

Courtesy of The Asheville Citizen Times, 2012. Bobby
Cremins and Eddie Biedenbach, during the Eddie Biedenbach
Celebrity Golf Classic at The Cliffs at Walnut Cove

I met Jon and his family through my friend and former assistant coach, Bill Burrows. The life story of Jon's youngest brother Brett is an inspiration to all. The stories from Jon's life and from this book are great examples of how dreams, hard work, and faith can lead to success in any sport and in the game of life!

CHAPTER 6

Promises Kept

"Now on the next day, the day after the prepa-
ration, the chief priests and the Pharisees gath-
ered together with Pilate, and said, "Sir, we
remember that when He was still alive that
deceiver said, 'After three days I am to rise
again.' "Therefore, give orders for the grave to

be made secure until the third day, otherwise His disciples may come and steal Him away and say to the people, 'He has risen from the dead,' and the last deception will be worse than the first." (Mathew 27:62–64)

On this day, the third day, the chief priests, the Pharisees and even the guards who brutally tortured the Son of God learned that Jesus was a man of His word. On this the third day, the world learned the truth; that Jesus lived a life with promises kept.

On February 28, 1972, my youngest brother, Brett, was born in Bryson City, North Carolina. There was an air of anxiety around our home because my parents were concerned that Brett would be a leap-year baby. Not that we were aware of any superstitions or folklore, but my brother Michael and I thought it would be cool for Brett to be born on the twenty-ninth, so we were moderately disappointed when he was born a few hours before. Even at such a young age, we realized there was something special about welcoming home a newborn. My eyes must have resembled saucers as I gazed at my little brother. I was just that excited witnessing the wonders of nature. It takes a village to raise a child. In addition to family, Brett's village included members of the golf course, our local church and close friends. Partly through sports and athletics, Brett has met many influential people who have had a profound impact on his life. They have provided inspiration for Brett, influencing his life through kind acts, thoughtful gestures, and more importantly, promises kept.

Proud father with his youngest son.

Brett and my great-grandmother, Dee Dee

When Brett was three years old, our parents noticed he wasn't speaking normally, so they took him to specialists to test his speech. Brett's early diagnosis was delayed speech. As Brett entered high school, he was tested again. The diagnosis this time was high-functioning autism. This diagnosis was significant because it allowed Brett to take special classes and graduate on time, like his older brothers, from Charles D. Owen High School in the spring of 1991. Brett's diagnosis didn't keep him from getting a job at McDonald's in high school. He cooked fries with the determination to be the best employee possible. His work ethic drew praise from his supervisor. Brett is very structured in a work environment. Teach him the job and he will do it exactly as you instruct. However, adapting to change in that environment proved to be more difficult.

Brett had normal motor skills but was very shy and reserved socially. He had an amazing ability to memorize dates and scores from competitions. For example, he could remember all the scores from the Wake Forest football games. You could ask him, "Brett, who won the 1932 game between Wake Forest and William & Mary?" And Brett could give you the score. It was amazing! Brett learned to play golf and would join the rest of the family for outings after church. Eventually, he developed a passion for the game, which brought a smile to my face every time I thought about a younger sibling following the path I had taken. Brett had normal childhood interests. He enjoyed shooting basketball, loved fireworks and was consumed with the weather, especially snow. Like all teenagers, he learned to drive a car. What distinguished him from most of his peers were his exceptional and cautious driving skills. He became an excellent driver, very safe and aware of his speed, turn signals and gas mileage. These skills would help him later in life as he learned to proficiently drive a forklift for Ingles Supermarket warehouse.

Brett's athletics background was typical of most boys. He played some organized sports including little league and youth basketball. In high school, he played on the golf team and was voted Most Improved Player his senior year. I remember how proud Brett was as he received his award at Owen High's annual sports awards banquet. Our family was awash with pride as we witnessed his special moment. Mom and Dad couldn't hold back the tears, and I was just slightly more successful. Brett seemed unfazed by all the attention except to flash a one-thousand-watt smile that warmed the entire room. Brett also loved basketball mostly as an observer. Often though, we would see this lone figure shooting baskets in our driveway, and every now and then, he would even join his older brothers in a family scrimmage there. Basketball was as much a Decker family staple as pancakes on Sunday morning. Mom played at Wake Forest; Dad played in the North Carolina State Championship in high school, while Michael and I played on Owen's varsity team.

At the start of my junior year, I decided to quit basketball and focus solely on golf. Coach Burrows confronted me about my decision. He knew golf was my favorite sport. Frankly, I was nervous about playing for him. Teammate Brad Johnson came up to me in the hallway before class seeking answers, too. "Are you playing basketball this year, Jon, we need you?"

"No," I said with as much conviction as I could muster considering I directed it to one of the best athletes in school history. Then fate stepped in and Coach Burrows unexpectedly resigned from teaching and coaching at Owen to become an assistant coach for Georgia Tech, working under Coach Bobby Cremins. The move sent shockwaves throughout the tight-knit community. After all, Coach Burrows had been responsible for the Warhorses' transformation into a powerhouse program in Western North Carolina. On the flipside of the unexpected news was our excitement for junior varsity coach Bruce Arrowood, who filled the position vacated by Coach Burrows. I almost quit out of plain fear, but quitting has never been in my nature. I decided to play basketball—one of the best decisions I've ever made.

Brett attended every game and watched his big brother bang shoulders and elbows with much bigger players in the middle. At six foot four, I was an undersized center, although unafraid to stick my chin in the fray. One of my pregame traditions was to scan the stands for Brett. He was always there with a wave and smile—my personal motivation—chomping at the bit to be in combat alongside us. What Brett lacked in size as a twelve-year-old, he made up with feistiness. Coach Burrows developed a soft spot for Brett, allowing him to take a few shots after practice and games. Brett might have been timid socially, but he was not afraid to shoot the ball. The summer after my junior year, our family was going to Atlanta to see a Braves game. Brett made a simple request to Coach Burrows, "Can I shoot at Georgia Tech's Memorial Coliseum when we go to Atlanta?" Coach Burrows laughed but realized Brett was serious. So he called his friend Bobby Cremins and received an immediate okay. "Sure" came the reply over the phone, leaving our family in total disbelief.

On a warm, summer day, our entire family drove to Alexander Memorial Coliseum in Atlanta. I was very excited to be reunited with Coach Cremins. I had attended the Appalachian State University basketball camp in Boone, North Carolina. conducted by Coach Cremins during his stint at the NCAA Division I school. I loved his enthusiasm and his thick New York accent. Upon our arrival, one of the assistant coaches met us at the door to the coliseum. He had a worried look on his face. Then he delivered the bad news. "This morning the coliseum floor was refinished," he said. "No one can go on the floor until it dries." I knew Brett was hurting inside, yet he showed no emotion. It was a typical reaction from my little brother. "Coach Cremins would like to meet with you in his office," said the assistant. I couldn't believe it. Our entire family was going to meet with Coach Cremins, head coach of the Georgia Tech Yellow Jackets. What a moment!

Coach Cremins is notorious for his hand gestures, facial expressions and superfast vocal delivery. Our family was fascinated with his demeanor and transfixed on his gracious personality. He praised Coach Burrows and told us how popular he was with the current players. Georgia Tech's roster was deep in talent with future stars John Salley, Mark Price and Ivan Joseph. The players nicknamed Coach Burrows Wild Bill because he never stopped yelling, clapping or coaching. Television cameras seemed as focused on the sideline antics of Coach Cremins as with the on-court action what with Coach Cremins running up and down like a man possessed. In the meantime, Coach Burrows would be in a full squat, clapping and screaming. What a pair! They were a perfect, albeit lively, combination. "Brett, I'm sorry you didn't get to shoot today, but I promise you that if you come to a game this year, I will let you shoot on the coliseum floor before the game starts," Coach Cremins said. I nearly fainted! Such was my admiration and awe of one of college basketball's greatest coaches.

Later that year, Wake Forest traveled to Atlanta to play the Yellow Jackets in a pivotal Atlantic Coast Conference match up. Again the family loaded into our car for the trip south and Brett's appointed destiny. Basketball is big business with big rivalries in ACC country, akin to football fanaticism in many of the nation's other major conferences of yesteryear. Often students form long lines well before game time in a grand showing of team allegiance. We waited patiently outside the coliseum with everyone else. Suddenly, we saw a town car slowly pulling up curbside. Exiting were Coach Cremins and Coach Burrows. The students went crazy as Coach Cremins gave them a wave. He was like a rock star entering a concert. Coach Cremins' staff escorted us in ahead of the crowd. Of course, the seats were first rate, making us feel like celebrities. As Brett was being led down to the court, I noticed a familiar face along press row. It was Dick Vitale of ESPN prepping for the show. There were a few hundred people around the court as the students had not yet been allowed in for their open seating. Brett walked onto the court and started bouncing the ball. My heart was pounding because several people courtside turned around from the noise of the ball hitting the court. The cheerleaders were ready; the band was taking their seats, and Brett put up his first shot.

I really can't remember if Brett made that shot or not, but I will never forget what happened about thirty seconds later. The outside doors flew open and all the students started pouring into the coliseum in a mad scramble for seating. Within a few minutes the coliseum was filled to the rafters. Suddenly, Brett was shooting in front of a packed house. Frankly, I wanted to crawl under my seat. Brett took some dribbles and hoisted a long outside shot. Swish! Several people started clapping. Another shot, another swish! All of the sudden my little brother, the one who always came to my games and supported me, the shy kid who never said much was shooting in front of more than 8,000 people and they were cheering! Now I was on the outside looking in, supporting my younger brother. We had traded places. Brett was front and center! If the shot went in, the students cheered. Each miss was greeted with a resounding, "Awwww." For one brief moment in time, Brett performed as the world watched. Michael and I laughed and cheered. "That's our little brother, Brett," we bragged to the people sitting beside us. Coach Cremins not only made a promise to Brett, he delivered on his promise. Thank you, Coach Cremins. for your promise kept.

Years later I was working at Grand Cypress Resort and Academy in Orlando. Brett was twenty-four and working at Home Depot in Asheville. His main job was to collect the shopping carts and help customers with their purchases. Brett would always comment how people just randomly left their carts in the middle of the parking lot. Today whenever I have a shopping cart, I always return it to the cart return area and think of Brett. In 1996, that Home Depot store awarded Employee of the Year to Brett.

One day while I was working at Grand Cypress in the Academy Pro Shop, Arthur Blank came to take a lesson with our Director of Instruction, Fred Griffin. Mr. Blank was the CEO of Home Depot and a regular student of Fred's. He currently owns the Atlanta Falcons of the National Football League. After the session, Mr. Blank came into the pro shop to pay up. I was working behind the counter that day. "Mr. Blank," I said, "I'm Jon Decker. My brother Brett works in Asheville at Home Depot. Recently he was named Employee of the Year." I told Mr. Blank about Brett, about his job responsibilities and how much pride he took in his work. He reached in his pocket and pulled out a small organizer and pen.

"Now, what's your brother's name?" he asked. He jotted down some information and left for Atlanta.

Brett took off his twenty-fifth birthday and slept in. The phone rang and Dad answered. "Brett, you need to get up, your general manager from work just called," he said. "Mr. Blank is coming into the store today and wants to see you."

"But Dad, it's my day off," he said.

"Brett, get out of bed now. He wants to meet you!" When the two of them arrived at the store, all the employees were front and center in anticipation of Brett meeting Mr. Blank. Mr. Blank shook Brett's hand and said that while he was in Asheville he wanted to meet him. He congratulated Brett on the well-deserved honor. Brett still beams with pride when we retell that story. Although Mr. Blank never made me a promise, he made himself a promise the second he jotted down Brett's information. Mr. Blank's business success, fame, fortune and the prestige of owning an NFL franchise, will never overshadow the kindness and attention to detail he showed to my brother that day. And Brett will never forget his twenty-fifth birthday!

In 2012, I stood at the Peter Millar booth talking to a sales representative during the PGA Merchandise Show in Orlando. I looked up as a large, well-dressed group of people came walking into our area. The entourage appeared purposeful as if on a strict schedule. As they came closer, I recognized the main attraction. The elegantly dressed man was Arthur Blank. The Falcons logo pinned to his lapel caught my eye. "Mr. Blank," I said, extending my hand and referencing Grand Cypress to jog his memory. He smiled, gave me a nod, and we talked for several minutes about Grand Cypress and Brett. He was very gracious, inquiring about Fred and his family and Brett. I'm forever grateful to Mr. Arthur Blank for his kindness to me that day and his kindness to my brother, but, more importantly, for his promise kept.

In my journey as a Christian, I have stumbled many times. I have failed in a marriage. I have lived a life of mistakes and had my shortcomings. Through all these difficulties my faith has grown stronger. The Bible was written with many passages, countless stories and thousands of verses. However, what makes the Bible the most-read book in the world, the foundation for the Christian faith and the guide for mankind can be summed up in one promise. John 3:16 states, ***"For God so loved the world that he gave his one and only son, that whoever believes in him shall not perish but have everlasting life."*** Not all people keep their promises. The fact that my marriage failed ultimately means that my promise to God in the vows taken was not kept. But in this world of sin and sorrow, failure and despair, it is nice to know that some promises are kept. During these difficult times, I leaned on the Lord and His Word in scripture. John 3:16 is my rock because it embodies the ultimate promise kept.

On December 20, 2008, Brett married Claudette Peake. It was a day that our family thought might never happen. Six years later (on January 11, 2011), Claudette gave birth to daughter, TeriLynn. Like Brett's birthday being one day short of the leap year, TeriLynn was one day from my birthday of January 12th. As one would expect, Brett was front and center as he proudly held his baby girl. God gives us each a talent and purpose in life. It is up to each individual to make the most of this purpose, to fulfill their destiny and make the most of these gifts. Brett has made more with his God-given talents than most people in this world, including myself.

Coach Burrows, Coach Cremins and Arthur Blank all made a promise to Brett and then delivered on that promise. I made a promise to myself to not quit basketball out of fear and stuck to that promise. Although I have not kept all my promises and have often fallen short, I hold one thing dear to my heart. The ultimate promise came from God in the birth of His only son Jesus Christ. The belief in this promise ensures everlasting life, a guarantee stated in John 3:16. I know God will not fail in that promise and during difficult times, during the death of loved ones, during my divorce, during financial struggles, one promise holds true. God is with me always. God loves me. This I know is a promise kept!

L/R Claudette, Brett and TeriLynn Decker

CHAPTER 7

The Great Wall

"By the seventh day God had finished the work he had been doing; so on the seventh day He rested from all His work. Then God blessed the seventh day and made it holy, because on it He rested from all the work of creating that he had done" (Genesis 2:2–3)

As Mom and Dad sat at the kitchen table with pen and paper in hand, a family project began to take shape. The collaborative effort produced a tidy sketch of a retaining wall on the backside of our home perched along a Western North Carolina mountainside to level the backyard. The 155-foot railroad tie wall was something of an architectural masterpiece when one considers that my parents were mere novices with more creativity than learned skill. Dad's crude drawing needed manpower for implementation. That meant the Decker men, including three teenaged boys not totally adverse to hard labor but with a preference for athletic endeavors over heavy lifting. For most households, a family project might take up a Saturday afternoon, perhaps a couple of weekends for larger projects. From the sheer magnitude of our project, we put all other weekend activities on hold for the foreseeable future. The railroad ties were held together by steel spikes. Each tie had to be dragged by hand. We used steel cable to secure the retaining wall toward the house and held the cable with metal spikes, which were cemented into the ground. The wall stood more than eight feet tall at its highest point. When it came time to back fill the dirt, dump truck after dump truck delivered the cargo. When the wall was finally complete, we sowed grass and for the first time our home on Chapel Road had a true backyard, which only meant that I now had more grass to cut! This was no let's-make-a-trip-to-Home-Depot-and-pick-up-a-gallon-of-paint project. The project took more than two years to complete. This family project was my father's first real instillation of work ethic in his teenaged boys. I, for one, also learned the true importance of time management. I owe much of my work ethic today to the lessons learned in that two-year span of my life building the Great Wall.

During the early 1980s, our family moved into a beautiful and spacious home on the top of Allen Mountain in Black Mountain, North Carolina. The house jutted out the side of a mountain like something on a postcard. Our front yard was flat with some rolling terrain. However, the backyard dropped severely toward Allen Mountain Drive. During the summers, my brother and I built a three-hole golf course in the front yard. We would turn on the outside lights and play all evening with plastic golf balls. The front yard and driveway was ideal for football, basketball and golf. Conversely, the backyard was like walking down a wooded cliff. Over a stretch of two summers, my father's rule was very simple: "You can play golf all day during summer vacation, but at five o'clock you are to be here at the house ready to work." When Dad informed me of our new working arrangement, I knew my summer dream life of swimming, golf and television was over.

I was already an entrepreneur in the lawn care business. Since the age of ten, I mowed yards for my summer money. The best lawn job was the Klutz's yard a short distance from our house. They lived on the ninth hole at Black Mountain Golf Course. I would mow their entire lawn once a week for five dollars. But the big payday came after the work was done in the form of all the golf balls I found in the yard, which seemed to be an endless supply given the out-of-bounds stakes on the left side of the short, downhill hole and the propensity of players to hook tee shots OB. I also got to swim in their pool to cool off afterward. The job was more joy than anything. However, the family's home project curtailed my joy. There would be no afternoon swim or prized golf balls scavenged from the bushes. Worst of all, I was about to embark on a wage-less summer "vacation." I'm sure in today's politically correct world it might be frowned upon to make a child do manual labor at home. I often asked Dad if we were going to get any money for our hard work. His response was like the refrain to a song. "I will let you have dinner tonight," he would say. This five o'clock ritual continued for twenty-four months, including summer and weekends during spring and fall. It seemed like forever.

Dad's work ethic began as a child. His grandparents, Max and Cora Lee Decker, had sixteen children (an equal number of both sexes) including his father Clifford. My great-grandparents were teenagers when they started their family. During the Great Depression, their focus was narrowed on feeding those sixteen mouths. The Decker family farm raised cotton and peanuts for their cash crops and used that money for clothes and shoes. Each child had one pair of overalls for the year and a pair of shoes worn only during the winter months. The remainder of the year the children went barefoot. When the offspring reached their teen years, they began work at the various hosiery mills in Valdese, North Carolina. Money earned went into the family pot. Each child would use the money earned to give back to the family. Neither of my great grandparents could read nor write, but they began a family tree that continues to produce. Their story was so inspiring that during the 1930s, the entire family was featured in *Life Magazine*.

As a young boy, my father would work all day when he went to his grandparents' farm. The women would cook during the day as the men worked in the fields. After working, the family would thank the Lord for all their gifts. Then the family would partake in the feast. In building the Great Wall, my father had the opportunity to pass on similar work ethic to his three boys, allowing his children to work for their food. My parents believed in an allowance for their children as long as it was earned. My first allowance was twenty-five cents. Mom taught us to make our beds daily, take out the trash and clear the table after dinner. They were just a few of my many chores as a six-year-old. My brothers and I would keep our money in our piggy banks. When I turned seven, I finally got to mow the yard after several failed attempts at convincing Dad I was old enough to handle the lawnmower. The additional increased my allowance to one dollar and eventually five dollars. My parents also rewarded us for good grades on our report cards. They did a wonderful job of instilling the balanced relationship of work, making money and saving money.

I have never reared a child of my own. However, I truly appreciate the lessons learned through hard work. It is important to teach children that money does have value and that it must be received through hard work. I have also learned through my own experience as a child and through teaching junior golfers the very basic principle that most children will choose the path of least resistance. In other words, give your child the choice between playing on their computer and doing house work. More often than not, they will choose the computer. How about a Saturday afternoon of raking leaves or watching television? Most children will choose the latter. We have become an entitled society in America, where we want more things for less work. I, too, have fallen into this trap many times. Fortunately, my parents espoused a work ethic that has gotten me through these difficult financial times. I believe that it is the responsibility of parents, teachers and coaches to instill a work ethic in our children. Simple concept not so easily implemented.

Several years ago, I was speaking at our annual junior golf banquet. I related the story of my first personal experience with Tiger Woods. It occurred on June 17, 2002. The reason I remember this eventful date is that Tiger had won the 102nd U.S. Open at the Black Course of Bethpage in New York the day before. I was working at the Grand Cypress Academy of Golf in Orlando and for two weeks prior to the U.S. Open, a construction crew built a movie stage house on one of our three academy holes. Tiger would be shooting a commercial for Buick, and the house was part of the movie set. It was amazing to watch the construction. I knew the commercial was going to be shot soon, but I didn't know the actual day or time. On the morning of June 17, 2002, I arrived at work at 7:15 to set up the video cameras for a video computer lesson with a new student, a gentleman from Brazil. As I was setting up the video cameras, I looked out onto the driving range tee and saw that it was empty. Suddenly, through the bushes, I saw the figure of a man. It appeared to be Tiger Woods. Back then when Tiger filmed a commercial, the production company would employ a body double—a man who looked very much like Tiger, especially from a distance. Although this body double looked like Tiger, he certainly didn't swing like Tiger. He wore the exact same clothing as Tiger each day of the shoot and helped with the camera positioning, which enabled the lights and cameras to be perfect. Then Tiger arrived and the crew was ready to shoot the commercial. The reason I know this is because I gave the body double a golf lesson while he was at Grand Cypress.

My skepticism peaked when the figure appeared from the bushes. "That is probably Tiger's body double because no way is Tiger showing up at seven thirty for a commercial shoot the morning after winning the U.S. Open," I thought to myself. "I'm sure he's resting." Suddenly, the man took a few practice swings. "That's no double, that's Tiger Woods," I said under my breath. As Tiger was hitting balls on the driving range, a golf cart pulled up to the tee. An elderly gentleman got out of the cart and started walking directly toward Tiger. I did not recognize the man, but I knew he was most likely my eight o'clock lesson. A large lump grew in my throat as I approached the two men. One was the most recognizable athlete on the planet, a man who had just won the U.S. Open. The other was my next student. Neither man spoke a word as I approached. I stuck out my right hand and said to my presumed student, "Hi, my name is Jon Decker. I will be your instructor this morning."

As the gentleman extended his right hand in my direction he proclaimed very loudly in broken English, "I don't believe it. I come to America to take my first golf lesson of my life and look who is here, Tiger Woods!"

Without hesitation I responded, "He usually shows up for all my lessons." Suddenly, Tiger turned to me and gave me his classic smile. What a relief! The ice was broken for a very uncomfortable situation. I finally pried my new student from Tiger's spell and we both walked toward the video area to begin our lesson. I was excited to see Tiger hitting balls in person. However, I respected his privacy. Tiger never spoke a word too me, but his smile said, "Thank you."

My student was still on cloud nine when the lesson began. Afterward, he drove to his villa at the resort in haste and proclaimed, "I am going to call all my friends in Brazil." The next day I was driving to the employee cafeteria in my golf cart. I saw my student with his wife driving in a cart in my direction. He slammed on the brakes, jumped out of the cart and yelled, "You tell my wife, you tell my wife, I saw Tiger Woods!"

None of his friends in Brazil—not even his own wife—believed the story of his first golf lesson in America. I looked at his wife, smiled. and said, "Yes, your husband did see Tiger Woods."

When I told this story at the junior banquet, I asked the young golfers how many of them aspired to becoming a PGA Tour player. Nearly half of them raised their hands. "Well, this is who you are all chasing, Tiger Woods," I said to the wide-eyed group. At the time, Tiger was the number one player in the world, and less than twenty-four hours after winning the U.S. Open, he was practicing! I told the juniors and their parents, "Honestly, if I had just won the U.S. Open, I would probably have just been getting in bed at 7:30 a.m. after celebrating all night." Regardless of your personal opinions of Tiger Woods, there is no doubt of the man's work ethic. On that memorable morning, Tiger was hitting low punch shots on the range. I suspect in the U.S. Open he hit a shot that wasn't up to his expectations and was determined to work it out on the range. That's what I love about golf. There is always something to work on.

I am not a big fan of the swing changes Tiger made post Butch Harmon. The Tiger I saw that day on the range was a player at the top of his game hitting golf shots creatively with instinct. He wasn't making some robotic, stack and tilt, hold-on swing move. He was hitting golf shots. In his mind first, the place where all shots are played before the club is ever drawn back, Tiger was looking at his target and hitting a particular shot. He was a shot maker! Every shot was low, boring through the air and perfectly struck. Each shot looked like one that would be played into a strong wind or a shot from beneath some trees. It was magnificent to watch. In retrospect, perhaps Tiger was preparing for the British Open about a month out on a links course that demands a low, boring shot. Preparation is not only necessary for tournament golf but also an important part of work ethic. It doesn't assure success, but it sure does increase the odds of it.

I told the audience at the junior banquet that story for one reason, to inspire them! I try to instill a work ethic into all my students, whether their sport is tennis or golf; whether they aspire to be the next president or make the A–B honor roll for the first time. They must be pushed and they must learn to work. God did not form us in his image to walk on this Earth to be ordinary. We are to be extraordinary!

During our junior camps one summer, I spent way too much time picking up after all thirty of our kids. Every day, campers would leave their clubs, gloves or clothing behind. One day I had a child leave his bicycle behind. How do you leave your bicycle? I sat the kids down and established a new rule for the camp, a rule that is still in effect today at the New Albany Golf Academy. The rule is very simple: If a child leaves something behind, and I find it, the child must vacuum my office to get it back. After explaining the camp's new rule, one child asked me, "Why do we need this new rule?" My answer was very simple. "Your parents worked to make the money to buy you these clubs, and you must work to get them back," I said. The next day my new rule went into effect after one of the children left their club behind. My office floor was spotless the next day. During the junior banquet, I asked all the children, "How many of you had to vacuum my office this year?" Half the room raised their hand. After the banquet, many parents came up to me and thanked me for establishing this new rule. It truly does take a village to raise a child.

In life, we are all held accountable for our actions. The sooner a child understands this concept, the sooner they will adapt to the realities of this often cruel world. In building the Great Wall, my father defined guidelines that he expected to be met. We were given the freedom to choose our leisure activities. In my case, I chose to play golf over swimming and television. I knew that I needed to get up early, get to the golf course and start playing. Those summer days I played 36 holes per day, got myself home, had dinner with my family, and then went out to work until dark. Although I often resisted my father's authority, there is no doubt that this two-year span taught me to cherish my leisure time. It also gave me an understanding of the importance of time management. And it made me accountable. Hebrews 12:11 states it best, *"Now, discipline always seems painful rather than pleasant at the time, but later it yields the peaceful fruit of righteousness to those who have been trained by it."*

In my research for this book, I found more than sixty verses in the Bible relating to work. My work ethic, plus my passion for teaching, has enabled me to produce a good living—a true gift by the grace of God. I am blessed to have a career for which I have a passion and love. However, with every blessing and gift from God comes responsibility. My greatest regret from my failed marriage is that I became a workaholic. Every golf lesson represented income; income paid the bills and as I advanced in my career my mortgage and bills increased. I became a slave to my house for many reasons. As I have grown in my Christian faith, I have learned one very basic principle: With work, you need a day of rest. On the seventh day, God chose to rest. On the seventh day, I chose to work. I became addicted to my production and set myself up for eventual failure. It took years for me to learn this lesson; years I will never get back. Although the golf business fuels my passion for the game, teaching and helping others, the golf business can be very cruel. Weekend and holiday play increase revenue. Whenever a young adult comes to me and asks about the golf business for a career choice, I always reply with a question. "Do you like your weekends and summer holidays?" I ask.

For years I told myself, "I believe in Christ. I will just pray." Prayer is good and very important to the Christian faith. However, there is no substitute for Sunday worship. Although it is rare when I get an entire Sunday off, I mark off my mornings and now go to church. In 2013, I only missed one Sunday service. I have also learned that it is all right to say no when a student asks for a Sunday morning lesson time. My response now is "I go to church on Sunday mornings." I certainly don't have all the answers to the balance of work and rest, but I do know that both work and rest are essential. Don't give your child everything he or she wants. Make them earn it. I remember the pride of paying off my first car. Teach them to work, teach them to save, and teach them to work for the glory of God. Excellence is the payoff. Teach your children to worship on Sunday, to enjoy the Sabbath with rest, fellowship, and rejuvenation. After all, even God needed one day of rest

My teenage years will be defined by many experiences, some good and some bad. But no experience taught me more about the realities of life than the building of the Great Wall. Several years after the wall was finished, my father announced to the family that we would be building a new home in Black Mountain. In 1987, the building of our new home was complete. I took particular pride in the new home because I had helped build it. I spent one summer clearing the land where the house now sits; this time for wages. The next winter, I worked with the construction crew assisting in the framing of the house. Although I took pride in both these jobs, the completion of the Great Wall for no money in exchange gave me more in return. When we moved from that home on Chapel Road,

I thought to myself, "All that work for nothing." As an adult, I now know that the lessons learned from building the Great Wall will endure. They will be passed on to my students and maybe one day to children of my own. The irony of building the Great Wall was that our family never really enjoyed the benefits of that level backyard. The real winners were the new homeowners. The Great Wall represents what God has in mind for everyone, work for excellence in God's name so that others will benefit. The Great Wall was worth the work and effort after all!

As Seen Through My Eyes

Coach Kenny Ford, retired head football coach at Charles D. Owen High School

Courtesy of the Black Mountain News

In 1985, I was the head golf coach of McDowell High School in Marion, North Carolina. In the spring of that year, Ann Marie Decker became the coach for Charles D. Owen High School. "Wow!" was my reaction upon hearing the news. I was very aware of what Mrs. Decker was going through coaching an all boys team. Being from "the Valley" and an Owen alumnus, I knew all the boys she was coaching and respected what she was doing. She was sacrificing herself for her family, their school and the community.

The coaching fraternity for high school sports is an "all men's club." At each match, all the men would pair up and have their own "tournament" where cash was sometimes exchanged after a day's work. The pecking order was dominated by the larger schools of Buncombe County. I remember Ann Marie as being more or less an outcast. I really felt no obligation to play with her but wanted too. I always enjoyed playing golf with her and having the opportunity to talk about the kids from our home town and what they were up too. I wanted to take care of her.

The Swannanoa Valley was a very special place to grow up, and I am very proud to show it! Through the stories in this book, Jon has brought back memories from my career as a teacher and coach that makes me thankful to call Black Mountain home.

CHAPTER 8

Coach Mom

10   Asheville East, Wednesday, June 1, 1983

Owen Golfers 'Best Ever,' Says Coach

The Owen High School Golf Team shot a 325 at Etowah Golf Country Club to win the Western North Carolina state sectional on May 16. Hendersonville High School placed second in the western sectional.

Owen's score qualified its golfers to participate in the state title games at Chapel Hill on May 23-24.

At Chapel Hill, Owen finished 17th in the state. David Ballard and Jim Davis both shot 163 to lead the Owen team in the second day of the tournament.

"The boys were a little jittery," said coach Ralph Singleton, "but played better the next day and gained some valuable experience." Coach Singleton said he was pleased with his young team.

"There are around 200 high school golf teams in the state," he

WINNERS- The Owen High School Golf Team won the WNC members are (L-R): Scott Tuttle, Jim Davis, Michael Decker, David Ballard, Daron Slone and Jon Decker.

Courtesy of the Asheville Citizen Times

"If you forgive anyone's sins, their sins are for-given; if you do not forgive them, they are not forgiven" (John 20:23).

My classroom for the game I love was the Black Mountain Golf Course, the perfect sanctuary for fledgling golfers seeking to become battle tested in money games. Among an eclectic group of players from a variety of backgrounds, I lost my innocence of adolescence and learned the practical but harsh realities of being street smart. The short (by today's standards), municipal layout took local knowledge and a unique arsenal of shots to master; to the locals this playground was simply known as "the rock." During my first three years at Charles D. Owen High, I spent many hours in the city course's classroom expanding my vocabulary with colorful words like *press, bloody nine,* and *Vegas*—gambling terms unfamiliar to most high school students. As members of the dominant prep team in Western North Carolina, my teammates and I were privy to both the nuances of the golf course and the competitive idiosyncrasies of those who played in the daily gang-some—a team competition headed by an appointed captain. Individual side bets were arranged between competitors with the better player often giving strokes for the sake of fairness. My teammates and I became better players. We played in the gang-some on weekends. The pro shop was run by city employees, including the late Wilburn Waters and the late Bromo Burrell. Bromo would often loan me money when my game was off, to pay my debt. He obliged with an interest free loan that was always paid back in expedient fashion. The young guns of the Owen golf team were frequent gang-some players, along with David Ballard, Scott Tuttle, Jim Davis, Daron Slone, Tim Maxwell, Mark and Mike Marett and my brother, Michael. We were playing against seasoned veterans, who were not ready to give up their place atop the throne. Although they had various skill levels, the competition was always heated and friendly—win or lose. Many of those fellow competitors are still my friends today. Many of them shaped who I am as a man. However, my senior year in high school would eventually be influenced not by a man but by a woman, my mother. In 1985, my high school golf coach went by the simple title, Coach Mom.

OHS Golf Team Going Great Guns

The 1984 Charles D. Owen Golf Team has steadily improved since the opening of the season. Eight matches have been played and the team has won five first places, two second places and one third place.

The team has been sparked by returning players Scott Tuttle and David Ballard. Owen's golf team is coached by Ralph Singleton.

The 1984 Owen High School golf team is pictured above. Kneeling are [l-r]: Mar Marett, Michael Decker, Jon Decker; [standing, l-r]: Jim Davis, David Ballard, Sco Tuttle, Tim Maxwell, Daron Slone, and Coach Ralph Singleton.

Courtesy of the Asheville Citizen Times

Coach Ralph Singleton guided Owen High's golf program for years. The veteran coach and longtime high school teacher loved to play the game. Prep coaches have never been known as high-wage earners for the many hours they spend with student athletes. That's particularly true with coaches of "minor" sports like golf. However, Coach Singleton reaped other benefits, including free golf several days a week and an escape from the classroom for an early tee time. It was a perfect fit for Coach Singleton's lifestyle. The coaches organized the team, made the team schedule, chaperoned the team to the matches and then played golf among the other coaches. At the end of the day, the scores were totaled, and we all went home excited. The highlight for me was looking in the box scores of the *Asheville Citizen-Times* the next morning. We got very little press at first, but over time, our dominance started getting write-ups; people took notice and golf became relevant in the Swannanoa Valley of Western North

Carolina. The morning after the match, Principal Charles A. Lytle would announce the scores over the public address system. Suddenly golf was *cool* at Owen. It was one of the most memorable times of my life. I often draw from those memories when I teach high school players.

The teams from 1983–1985 rewrote the record books for golf at Owen High. In 1983, our team was the first in school history to win the WNC Sectional Championship and qualify for the state tournament in Chapel Hill. During my first two years of high school, my game struggled. However, through hard work and dedication, I managed to make All-Conference my sophomore year. I started to blossom as a player my junior year. My first match that year was memorable for a couple of reasons. I had broken my wrist during basketball practice, forcing me to miss the final month of the basketball

Owen golf team going to state finals

Congratulations to the Owen golf team for winning the Little Mac Conference championship played at Etowah last week. Owen beat Hendersonville by six shots for the title.

Scott Tuttle, David Ballard and Jon Decker made All-Conference with their play. Coach Ralph Singleton says that this is the finest group of golfers that he has seen at Owen in his twenty-four years of coaching there.

Coach Singleton wants to thank the men who have supported the golf team this year. The conference tourna-

ment was a great success due to the contributions of Carl Bartlett, Steve King, Tom Blizard and Chuck Henderson.

The conference scores are as follows: Owen, 628; Hendersonville, 634; West Henderson, 640; Mitchell, 901.

Individual scores were as follows: Jon Decker, 83; Jim Davis, 79; David Ballard, 76; Daron Sloan, 92; and Scott Tuttle, 87.

The team will compete in the State Finals on Monday and Tuesday, May 23 and 24 in Chapel Hill. Good luck to all the team members.

Courtesy of the Asheville
Citizen Times

Page 4--May 19, 1983, Black Mountain News

SPORTS

The Owen Golf Team will be competing in the state play-offs next Monday and Tuesday, May 23 and 24. Pictured with their plaque from the Little Mac Tournament played last week are: [l-r] Coach Ralph Singleton, Mike Decker, Jon Decker, Jim Davis, Mark Marrett, David Ballard, Daron Sloan and Scott Tuttle.

Courtesy of the Black Mountain News

season. We opened the spring golf season with a dual match against our bitter rival, A.C. Reynolds, one of the largest schools in WNC. The Rockets might have been a much larger school but we dominated their classification in head-to-head matches that season.

Before the match at our home course, Black Mountain GC, I went to Coach Singleton that early spring morning and informed him that I was ready to play. "Jon," he said, "you still have your cast on."

"Don't worry, Coach, I'm getting it taken off today," I said. My mother picked me up from school and drove me to the doctor. After six weeks of my wrist being immobile, the cast was removed. Mom then drove me to the golf course and Coach Singleton taped up my wrist and forearm. Coach Singleton applied enough tape to form a soft cast immobilizing my right wrist again. The temperature on that March afternoon *rose* to the 50s but felt much colder with a 20-mph northwesterly wind. As the sun set that afternoon, the temperature plummeted, making the golf ball feel like a rock. I hit my approach shot on the 15th hole *fat*. I doubled over in pain and began to cry but refused to quit. When the round was over, I had carded an 85. Coach Singleton cut the tape off of my arm, and I became nauseous. My arm looked grotesque and many of the players turned their heads at the sight of my black-and-blue limb. My arm was weak without the support of the tape and seemed smaller in size compared to my healthy left arm. Despite the pain, I was joyful because my score qualified as one of our four counted toward the match. Our score was good enough to beat Reynolds, mission accomplished! We had won our first match of the year! I will never forget that match and the comments from one of the Reynolds seniors, Mike Dill, as he spoke to his teammate, "I just got beat by a guy who played the last three holes with one arm."

The season of 1984 was magical for many reasons. For the second straight year, I made All-Conference and our golf team won the Little Mountain Athletic Conference Championship, and for the second straight year, our team won the WNC Sectional Championship. We advanced to the state tournament in Chapel Hill and an opportunity to redeem the previous year's poor performance. When we arrived in Chapel Hill, Roy Williams greeted us. Roy had coached varsity basketball at Owen and was good friends with Coach Singleton. Roy, who has coached the North Carolina Tar Heels to two NCAA Division I championships, is in the Charles D. Owen High Hall of Fame. He played freshman ball at UNC and served as an assistant to legendary Carolina Coach Dean Smith for a number of years before taking over the basketball program at the University of Kansas and eventually returning home to UNC. Roy not only spent time with our team but for two days followed us and supported Coach Singleton.

Several times in the round, the two coaches came by my group and offered words of encouragement. To hear Coach Williams yell, "Good shot, Jon!" gave me confidence. I played great for two days, and in the end was the low man for our team finishing 21st in the state individually while our team finished in a respectable fifth. As one of the smaller schools competing against the big boys from Raleigh and Charlotte, we had held our own. Many of my fellow competitors in that state competition would become close friends of mine in college.

At the end of the 1984 golf season, Coach Singleton retired from Owen High. We also lost three seniors to graduation. Only Jim Davis and I returned as starters. We had a strong team but no coach. There was no one available from the high school to coach the team, so some of the parents including Ellen Johnson, mother of Brad Johnson, encouraged my mother to take over the coaching duties. Reluctantly, Mom said, "Yes." I had mixed emotions at first, but knew our team needed a coach. Jim and I were a strong one-two punch. Overall, he was the better junior player than I after three years of high school, but my game was improving. Eric Morgan was another highly skilled player at Enka High School. However, Enka's team didn't have the support and depth to consistently beat us. I was pretty confident that Jim and I, along with a cadre of talented prospects in Tim Maxwell, Mark Marett and my brother Michael, were a formidable team that could make a third trip back to Chapel Hill.

Several days before the first match of the 1985 season, I ran into Tim Maxwell in the hallway before class. "Did you hear the news? Jim transferred to Reynolds!" I couldn't believe it, but it was true. Jim and his family made the decision for him to change high schools during the spring of his senior season. At first our friendship was fractured. I was angry and disappointed to say the least, but I knew that I needed to put my personal feelings aside and move on. This was my senior year and I was going to make the most of it. I have never been more focused or more *in the zone* than I was from March through May of 1985. I was medalist in almost all my matches, and our team was playing well. Reynolds was in the Big Mountain Athletic Conference. With the addition of Jim Davis, their team on paper was certainly the one to beat. One of the highlights of my senior year was at Etowah Golf Course during a big conference match. I made a hole-in-one on the par-three 17th hole with a 6-iron to win the tournament by a shot. Our team was on a roll and I felt like we could compete with anyone on the road to Chapel Hill.

Coach Mom inspired our team. She insisted that we learn the rules of golf. The year before in Chapel Hill, I had made a bad drop that cost me one stroke and possibly a top-10 finish. The rules of golf are designed to help a player not penalize them. The more familiar with the rules, the better decisions the player will make during a round or tournament competition. My mother understood the importance of the rules and had the team attend a rules seminar. Mom was an 11-handicap player herself. Her assets included organizing the team, her positive attitude, and insistence that her team know the rules. This leadership paid dividends as the season progressed.

Mom was also adamant about our dress code. Before Mom, we were allowed to wear jeans during matches. Mom championed school spirit and demanded that our team dress as gentlemen. Matching slacks or shorts along with our maroon golf shirts were worn to all our matches. Her coaching style was met with some resistance, but I didn't care. Owen was winning matches!

I am fairly confident that in 1985, my mother was the only female high school golf coach in the entire state of North Carolina, coaching an all-male team. Heads often turned as our team pulled into the parking lot, but over time, the other coaches were cordial to my mother. Most of the other coaches treated Mom well and with respect, especially McDowell High's head golf coach Kenny Ford. Coach Ford always welcomed my mother and often asked her if she would like to join his group. I will always be grateful for his hospitality toward my mother, a graciousness that my mom just recently told me about more than thirty years later. However, some coaches were not as accepting of my mother's presence. I knew this fact and who those coaches were which only hardened my resolve to focus more. In golf, your opponents are the golf course and your mind. My play only got better the worse the other coaches treated Mom.

My relationship with Jim during the 1985 season began to improve. As young boys, we played golf, basketball, football, tennis, had sleepovers, went on beach trips together and shared classes. On the golf course, we were fierce competitors and would often pair up and play matches against much older men. Alongside Jim, I learned how to gamble. I remember one day I showed up at the course and Jim said, "I've already made our side bets." I looked on the sheet of paper, and we had more than seventy different bets. During these matches, we would often say to each other when putting for birdie, "If you knock this in, I will get it out of the hole for you." It was our way of rooting for each other. When a birdie was made, we would scream so loud it would echo throughout the mountains. Those gambling days taught me both good and bad life lessons.

Jim's transfer created a great divide that also impacted our matches at Black Mountain. We stopped teaming up against other players. I would often see Jim practicing at the Black Mountain, and we would have brief conversations that slowly began to repair our friendship. As expected, Reynolds won the Big Mac Championship, but our team didn't play its best golf and came in second during the Little Mac Championship. The sectionals were next at Connestee Falls Golf Club and an opportunity to return to Chapel Hill for the State Tournament. The pairings came out, and for the first time all year, I was paired with my lifelong friend, Jim Davis. As I walked into the locker room an hour or so before my tee time, I felt totally at ease and mentally ready for the challenge at hand. The entire Reynolds team was sitting in the locker room. "Hello," I said to no one in particular. The inner peace I felt proved an early sign that I was going to play well. Golf is a game of confidence, and the sport is ultimately played in the mind. The fact that golf is much more than a physical skill is the reason for the game's immense popularity. As I came off the putting green and walked to the first tee, I knew this day would be special. It would be a day to remember.

On the first hole, my drive split the fairway. I got off to a fast start and felt like I was in complete control of my game. Jim struggled that day, but I did not pay attention to anyone but myself. I talked very little and took every single shot one at a time. I turned the front nine in even par but started to struggle on the back nine. As I stood on the par-3 17th hole, I was four over par. I needed to make a birdie. A solid iron shot produced a 30-foot birdie putt, giving me an outside chance for birdie. As I got to the green, I noticed the coach for Western Carolina University walking up to the green. He was recruiting Jim. I stood over the putt and as soon as it left the putter I knew it was solid. It rolled right in the heart for a birdie! Three-over-par might qualify me individually for the state tournament, but I wasn't sure.

My approach shot on the par-4 finishing hole left me with an extremely difficult downhill, 22-foot, left-to-right breaking putt. The putt was so fast that all I had to do was touch the ball. Many of the players were putting the ball off the green that day. Par would be a great score. Mine was one of the last groups that day and a small gallery of players and coaches—some college coaches scouting prospects—stood around the green. Coach Mom stood anxiously behind the green. I walked over to her, and for the first time during the entire round, I uttered something other than "nice shot" or "thank you."

"Mom, what is the low score?" I asked.

"I don't want to tell you, Jon. Just putt," she said.

"Mom, what is the low score?" I demanded.

"Seventy-four," she said reluctantly. I had to hole the putt for a tie.

I surveyed the putt from every angle. Surprisingly, I wasn't nervous as I assessed the most important putt of my life. This putt was for our team and for my mother. I visualized the ball going into the hole from the top left corner, so I aimed well left, made a very small swing, and let the momentum of the putter touch the ball. The ball started slowly moving. As soon as the ball got halfway to the hole, I started walking to my right. The putt was rolling so slowly that I could have walked to the hole as it entered the left side of the hole. As the ball entered the cup, I screamed, "Woohoo!" What happened next represented one of the greatest acts of sportsmanship I have ever experienced. Jim walked to the hole, reached in and got my ball out of the cup. Tossing me the ball, he laughed and said, "Great putt, Jon!" It was like we were gambling with the older men at the Black Mountain GC in the gang-some and had just hustled two dollars. I had finished birdie-birdie and was tied for the lead!

Due to limited daylight, the officials checked with the remaining two groups behind our foursome. None of the players in the groups yet to finish was going to tie or beat 74. Eric Morgan and I were set to begin the playoff on number 10 immediately. I hit a 2-iron in the middle of the fairway while Eric's tee shot found the right rough. After he missed the green in a difficult spot, I knew that keeping my ball below the hole was paramount. I hit a sand wedge short of the hole leaving myself a nice uphill putt. Eric got on the green, missed his par putt, and tapped in for bogey on the first playoff hole. I had a birdie putt straight uphill from about 20 feet. I knew all I needed was a two putt and purposely made sure not to race the ball by the hole. I lagged the ball several inches beneath the hole and tapped in for the win. Till this day, I have never been more satisfied over a round of golf. Although I have had much better scores recreationally and professionally, that round was about the team and was played for my mother. I knew I would be going to Chapel Hill as an individual but wondered how our team had done.

As the gallery watching the playoff walked back to the clubhouse, a beaming Mark Marett quickly approached. "We did it, Jon!" he said. "We beat Reynolds and we are going to Chapel Hill!" I couldn't believe it. We celebrated on the van ride home. My teammates said that Jim took the time to congratulate them and wished the team well at the State Tournament. Our team drove straight to the Black Mountain Golf Course to let the members of the gangsome know we were going back to Chapel Hill for the third year in a row. Indeed, it was a very special day.

I often reflect on the lessons learned during the 1985 golf season. Lessons that add substance to what I have learned as a Christian man. Personally, the most difficult part of being a Christian is forgiveness. No greater example of this is when Jesus was on the cross. Jesus spoke, ***"Father forgive them, for they do not know what they are doing"*** ***(Luke 23:34)***. I am as guilty as most in holding a grudge, and I can be very stubborn. When I first learned of Jim's transfer, I was angry and used that anger to fuel my golf game. Whether this helped my game or not really doesn't matter because inside I was hurting. As I began to forgive Jim and simply let go, I actually believe that I received inner strength, the strength of the Holy Spirit. When we as humans act in God's way, we don't always receive the gifts of the world, but we do always receive His grace and comfort. Forgiveness allows your soul to be free and not bound to the past trespasses of others. Forgiveness allows your soul not only to be free but for your soul to grow in strength; slowly the pain and hurting turn to strength and resolve.

Jim and I eventually became the best of friends again. That summer, we went on a trip to Myrtle Beach together and after Jim's stint in the Navy, he moved down to Orlando where we were roommates. It was like old times again. Jim has been such a good friend to me during the years. He was in my wedding party and always lends a hand when help is needed. He has also loaned me money when I was in need. Many years ago, my mortgage was due. I had the money but unfortunately would not be paid until Friday, two days after the due date. Without hesitation Jim loaned me the money, which I repaid on Friday. True friends in life are difficult to find. I am fortunate to have Jim Davis as a friend.

Courtesy of the Asheville Citizen Times

Our team played poorly at the State Tournament in 1985. But for this senior and the rest of the Warhorse golf team, it really didn't matter. Once again, heads turned as my mother led us to Chapel Hill. The *Asheville Citizen-Times* did a nice story about my season and the relationship with Coach Mom. I am blessed to have two wonderful parents that have given of their time, resources and support for the betterment of their children's lives. When I was twenty-seven, my parents divorced. I was not very happy and frankly, shocked because I had no idea there was even a problem. The lessons I learned from golf in my 1985 season helped me through this most difficult time. Once again my stubborn, hurt self harbored the anger, built a wall and drew a deep line in the sand. Once again inside I was hurting and thought only of myself. "How was I going to move on in life with my parents now divorced?" My friends rallied around me, including Jim while we were roommates in Orlando.

It's funny how at that moment in my life, God put me with someone who had taught me the importance of forgiveness, when I needed to forgive the most. Once I forgave and accepted my parent's divorce, I began to look at them both as individuals instead of as a team. As a couple, they parented as a team. As individuals, I got to know them both on a more personal level. Relationships are always growing. Either you are growing together or you are growing apart. To grow together in any relationship, it is imperative that you forgive those that ask for forgiveness. This concept is not easy. However, it is critical for any relationship to truly last. I have learned in life that being a Christian is not easy.

In the end, forgiveness is very simple. Jesus Christ died on a cross for our sins. By believing in Christ and asking for forgiveness, we are forgiven. As the three men were hanging on the crosses together, one criminal still mocked Jesus, "If you are the King, why do you not save us?" The other criminal spoke up, "How can you judge him, he has done nothing wrong." The other criminal then asked Jesus, "Remember me in heaven." At that moment, the criminal was forgiven because he believed. Jesus didn't try to save his own life or the lives of the criminals. He died on the cross that historic day so that we all would be saved from our sins. If Jesus can die so that my sins are forgiven, the least I can do is to forgive others.

In June of 1985, I graduated from Owen High. I learned some difficult lessons that year and began a new chapter of my life. Coach Mom would go on to be the coach for the 1986 team that included my brother, Michael. Jim would go to Appalachian State University on a golf scholarship, and I was headed to East Carolina University. That year, I learned the importance of inner peace and letting go. The fact that I forgave my friend allowed me to move on and play some of the best golf of my life. I also learned the importance of lifelong friends. God gives us our parents but we choose our friends. These friendships take time to evolve and are never to be taken for granted. In the end, I learned that a mother can coach her sons, lead by example and inspire a group of young men. Coach Mom's belief in our team will never be forgotten. Thank you Coach Mom. I love you!

CHAPTER 9

Failure

"The woman said to the serpent, 'We may eat fruit from the trees in the garden, but God did say, 'You must not eat fruit from the tree that is in the middle of the garden, and you must not touch it, or you will die.'" "You will not certainly die," the serpent said to the woman. "For God knows that when you eat from it your eyes will be opened, and you will be like God, knowing good and evil." When the woman saw that the fruit of the tree was good for food and pleasing to the eye, and also desirable for gaining wisdom, she took some and ate it. She also gave some to her husband, who was with her, and he ate it." (Genesis 3:2–6)

In August of 1985, I was resting comfortably on my bunk bed in Belk Dorm room 303-C. Classes for my freshman year at East Carolina University were scheduled to begin the next week, and I was in relax mode adjusting to college life. The heat from a searing summer sun sent the temperature in our room soaring north of 80 degrees, which caused an abnormal amount of heaviness in my eyelids for so early in the day. That and the sound of the mostly ineffective window fan induced a light sleep. As I started to fall off, I heard our suite door open and the sound of footsteps approaching down the hallway. After several seconds of silence, I heard the footsteps retreat back down the hallway and the suite door came to a close. In unison, the doors throughout the suite swung open and the new group of freshmen recruits came running out of their rooms—all of the recruits but me. I was prepared for the worst news, although I hoped and prayed for the best. Some of my suite mates would make the golf team that night while others' dreams would come to a screeching halt. I knew it would be a difficult decision for Coach Bob Helmick, but I thought, "Maybe I *will* be chosen for the team." I lay in bed and asked very loudly, "Did I make it?" The response came through the closed door. "I'm afraid not, Jon," said my new suite mate Mike Nadeau. "Thank you," I said, turning over on my side. The door opened and my new roommate of two weeks, Jeff Davis, walked in and patted me on my shoulder as I began to cry. "It will be all right, Jon," Jeff consoled. He was among the freshmen making the team. I, on the other hand, would suffer through a very long, sleepless night. As an eighteen-year-old kid, I wrestled with the fact that for the first time in my life, I wasn't good enough. I looked into the mirror of self-reflection and saw failure staring back at me.

During my senior year of high school, I had been recruited by quite a few small universities and accepted by the University of North Carolina at Chapel Hill. A good performance at the state tournament that year had been paramount for an opportunity to play at Carolina. My poor play at state had removed that option and meant that I would have to walk on as a member of the Tar Heels—problematic at best. East Carolina had been an excellent second choice as it satisfied my desire to attend a large university. Besides, I had fallen in love with the Division I school during a visit. Plus, I had a passion for its highly touted football program. To the surprise of my parents, I had turned down the Tar Heels and became a Pirate that May. Now my dream of playing as a freshman had turned into a nightmare.

In retrospect, my becoming a Pirate was part of God's plan for my life. That summer, Coach Helmick called me several times to check on my game. My golf game, especially my short game, was getting razor sharp through rigorous, daily practice sessions. I was the first freshman to arrive in Greenville, North Carolina, in August, two weeks before classes would begin. In my eagerness to begin my college experience, I trucked along the major highway toward Greenville without regard for speed limits or the highway patrolmen on the lookout for fresh-faced newcomers to the area. As I sped through Wilson, North Carolina, one of those patrolmen blue-lighted me as I was exiting the city limits. As he approached the driver's side of my car, my palms became sweaty and a lump formed in my throat, similar to facing a long greenside bunker shot with money on the line. Still, I managed to remain calm as he informed me of my transgression. The speeding ticket not only got my college career off to an ominous start but surely raised Dad's ire. The salve for my wound came the next day from a story in *The East Carolinian*, expressing Coach Helmick's excitement over his freshman recruits. I couldn't help but smile as I read my name.

4 Purple Report - August 1985

GOLF TEAM ADDS SIX RECRUITS

East Carolina golf coach Bob Helmick has announced the signing of six athletes to join the Pirates for the 1985-86 season.

Mike Nadau and John Chapman led Raleigh Millbrook to the 1985 North Carolina state championship and each finished in the top five individually. Chapman was the North State Golf champion winning the tournament earlier this summer.

Chris Winkel will transfer from the University of Arkansas and the Algoona, IA native will be eligible to play in the fall and will be a freshman eligibility wise.

Jeff Davis of Sycamore, ILL, Pat King of Doylestown, PA and Jon Decker of Black Mountain, NC round out the Pirate recruits for 1985.

The Pirates return all-conference performer Mark Arcilesi and two-year Most Valuable Player Mike Bradley, who along with Paul Steelman give ECU a powerful line-up of juniors.

"We'll be as talented as we've ever been," said golf coach Bob Helmick. "You can't place talent on the scoreboard. You must produce and that is where we have failed in the past."

East Carolina will play four fall tournaments which include: the MacGregor Golf Classic in Pickens, SC; the John Ryan Memorial Golf Tournament hosted by Duke University; the Wolfpack Collegiate Invitational and the UNC-Wilmington Fall Invitational.

Courtesy of The East Carolinian

I practiced at Brook Valley Country Club every day. For the first time, I had a driving range at my disposal. Life was great. Prospects seemed endless. I was poised and ready to begin tryouts. My suite mates seemed to stream in daily starting with my roommate, Jeff Davis. Then Mike Nadeau, John Chapman, Chris Rodgers, TJ Jarrett, Pat King and Paul Kruslock all arrived. We were ready to get tryouts underway. It was one of the most memorable times of my life because of the lifelong friendships I would soon develop and the difficult lessons I was about to learn.

I was devastated upon receiving the news that I had failed to make the team. I had never been cut from a team in any sport, let alone the one to which I had dedicated the most time and effort. I was always among the first chosen when picking teams during recess. I was also captain of both my high school basketball and golf teams. This was unfamiliar territory for me, and all I could do that entire night was cry. The next morning, I made up my mind that I was going to transfer to Appalachian State University. At that moment, I believed I had made a mistake coming to East Carolina. Tryouts had been four days that week on three different golf courses, one of which I had never before played. The entire class of freshman recruits, along with the current team, was divided into three groups. All three groups played on three different venues for four straight days, playing the home course of Brook Valley Country Club twice. The first day I played well at the Greenville Country Club—a course I had never seen—and was tied for the lead, beating all the upper classmen and tying freshman T.J. Jarrett with a score of 75. I would later discover that T.J. was first cousins with NASCAR driver Dale Jarrett. I struggled the next two rounds, shooting 87 at Ayden CC and 84 at Brook Valley. My confidence was shattered and I second-guessed nearly every shot. I rebounded with a 78 (tied for low round that day) at Brook Valley the final day, but the bad rounds took their toll in the court of coaches' opinion. The staff decided to go with the more consistent performers.

Several days after the cut, I received a phone call from Coach Helmick. He wanted to talk with me in his office. Coach Helmick told me that he was surprised I got cut because on the first day, he followed me for most of the round and liked what he saw. I played solid that day, but during those four days of competition, my swing flaws were evident compared to the other freshmen on the team. I knew the issues of my game and was always self-conscious about my overall swing. Coach Helmick didn't want me to transfer and asked that I keep working on my swing technique. However, eventually the college lifestyle caught up with me. I began to give in to temptation, enjoying the parties more than the classes. In the process, I became more enthralled with ECU coeds than hitting golf balls. It was a fool's paradise for sure.

One day when I came back from class, the phone rang in our dorm room. I picked it up and it was my roommate's mother, Sally Davis. It was the first time we had ever spoken. We exchanged greetings, then I told her Jeff was not there and asked if I could take a message. "No, I wanted to talk with you," she said to my surprise. "Jeff's father has been diagnosed with leukemia," she said, "and Jeff has no idea anything is wrong. We wanted to call Jeff tonight to tell him but decided to first prepare you. I called your mother today and asked if you would be able to handle the situation and she assured me that you would. Please do not tell Jeff anything. When the phone rings tonight, please make sure Jeff has privacy." Time stood still; I will always remember that moment as the longest day of my life.

I prepared my suite mates because everyone was in our room that night watching *Monday Night Football*. I was so nervous waiting for the inevitable. Suddenly, the phone rang. "Everyone get out of the room," I said as Jeff answered the phone. We all exited the room, my heart aching uncontrollably. In one short month, Jeff and I had become great friends. I knew the heartache that was ahead, even before Jeff knew, feelings I had never really experienced. The conversation on the phone was very brief, and I heard Jeff say, "No way!" As I walked back into the room, Jeff told me the sad news. He was visibly shaken. His eyes welled with tears. Now it was my turn as consoler. I hugged him tightly and assured him that everything would be all right. I know God put us together for a reason. God knew I was going to fail in my attempt to play at East Carolina, and Jeff would be there for me. God also knew Jeff's father was going to die of leukemia and I would be there for Jeff. During the Christmas holidays, I flew to Chicago to spend a week with Jeff and his family in DeKalb, Illinois. I had a blast in Chicago as the Chicago Bears were making their historic Super Bowl run. I loved meeting Sally and Jeff's father Alan. We had a wonderful visit as they truly made me feel at home. Nearly a year later, on November 8, 1986, Alan lost his fight. Jeff and I hugged again—this time in our new apartment the autumn of our sophomore year.

My freshman year was one of the most amazing years of my life. I experienced life and death, success and failure and made friends who would later be in my wedding and know all my secrets, both good and bad. My college career started with failure. I received a speeding ticket before I had stepped foot onto campus. Two weeks later, I was cut from the golf team. Looking back at my college career and my career as a PGA golf professional, God used my freshman year to teach me some difficult but necessary lessons. I would try again several times to make the team, but my heart wasn't into it anymore. I loved the college life and for five years—yes, five years—I relished every moment, made lasting friends, was president of Phi Kappa Tau Fraternity and lived the college life. Had I played golf at East Carolina, my experiences would have been much different. I am around golf every day. College gave me a break from the game and allowed me to live my life as a normal college student. Not making the golf team also made me aware of my swing issues. My short game has always been my strength, especially in competition. Being cut at East Carolina gave me the resolve to improve my full swing. God would lead me to Florida eventually. At the age of twenty-five,

I would completely break down my swing and start from scratch. Golf is a great way to learn the lessons of life, to take one's weakness and through hard work, faith and patience, turn that weakness into strength. *"My grace is sufficient for you, for my power is made perfect in weakness." Therefore I will boast all the more gladly of my weaknesses, so that the power of Christ may rest upon me" (Corinthians 12:9).*

Fifteen years later, after moving to Florida and rebuilding my golf swing, I played in a United States Open qualifier at MetroWest Golf Course in Orlando. My game was on autopilot during the 18 hole qualifier as I stood on the tee box of the ninth hole, my final hole. Even par for the round, my confidence soared as I surveyed the par-4 bordered by a lake on the left side of the fairway. Normally for the local qualifying spot at MetroWest, even par is in a playoff and one-under-par is a *lock* for one of the eight qualifying spots. Number nine can stretch out to 405 yards as it wraps around the lake. It is significantly shorter, however, as the crow flies. On the tee box is a plaque memorializing where John Daly drove the green on the fly during an exhibition round when the PGA Tour major championship winner was playing in a charity event. This hole poses several problems because of the water on the left. Also a shot down the right side can run through the fairway and be blocked by trees. In the past, I tried to hit three-wood off the tee but noticed that the landing area for the three-wood was very tight. If I hit the driver, my landing area was much larger, but hitting the driver meant I had to challenge the water. The wind was blowing off the lake from left to right. I was swinging confidently and pulled the driver out. I hit my best drive of the day, hitting a slight draw (right-to-left shot) against the wind. The ball straightened out, flew over the left side of the lake and landed in the middle of the fairway more than 300 yards away. I was in complete control of my game.

As I walked down the fairway with my caddie Chevis Earle, the wind began to really pick up. The air was hot and dry that May afternoon and exceeding 20 miles per hour. As I walked around the dog-leg to my golf ball, I relished the impending approach shot. Although the pin was tucked in the left-hand corner of a green that jutted out into the water, it was in a favorable position with a slope behind the hole. A ball hit past the pin would funnel back to the hole. The ball was slightly above my feet, which allowed for a natural right-to-left ball flight, and the wind was blowing in my face from left to right protecting me from the water left. I told Chevis, "I am going to aim 20 feet right of the hole and hit a draw, even if I over draw it the wind will hold it." I had 123 yards so I chose a 9-iron factoring in the wind speed. I saw the trajectory of the shot in my mind, felt the shot in my practice swings and knew that I had the correct club to cover the lake in front.

A small gallery of about twenty fans was sitting behind the green, including former PGA Tour player Steve Lamontagne and my wife. The wind was howling and the flag rippled so much that I could hear it from the fairway. I honestly wasn't nervous. I had worked my entire life to hit this shot and the conditions were ripe for me to be aggressive and let it go. I took one last look at my target 20 feet right of the hole and made my swing. As I hit the ball, I had a sincere feeling of ecstasy, because it was perfect. As the ball bore through the air, it started to move from right to left from my natural shot shape and the slope of the fairway. I said to Chevis, "That's perfect!" The wind caught the draw and straightened the ball's flight. It hovered straight at the flagstick. While the ball was in the air, I knew I was advancing to the next stage. I knew that my game had held up under pressure and that I was going to make birdie. I was so excited watching the shot that for an instance eagle popped into my head. The ball came down and I wondered if it might fly in the hole. Suddenly, I heard a loud clank and the ball disappeared for a second. The entire group screamed and Steve yelled, "It hit the flag!"

I looked up in amazement as the ball hit the top of the flagstick and flew vertically back into the air some 20 feet above the flagstick. My heart came out of my chest because it appeared from my angle to fly straight up in the air. I thought to myself, "That's all right. It will roll back down the hill toward the hole." Unfortunately, the ball flew too far forward, over the green and lay inside the water hazard on a patch of St. Augustine grass, six inches from the water. I threw my hat down in disgust and let out several profanities. There was dead silence from the gallery. Chevis asked, "Did that ball hit the pin?" We were both in complete shock!

I walked over to my ball and faced the inevitable shot ahead. I had to take my right shoe and sock off and roll my pants over my knee and climb into the murky water. I took out a lob wedge, gripped down to the steel shaft and popped the ball onto the green. A small smattering of applause came from the group, as if they were saying, "Great job, Jon, you just got screwed!" I then took the time to dry off my right foot, put on my sock and my shoe and walked down to my ball, which had raced 30 feet past the hole on the lightning-fast green. The only chance I had to qualify was to make the long par putt and hope to advance in a playoff. In my attempt to make my par, I hit the uphill putt too hard and it raced four feet past the cup. I now had a difficult downhill putt for bogey, which I missed. I tapped in for double bogey, walked to the scorer's tent to sign my 74 and was on the verge of tears. My wife came over to console me. Then Steve sat down beside me at the scorer's table and said, "Jon, I played on the PGA Tour for four years and that is the worst break I have ever seen." I shook his hand in appreciation of his kindness, but my body and mind were in total shock. I couldn't sleep for a week and wondered why this was happening to me. I asked God, "Why do I keep trying and always seem to come up short? I did everything right this time, yet I still failed. For once can I not get a break to go my way?" A week later, I mustered up the strength to play in a mini-tour event on the Moonlight Golf Tour. As I stood on the first tee waiting to tee off, a player in the next group said to one of his playing partners, "Did you hear about the guy last week at MetroWest who hit the flag stick at the U.S. Open Qualifier?" I shook my head in disbelief. In life, we all want to be recognized for our accomplishments. In one swing, I was now recognized for my misfortune. Golf is very much like life. Every shot is like a day of your life. Some are good, some are bad, some will make you angry, and some will make you rejoice. The key to golf and the key to life are really very simple. In golf, the player controls one shot at a time and in life, an individual controls one day at a time. That's all we can handle as human beings.

I look back at my playing career and now realize in many ways my personality is not suited for the PGA Tour lifestyle. Several years after my misfortunate break at MetroWest, Steve Lamontagne and I played in a pro-pro event at Grand Cypress in Orlando. Individually I shot 71, and as a team, we came in fifth place. After our round, I said to Steve, "Can I have a moment of your time?"

"Sure," he said. We sat in our cart for about an hour as I picked his brain.

"Steve, what do you think about my golf game? Please be honest."

"Jon," he said, "you have a great swing. You hit the ball over tour average. Your short game is solid and you have a great touch with the putter." In my mind, I jumped for joy. I thought to myself, "My hard work must be paying off." Then Steve said something that I will always remember. "Jon, if I did a psychological evaluation of every tour player, 90 percent of them would be a type B personality. The majority of tour players are laid back, and if they hit a bad shot, they say to themselves, 'I'll get it back on the next shot.' You shot 71 today, but you should have been much lower. You were not aggressive enough on your wedge shots, playing too safe. When you hit a bad shot, you let it bother you over the next shot."

"The last time I was aggressive with an approach shot, I hit the flagstick at MetroWest," I said. We both laughed. I was stunned by Steve's remarks, but knew deep down that his assessment of my game personality was correct. I needed to focus on the now and not let the past frustrate me or the future worry me. Mathew 6:34 says, *"Therefore do not worry about tomorrow, for tomorrow will worry about itself. Each day has enough trouble of its own."* In golf speak, each shot has enough worry of its own as well.

My failures in life did not start when I was cut from the golf team at East Carolina University. Like most folk, I have had times of failure my entire life. Many of these failures have been through sin. Some of my sins were cheating on a test in grammar school, receiving a DWI at the age of twenty, and experimenting with recreational drugs in college, just to name a few. Many people, including my parents, would ask, "Why would you write about your personal sins to the entire world." The reason is very simple; those sins are in the past. I know that God has forgiven me of those sins. How do I know this? Because I asked for God's forgiveness of those sins many years ago, and through the death and resurrection of His son Jesus Christ, I was forgiven. I am not proud of these mistakes. However, I am now comforted because I have already been washed of my sins through Christ. Acts 2:38 says it best, *"And Peter said to them, 'Repent and be baptized every one of you in the name of Jesus Christ for the forgiveness of your sins, and you will receive the gift of the Holy Spirit.'"*

Pastor Mike Bowie of the Stonybrook United Methodist Church spoke on a similar subject during a Sunday service in 2013. "Ten percent of life is what happens to you, and 90 percent of life is how you react to it." God has used my past mistakes, failed relationships, failed marriage and poor decisions to sharpen me, to strengthen me, and to make me a better man. When I teach a junior camp, I talk about my failures to help inspire young people to be accountable for their mistakes. When a student is getting ready to hit a shot, which I consider risky or of poor choice, I allow them to hit the shot, then I correct them and show them the proper shot or technique so they will learn from it. Through their weakness, they will grow stronger. When a student complains about a bad break or unfortunate situation on the golf course, I tell them my story of misfortune.

In golf, "rub of the green" describes a bad bounce or bad luck. All golfers have experienced this. Most human beings are also well acquainted with it, too. When I hit the shot on my last hole at MetroWest, I did everything correctly. My thought process was spot on; my swing technique was fundamentally sound and my mind-set was confident. My 10 percent was perfect! I had taken all of what God had given me and executed it to the best of my ability. I factored in everything for that one shot, everything except "rub of the green." As soon as my ball disappeared into the hazard, the 90 percent took over. I threw my hat to the ground, said the Lord's name in vain, threw a pity party in the fairway, hacked it out of the hazard, three-putted and lost sleep for a week, 10 percent perfection and 90 percent failure. In golf or in life, you cannot afford to mess up the 90 percent! It wasn't until writing this book that I realized why God permitted "rub of the green" to happen in my life. God wanted to see how I would react with my 90 percent. I failed miserably that day. However, over time, I grew stronger from that moment and now can use that experience to motivate my students when "rub of the green" occurs on the golf course or on life's course.

I like to think of my Christian faith as a work in progress. I know what I should do, how to do it and the consequences of not doing it. Still I often lack faith and patience. As I have grown in my Christian faith, I have tried my best to put a positive spin on life's inevitable failures and disappointments. When things now aren't going my way at work, I say, "Thank you Lord for my job." When a relationship fails, "Lord, you must have someone really special waiting for me," I declare. When I am having financial difficulties, "I am so fortunate to be healthy and able to work," is my evaluation. Quite frankly, this is not always easy, yet being a Christian is not supposed to be easy. Throughout the New Testament, Jesus speaks of this inevitable conflict we all face while living on this earth. Romans 5:3–5 says, *"More than that, we rejoice in our sufferings, knowing that suffering produces endurance, and endurance produces character, and character produces hope, and hope does not put us to shame, because God's love has been poured into our hearts through the Holy Spirit who has been given to us."*

I failed in my attempt to make the golf team during my freshman year, but now I teach collegiate and professional golfers on a regular basis. I've taught at the 2007 Women's U.S. Open and at four PGA Championships to date. I now teach my old suite mates who did make the golf team in August of 1985. I have given regular lessons to my past suite mate Mike Nadeau. I was best man at his wedding. I'm also godfather of his children, Amber and Nick. I have also taught my former roommate Jeff Davis and suite mate John Chapman, along with John's sons, Zach and Kyle. God closed the door on my collegiate golf career and opened the door to my professional teaching career, bringing me back to my dearest friends and their families on a regular basis as a guide to their development and improvement as players. As promised in the Bible, I will continue to have disappointment and failure in my life ahead, but I now know that life is more about how I react to disappointment and failure than worrying about what misfortune is coming next. My failures may come through choice, as in sin, and other times by God's choice, as in difficult life lessons. When I sin, I pray to God to forgive me from my sins and help me resist future temptation. This leads to my continued evolution as a Christian man. When God allows failure to happen in my life, like not getting a job or losing a girl to someone else, I now look at that failure as God's will. Either way, I am better off because I am in God's hands, following God's lead to an everlasting life where failure doesn't exist!

As Seen Through My Eyes

Fred Griffin, Director of Instruction for the Grand Cypress Academy of Golf/ Top 100 Teacher

When I first met Jon, I was on vacation in Hilton Head, South Carolina, with my family. He was working at the Hyatt Regency Resort as a camp counselor. A couple of years later, Jon shows up at Grand Cypress and applies for a job at the academy.

The academy was growing and very busy, so it was a great opportunity for Jon to start his career in the golf industry. He began working as a range and retail attendant. He would pick the range, set up for the golf schools, and work in the pro shop registering guests. It didn't take me long to realize that Jon was very passionate about teaching golf. For countless hours, he would observe me and Phil Rodgers teaching and always want to learn and ask questions about some of the lessons he observed. Jon also liked to play, and a good

126

way to learn how to teach is to take lessons and work on your swing. Phil and I worked with Jon to help him improve his game but also to help him learn as a teacher. As with everything, Jon worked diligently on his game and developed into a very good player. With Jon's energy, passion, and work ethic, I quickly realized he would be a great addition to our teaching staff.

Because of the long hours in the golf business, you spend a lot of time together as a staff. That was the case at Grand Cypress. This gave me the opportunity to get to get to know Jon on a personal level. As both of us are Christians, we were able to discuss our faith and how important it is in our lives. I was involved with a men's ministry, the gathering of men through my church, and I invited Jon to an event that would feature one of my favorite Christian speakers, Tony Campolo. Tony's message really hit home with Jon, and the next day, Jon wrote me one of the most heartfelt letters I have ever received about how he was impacted by Tony's message. As with teaching, Jon is very passionate about his faith and how it is the cornerstone of everything he does on a daily basis. As you will read in this book, he shares in an intriguing way the importance of hard work, faith, family, and giving back to others. I have thoroughly enjoyed reading this book, and I'm confident it will inspire you to examine your life and focus on what is important and what it is that God has planned for you.

CHAPTER 10

Coincidence

"Therefore the Lord Himself will give you a sign: The virgin will conceive and give birth to a son, and will call Him Immanuel. He will be eating curds and honey when He knows enough to reject the wrong and choose the right" (Isaiah 7:14–15).

More than seven hundred years before the birth of Jesus Christ the prophet, Isaiah, foretold the coming of the Lord. His prophecies illustrate God's ultimate plan, one with precision in every minute detail. God's order and timing is something mankind will never grasp. We as God's children are only asked to trust. *"For we live by faith, not by sight" (2 Corinthians 5:7).* Of all the stories and parables I read in the Bible, Isaiah's prophecy of Jesus Christ's birth had the most significant impact on my understanding of God's plan. In fact, it gave me goose bumps during my initial reading. I was astonished at how carefully God planned the birth of His son. It made me realize the magnitude of God's time-table. To the unbeliever, Isaiah's prophesies could be viewed as a coincidence or lucky guess. Coincidence is defined as "a remarkable concurrence of events or circumstances without apparent casual connection." This leads one to believe that luck or happenstance sometimes gets us through life. My motto has always been *"The harder I work, the luckier I get. Luck is when hard work and opportunity meet."* God's plan never involves luck; only His daily grace for His children. God's plan for His son Jesus Christ was laid out since the beginning of time, time that seems insurmountable to human beings, yet it is only a moment to God. God's plan for Jesus Christ and for all His children is a well-orchestrated masterpiece revealed one precious second at a time. Coincidence? I think not.

The year was 1991 and I was completing an internship from East Carolina University. The internship was with the Hyatt Regency in Hilton Head, South Carolina. I worked for the spa and fitness center at the Hyatt, working on the pool deck, running youth activities, and babysitting in the evenings as a part-time job. The concierges enjoyed booking me business because I was the only male babysitter for the hotel. I became a hit with most of the boys because I was active, taking the kids to the pool, the beach or on bike rides. It was fun and a great way to make some extra money. Although I enjoyed my internship, personally I was struggling. I had just broken up with my college sweetheart. Uncle Jon, the man for whom I was named, had succumbed to AIDS six months earlier and his brother, James, was dying of cancer. James died almost a year to the day of his brother's death. To say my life was in turmoil is putting it mildly. Hilton Head's nightlife proved the perfect medicine for my emotional and mental ailments. Drinking allowed me to blow off some steam and temporarily forget my problems. Although I prayed every day, I hadn't attended church in years and I often thought, "God hears my prayers, why do I need to go to church?" My life seemed to be spiraling out of control.

Although I was low, making poor decisions and feeling like I had no clear path ahead of me, I continued to pray. At the end of every prayer, I asked God to "please lead me. Show me the way." That summer, God answered my prayers by bringing a five-year-old girl named Haley into my life. The extremely shy young girl had long, dark hair. Cute as a button, Haley was the only child that signed up for Camp Hyatt that week and I was scheduled to be her counselor. When her parents brought her to the first day of camp, her ashen face resembled the timidity of a preschooler being dropped off at kindergarten. Mom and Dad were reluctant to leave their little one with this strange man, too. Even though I wasn't a parent, I believe I was gifted with an innate caring that puts most children at ease. So it was with Haley.

I took my young camper to the beach then the pool and for bike rides. However, our favorite activity was crabbing. We sat on a rock under a bridge and caught crabs, one after another. Soon Haley began to warm to me and on the last day of the camp, both her parents came to pick her up for their family's departure. Haley gave me a big hug, and with it, a strong connection was completed. At that moment, I believed we were destined to meet. Her father Fred and I talked for the first time that afternoon, and I asked him what he did for a living. "I am the director of instruction at the Grand Cypress Academy of Golf in Orlando," he said, also mentioning that the resort was across the street from the Hyatt Grand Cypress Hotel. I had heard of this wonderful hotel and the resort, but it had been years since I had been to the Disney area. I said good-bye with no thought of ever seeing Haley or her parents again.

I said good-bye to Haley, God said "until we meet again."

I was still struggling with work and was near rock bottom emotionally. I was stuck in neutral, running in place with no apparent destination in mind. I was rotating jobs for the Hyatt. One day I'd clean the hotel rooms; the next I'd book reservations or work the spa. Of course, the babysitting was a constant. I was just getting by financially and couldn't seem to grasp what direction I wanted for my life. I often asked God, "Where do you want me, God? What is it you want me to do?" I don't know how I made it, but God finds a way to bring people into your life just when you need them most, rams in the bush to guide you, change your thoughts or give you a different perspective. In April of 1992, God brought Payne Stewart into my life.

Some coworkers offered me weekend passes to the Heritage Classic, the PGA Tournament played in Hilton Head at the Harbour Town Golf Links. I couldn't contain my excitement for I hadn't been to a tour event since going to the Masters as a child. Payne was one of my favorite professional golfers. I loved the tempo of his golf swing, his calm demeanor, and of course, the stylish knickers (Plus-Fours). As I approached the tournament parking area, a security guard stopped me. Patiently waiting for the crowd to clear so I could proceed to parking, I glanced to the left and there was one of my favorite players, Payne Stewart, hitting a tee shot. To my right was Billy Mayfair rolling in a birdie putt. Gripped by exhilaration and anticipation, I could hardly wait to get out and walk the golf course for the first time. After parking my car, I caught up to Payne's group and followed him for the remainder of the day and on Sunday, as well. Davis Love III would win the tournament as I stood and watched from the fairway of the 72nd hole. However, Payne had captured my heart that weekend. Seeing him stirred up my golfing juices. I felt reborn. Sitting on my bed that night, I felt the warm tears streaming down my face, tears of sadness and realization. I knew that golf was supposed to be a part of my life. I knew I was going down a path that wasn't what God had intended for my life. I had gotten away from my passion in life. More importantly, I had gotten away from my faith.

As my struggles continued, I began to alter my course. I met with the sales team for the Hyatt and considered joining them. Mr. Fox, the general manager, liked the idea. He also wanted to learn to play golf. Word got to him that I was a good player, so he invited me to play with him on several of the island's best courses. It was my first real experience teaching. After our playing lesson, Mr. Fox offered to move me into a sales position. With the offer came a ray of hope that God was guiding me along His intended path for my life. I began playing golf with Mr. Fox on a weekly basis.

Often with God's plans, circumstances are used as beacons to change one's course in life. Several weeks after playing golf with Mr. Fox, the Gulf War broke out. The immediate impact on tourism took a devastating toll on resorts, including my employer. People stopped traveling, and the island's hotels were desperate for vacationers. I set up a meeting with Mr. Fox in his office. I will never forget his words, "Jon, I can't move you into sales. The Gulf War has us under a hiring freeze." Upon hearing the bad news, I looked Mr. Fox in the eyes and said, "I appreciate all you have done for me Mr. Fox, but I am moving to Orlando." With no job lined up and no career path in mind, I took the greatest risk of my life. I had five hundred dollars in my savings account, a car, some clothing, odd pieces of furniture, and some dishes. Fraternity brothers Mike Nadeau and Rich Thurston lived in Orlando. God was calling me to move and I listened!

That November, I left Hilton Head for Orlando. One of my best friends, Scott (Skillet) Studenc, helped me pack my car and his truck and we headed south. When we arrived at Rich's house, I handed him three hundred dollars for the first month's rent. Down to my last two hundred dollars, I had no bed and slept on the floor of the room I was renting for three months. On that initial night, my frat brothers and I hit the town and partied to celebrate my big move. Without a job or prospects, I woke up the next day with only a headache and a mouth dryer than sawdust. I needed a job! I applied for a front desk position at the Hyatt Orlando and was hired immediately. Although I was happy to be working, I was not happy with my career path. I was so nearsighted as to my current circumstances that I couldn't see God's plan for me was well underway. *"God will instruct me and teach me in the way I should go. He will guide me with His eye"(Psalm 32:8).*

One day Rich said to me, "Jon, you should apply for a bag room position at Grand Cypress. My sister, Julie, works on the beverage carts. She will give you a referral." Since arriving in Orlando, I had worked several jobs but still wasn't happy. I decided to take Rich's advice and applied for the bag room position. During my interview, Director of Human Resources Kim Kimble asked a most thought-provoking question. "Jon," she said, "you seem to have a great personality. Have you ever considered working at our Academy of Golf?"

"What is the Academy of Golf?" I asked.

"Our golf school," she said. "I think you would be perfect for the job." After thinking about it for a second or two, I assured her that I would work wherever there was a need. That moment in time changed the course of my career and my life forever. In my shortsighted mind, I was getting an entry-level position with a large company and could then move on from there. God, however, had much bigger plans for me. He was fulfilling His promise to me by answering my prayers.

After several days of work at the academy, I knew that being a teaching professional was my true calling in life. I remember standing on the range and watching the other instructors teaching and thinking to myself, "This is what I want to do with my life." My first day on the job, I met Fred Griffin, the Director of Instruction for the Grand Cypress Academy of Golf for what I thought was the first time. Several weeks later, Grand Cypress hosted a party for the staff members and their families. Fred brought his family and I immediately recognized his oldest daughter, Haley. I couldn't believe it! I had met Fred briefly in Hilton Head, but I recognized Haley immediately. The certainty of God's planned career path for me crystallized. I saw it clearly unfolding for the first time.

After working several weeks, I got more great news! Payne Stewart was coming to take a lesson from Fred. The funny thing is when Payne showed up for the lesson, he was wearing tennis shorts. I thought to myself, "Where are the knickers?" Payne said he could go into any grocery store in shorts and no one would ever recognize him. Those colorful knickers (Plus-Fours) were his calling card. I sat and watched every shot of the lesson. Fred was using the Modelgolf video technology (now known as SwingModel) during the lesson. The technology was developed by Dr. Ralph Mann. The video enabled me to see a tour player's swing frame by frame for the first time. It was spellbinding. Surprisingly, the technology revealed that Payne's swing was not perfect. I ached to point out this revelation, but fear of rejection silenced me. I said nothing as my eyes grew wide and my mind raced. During the next several years, Payne and his son, Aaron, often came to practice at Grand Cypress. One day I was on the putting green and I tried to strike up a conversation with Payne as he practiced his putting stroke. His response to me was rather short, and I realized he was at work, but deep inside, it hurt. As the years passed, he began to speak to me when he came out to practice. I have no older brother, so in many ways I looked up to Payne as a child might look up to an older brother. In many ways, Payne's presence in my life at Harbour Town steered my career, but I was too nervous to share my thoughts with him. After all, he was a PGA Tour player who would go on to win three majors. I was a struggling PGA apprentice just trying to make it paycheck to paycheck.

My playground was the academy. I hit balls
every day before or after work.

One day Fred announced to the staff that Payne was testing new equipment and would be using one of the academy's practice holes. The staff was instructed to give Payne and the club manufacturer privacy as they tested clubs. I watched him practice from a distance as I was practicing my own bunker game. At the end of the day, I saw a caravan of golf carts full of clubs coming my way. I knew the long day of testing new irons and drivers was over for Payne. As Payne drove by, he looked at me, pointed his finger at me, smiled and gave me a wink. It was the last time I would see Payne Stewart alive in person. A few months later, Payne won his third major, the U.S. Open at Pinehurst in the sand hills of North Carolina. A few months later, he was an integral part of the winning Ryder Cup team at Brookline in Massachusetts. By that time, Payne Stewart had changed as a man. He was blessed with fame and fortune, but more importantly, he was living as a Christian. I remember him openly stating his faith on television and making significant contributions to the Arnold Palmer Hospital in Orlando and to his local church. I noticed this change in the way he acted around me, too.

On October 26, 1999, Payne Stewart and five other people died in a tragic plane crash. The group was flying to Houston in a private Lear jet when the cabin lost pressure. The pilots passed out and the plane flew across the country on autopilot until it ran out of fuel and crashed in South Dakota. I was at work when I heard the news. I went into the pro shop and Fred was sitting in the chair watching the news. We were both speechless. Several weeks later, after Payne's funeral, Fred revealed an ironic fact to me that would take me years before I connected the dots. According to Fred, on the day of the accident, Fred's oldest daughter, Haley, that shy five-year-old I met at Camp Hyatt in Hilton Head, was having lunch with Payne Stewart's daughter, Chelsea, when the principal came in to get Chelsea. Haley and Chelsea became fast friends when their dads began their working relationship.

There were few remains at the crash site—the only identifiable connection to Payne was a bracelet he wore everywhere. The inscription WWJD (What Would Jesus Do) spoke volumes about his faith and the spiritual growth of one of professional golf's most endearing personalities. God gave Payne Stewart the greatest platform a professional golfer could hope for. He was the reigning U.S. Open champion at the time of his death. The acronym on his bracelet served as his final official message to the world.

The news of Payne Stewart's death rocked the sports world and dominated national news for quite a while. The golf world had lost a true champion in the prime of his life. I lost a spiritual beacon to the game of golf. Sometimes in life, you just have to move on, and move on I did. Years later, I was playing in the North Florida Section Championship at Disney's Magnolia Course. I went to the locker room to change my clothes and prepare for my tee time. Surprisingly, I was the only one there. I walked up to a random locker to change my shoes. As I got up to leave the locker room, I looked up and I was dressing at Payne Stewart's memorial locker. Disney had posthumously honored its 1983 champion with a memorial locker containing his picture, knickers and glove. The most surreal sense of peace came over me as I stared at that locker.

Several years after Payne's death, I got a second opportunity to thank the legend. Payne's son, Aaron, was standing at the counter of the Grand Cypress pro shop when I entered. After introducing myself, I told young Aaron that his father was the reason I was in the golf business. "He inspired my career and was one of my favorite players," I said. I felt a great sense of relief that I had finally gotten those words off my chest. Aaron thanked me as we both said goodbye. That day I learned a very important life lesson: Always tell those you love how you feel, because you might never get a second chance. I thank God for my second opportunity to say, "Thank you."

To the crime-scene investigator, all this evidence seems circumstantial or just a series of coincidences. However, I'm convinced that it was all a part of God's plan for my life and laid the foundation for this book, my journey in faith and my career path. God used Haley Griffin to bring her dad into my life. Fred's technical knowledge of the golf swing, friendship, and leadership helped shape my career over a twenty-year span. Like most people, circumstances in the world also affected my life. Who knows what would have happened if the situation in the gulf had been resolved peacefully through diplomacy instead of weapons of mass destruction? I may have gotten hired in sales at the Hyatt and taken an entirely different path in life. God used Payne Stewart to be a spiritual beacon and revitalize my passion for golf. Some will say that it was a coincidence that I met Haley that summer and that meeting had nothing to do with my career path. They might also conclude that the day at the Heritage meant nothing in revitalizing my passion for golf. To the cynic, the agnostic or the atheist, all these events are circumstances of nature or coincidence. After all, as Payne's Lear jet was flying through the air, Chelsea could have been eating lunch with anyone other than Haley. God brings people into our lives every day to shape our career, reunite us with family members, open a door of opportunity or simply rescue a stray dog and give it a home. The problem is that most people don't realize that God is giving them a gift at the time. It is not until years later that the gift becomes apparent.

The greatest lesson I learned from Payne Stewart was simple. At twenty-five, I was enamored of Payne Stewart's golf swing. I envied his career and his lifestyle. I also envied the talents, fame and fortune that God had given Payne, gifts that were so apparent the whole world knew him by the way he swung a golf club and dressed on a Sunday afternoon. As a Christian man, I now know that envying the gifts that God gives to someone else is wrong and sinful. As a man who has matured in his faith, I admire the fact that Payne Stewart turned his life over to Jesus Christ. I admire that even though he was a flawed man, like all of us, he eventually chose to walk as a Christian and spread the word of Jesus Christ, before he began his everlasting life. Payne's last official words to the world were "What would Jesus do?" As a Christian, I know that one day I will see Payne Stewart again and I will say, "Thank you." That is a guarantee from the Bible. I was wrong to envy Payne Stewart for his gifts because my gifts are so different from his. I learned through this experience that there will only be one Payne Stewart. That's the way God wanted it!

Kraig Kann, Chief Communications Officer for the LPGA

In golf, there are instructors, and then there are ambassadors. There is no game like it—where the mind is actually challenged as much or more than the body. The game is especially challenging for those who are new, potentially intimidated and insecure, and yet seeking positive memories that carry them to the next lesson and beyond.

Jon Decker is a leader. And he is a believer in people. He is an ambassador for the game and always carries the hope that goodwill must go along with it.

His teachings are sound and understandable. But where Jon separates himself is with his personal touch. He knows how to deliver his message in a way that inspires.

I'll never forget the work he did with my young son whose "perfectionist" qualities sometime got in the way of enjoyment and success which should be the ultimate goal for any junior player. Jon found something with him, and my son bought in immediately. He wanted more from his coach, and he chased results with a smile. Soon after that lesson, on a par-3 practice hole at Orlando's Grand Cypress Resort, Trent Kann laced a 7-iron and made a hole-in-one! A smile as big as Epcot Center came across his face. The rewards from work with Jon were there for the both of us to share.

Decker has the "it" quality that golf needs more of when it comes to instruction. Empowering people to believe they can achieve is a gift. And Jon knows how to do just that. The game is far better with him on the lesson tee.

CHAPTER 11

Foundation

Back: L to R Harry Zimmerman, Todd Meena, Gus
Holbrook, Adrian Stills, Fred Griffin and John Page /
Bottom: L to R Jon Decker, Eric Eshleman, Carl Alexander,
John Pinel. Photo Courtesy of the Grand Cypress Resort

"Very truly I tell you, the Son can do noth-
ing by himself; he can do only what he sees his
Father doing, because whatever the Father does
the Son also does" (John 5:19). In one simple
verse, Jesus Christ, the Son of God, laid out the
foundation to the world.

On a late spring day in Orlando, I was finishing up my last pick
of the afternoon at the Grand Cypress Academy of Golf driving
range. It was pick-clean day, which meant all twenty-three baskets
of golf balls had to be gathered and cleaned that afternoon. I looked
forward to heading home after a long day's work. Although I had
a college diploma on the wall, I was now driving a Kubota tractor
(the Rolls Royce of golf course maintenance equipment) for a living
and handling the lesson transactions for the academy's instructors. It
was not quite what my parents had in mind as dividends from their
son's college degree. I had just started my new career as a retail/range
attendant, a job more suited for a person with a high school sheep-
skin rather than one with much loftier goals. Still, I was thoroughly
enjoying the gig despite the meager (seven dollars an hour) wage. As
I was pouring the golf balls from the picker into the baskets, I looked
down the driving range tee and saw Brenda Pfeifer walking in my
direction. As sales manager, Brenda booked all of our golf schools
and private lessons. An extraordinarily pleasant woman, she wore a
huge smile as she approached. "Jon," she said, "I hope you're ready to
teach this weekend. We had several students add onto the golf school
and we are out of instructors. We need your help!"

"That's awesome!" I said, trying not to let my excitement betray
my confidence that I was up for the challenge. I have always had confidence working with people and knew my time had come. However,

my only experience in teaching was a few of the clinics the resort offered to novices. I had a great lead instructor in Adrian Stills and knew our personalities would mesh, but more importantly, I had confidence in a foundation of teaching that had already begun to form. It's a foundation that I rely on to this day.

In the golf business, the unavoidable rite of passage includes picking the balls from the driving range. I took pride in my work because of my upbringing and because for the first time in my life, I knew what I wanted to do with my life. I wanted to teach the game of golf. For me to reach my goal of one day being a head instructor at Grand Cypress, I had to start at the bottom and slowly scale my Everest. In one afternoon, though, that mountain became a much quicker climb. I had put in the extra personal time taking mental notes as the academy's lineup of talented teachers doled out advice on every aspect of the game. I had also begun certification classes to learn the Grand Cypress teaching system. I felt so fortunate because in my quest for knowledge, God had directed me to Orlando, and by His grace, He had deposited me at the knee of some of the best instructors in the world. After nearly a year and a half of paying my dues in grunt work and spending my own personal time observing the innovative teaching styles of some of the world's greatest instructors, I was ready to dive into the deep end of the pool with the other teaching pros. That spring day in 1994 is one of my cherished birthdays, for a dream became reality.

Every Thursday evening a new group of students would arrive at Grand Cypress for the weekend golf schools. The academy hosted a cocktail party so the instructors and students could meet, go over the itinerary for the weekend and digitize each student. What set Grand Cypress apart from other golf schools in the country was the wonderful teaching programs, exceptional instructors and world-class practice facilities. The research for teaching was headed by Fred Griffin and Dr. Ralph Mann. Dr. Mann, the founder of ModelGolf (now SwingModel) and Fred, the academy's director of instruction, filmed fifty-four tour players including Jack Nicklaus, Tom Kite and Greg Norman. The swings were put into a computer and Dr. Mann came up with a model of the similarities of all those great golf swings. The idea was based on one simple concept: Take what the best players in the world do in their golf swings and use that information to help the students improve their swings. For those students who might have been apprehensive, we had a solid mantra: "You may not be a PGA Tour player, but we can set you up like a one." The setup is the most important position in golf. It is the foundation of any golf swing, regardless of the player's ability. The tour-player model is built to the student's body frame through digitizing, a process of measuring the stature of a person and putting the measurements into the proper scale, creating the student's model. After a student hits a shot, the instructor takes the scaled stick-figure model and superimposes it over their body on the video screen. The result is a clear depiction of the setup and swing changes that need to be made. Subsequently, as the student's setup improved, the student's golf swing would subsequently improve.

Sixteen students attended this particular cocktail party, each one eager to begin the journey toward improvement. That journey began with digitizing, a time-consuming process that required patience and willing participants. Eight of the students might have been a little short on patience being that they were veterans of Wall Street—a most frenetic workplace not exactly conducive to the solitude required in golf instruction. However, the potential fun quotient was heightened by two facts. First, they were great friends. And second, there was an open bar.

I arrived early that initial morning of the school full of excitement and pure joy. As a rookie teacher, I might have had a slight bit of trepidation. There was also the uncertainty of how the New Yorkers would treat me. My fears were quickly allayed as the gregarious group embraced the opportunity to learn from someone whose accent dripped of Southern molasses. Like many of the other staff members, the New Yorkers all started calling me J.D. After a successful morning of teaching, I went to lunch and returned to the real world of picking the driving range. Attendants were required to wear knickers as part of our uniform, so during lunch, I changed into my knickers and went back to work. As the students returned from lunch to warm up before their round, I drove across the range on the tractor wearing my knickers. The New Yorkers, with extraordinary youthful exuberance, engaged in target practice with yours truly as the primary target. Fortunately, their aim on the range wasn't that accurate and the balls harmlessly whizzed past me. Boys will be boys, I guess. We laughed about it the next day; just part of paying dues when you're low man on the totem pole.

After the second day of the school, my new friends from up north made an offer I couldn't refuse. "J.D., you're going out with us tonight," they said. "Where do you live?" Of course, they didn't have to twist my arm. I gladly gave them the address to my apartment, and they picked me up in a van. Mickey's playground became ours for a night of fun. I love the social side of teaching and getting to know people. Even though the New Yorkers were older, more financially secure and had already paid their dues in the financial business world, they treated me as an equal and paid for everything. The icing on the cake came in the form of their testimonials as the evening came to a close. They genuinely appreciated my assistance with their golf games. "Tomorrow is our last day of the school and you will be given a questionnaire about your experience," I said when they dropped me off at my apartment. "Any positive feedback will go a long way." At the end of the third day, Adrian and I passed out the questionnaires, and I noticed many of the students writing extended comments. We all shook hands, exchanged hugs and I turned the comments into Fred. He stopped me the next day as I drove my golf cart back from lunch. "Great job J.D.," he said, shaking my hand. "I can't believe those questionnaires. Every one of the students wrote positive comments about you and Adrian!" Success in my first golf school was sweeter than I could ever have imagined. Later that month in our staff meeting, Fred read many of the comments from the New Yorkers. The entire staff congratulated me on a job well done. The encouragement from the other instructors proved ample validation that I was a good fit there. All of a sudden, the future looked really bright.

The knowledge I obtained while working at Grand Cypress is the foundation of my teaching philosophy. In many ways, the instructors there were the building blocks to my career. It started with my director of instruction, Fred Griffin. Fred has been a top-50 teacher with *Golf Magazine* and featured on *Golf Channel.* He's also taught PGA and LPGA tour players. A former Teacher of the Year in the North Florida Section, Fred often speaks at PGA teaching seminars. He began his career at the Grand Cypress facility in 1986 when it was the Jack Nicklaus Academy of Golf. Fred's technical knowledge of the swing and presentation skills greatly influenced my development as a teaching professional. He also is very active in his church and has strong Christian values. Fred's influence on my career is apparent in every lesson I teach. He is a true golf professional and gentleman, a great leader of veterans and young pros just cutting their teaching teeth.

Grand Cypress also gave me an opportunity to observe the genius of former PGA Tour player and academy staff member Phil Rodgers. Phil won six PGA Tour events. His clientele includes a long list of tour players who prospered as a result of his vast knowledge and unique style of teaching. I consider Phil my mentor as a teaching professional. Even as an amateur Phil demonstrated championship pedigree, winning the 1958 NCAA Division I Championship as a member of the University of Houston team. Five years later, he perhaps scored his biggest moment on one of golf's grandest stages—the British Open. Displaying impeccable ball striking, Phil tied Bob Charles at the end of regulation 72 holes. Charles won the 36-hole playoff, but his American challenger won the hearts of many fans back home. In 1980, Phil's longtime friend, Jack Nicklaus, asked him to come to his home in West Palm Beach to help him with an inconsistent short game. Two weeks of short-game work that winter propelled Nicklaus to titles in the 1980 U.S. Open at Baltusrol GC in New Jersey and the PGA Championship at Oak Hill CC in Rochester, New York later that summer. Nicklaus credited the improved short-game technique taught him by Phil as critical to his two major victories. During the years, Phil has spent countless hours of his own time working on my swing and mentoring me in my teaching career. I believe his teaching eye is second to none. Besides my parents, there has never been another human being in my life that has given me more of their own personal time, for the sole purpose of allowing me to grow in my chosen profession, than Phil Rodgers. Part of my confidence lies in the fact that I'm passing along knowledge that came from Phil Rodgers and his mentor, Paul Runyan.

My learning curve took a sharp turn as a result of Dr. Ralph Mann's legendary research into the biomechanics of the golf swing. His *model overlay system* has been used in track and field, major league baseball and the NFL. Ralph was a silver medalist in the high hurdles at the 1972 Olympics. According to him, it was technique rather than natural speed that secured the medal. Ralph saw the need for standardization in golf teaching because most teachers were trying to teach a feeling of what they do as players and had no scientific data to back up their teaching. The fear all students have at any golf school is to go to one teacher and take instruction and ten minutes later have another teacher tell them something different. Through Dr. Mann's research, I learned the technical aspects, science and the biomechanics of the golf swing. His SwingModel Video System is the best way to show a student their current golf swing and where it needs improving. Because of Dr. Mann's research, I now have a blueprint of the golf swing in my mind. I use this blueprint in all my video presentations.

My foundation for teaching while at Grand Cypress goes well beyond Fred, Phil and Dr. Mann. The entire staff at the Grand Cypress Academy of Golf was exceptional. I learned so much about the golf swing, presentation styles, teaching groups, and teaching individual lessons. I also made dramatic improvement in my own golf swing during my twenty-year career there. I have been blessed to be around many great teachers. However, some deserve special recognition. Head instructor Todd Meena is one of them. Todd is the kindest person I've ever met. Todd's own great swing—honed on the European PGA Tour—might be his best calling card. Patience is also one of his greatest assets. We share the commonality of autism —his eldest son and my younger brother. We've had many long and difficult talks during the years. He's a great friend, teacher and Christian.

Head instructor Gus "The General" Holbrook was an All-American at the University of Georgia. The General was easily the group's most colorful character. Despite his

Because of the wonderful Grand Cypress team, my personal golf swing began to improve. Photo courtesy of the Grand Cypress Resort.

penchant for retelling his catalogue of stories on numerous occasions, he made schools fun and enjoyable for all students. In fact, every once in a while I find myself chuckling at one of his tales. Gus is a true showman with the unique ability to keep a group entertained in various social settings. I loved working with Gus during rain delays because he could keep the group engaged while getting his message across. His fantastic short game rubbed off on me, too, especially bunker play.

Head instructor Harry Zimmerman (2000 Teacher of the Year, East Central Chapter) is also a wonderful teacher with whom I thoroughly enjoyed working during golf schools. We called him Harv because after one of our schools, his student wrote a long letter to our director praising Harry's instruction but referring to him as Harvey. Harry's wonderful sense of humor made every school fun and enjoyable; plus his instruction was very easy for his students to understand. Less is more for Harry, and it showed in the number of his repeat students. Harry also had the unique ability to play golf as a righty or lefty, something that still amazes.

In 2000, my goal of becoming a head instructor came to fruition. I spent the majority of my years teaching at Grand Cypress with Fred, Phil, Todd, Gus and Harry. However, there were many other teachers with whom I worked, including Eric Eshleman (2006 and 2010 Dixie Section Teacher of the Year). Eric, director of golf at Birmingham CC, and I started one month apart and became great friends. He has a trained teaching eye and understanding of the golf swing overall, but his real strengths are in his people skills. Eric's career has flourished, highlighted by a stint with U.S. Open champ Graeme McDowell.

Left Fred Griffin/Right Eric Eshleman and Carl
Alexander. Photo Courtesy of Carl Alexander.

Carl Alexander (2012 PGA National Horton Smith Award
Winner) has also been very influential in my teaching career. He is an
excellent player with great presentation skills and wonderful people
skills. The son of famed photographer Jules Alexander (*The Hogan
Mistique*), Carl matriculated to Purchase, New York, as director of
golf at the Golf Club of Purchase.

Lee Houtteman was another of the Grand Cypress teachers whom I admired for their teaching eye. Lee taught me the art
of teaching multiple students at once, a necessity when teaching
group clinics.

Adrian Stills (1985 PGA Tour Member) improved my teaching
as well as my game. Adrian gave me a true understanding of *working
the ball* against the wind to straighten out ball flight, how to lower
my ball flight and adjust yardages with uneven lies. He is currently
teaching at the Osceola Golf Course in Pensacola, Florida, and also
works with the First Tee Foundation.

Other building blocks of my career include Joey Hidock, Curtis
Cowan, Doug Lowen, Jason Bell, Dave Seeman, Kevin McKinney,

Brenda Pfeiffer, Cam Abascal, Bob "The Workhorse" Honohan, John Pinel, Kyle Phelps and John Page (See Acknowlegments).They have played a major part in my development as a teacher and ascension to my current position of director of instruction at the New Albany Country Club in New Albany, Ohio.

Although my teaching disciples taught the same thing, each had a different style. Personality, delivery, and presentation skills are vital to teaching the game of golf. In addition, social media has changed the way I correspond with students. I schedule lessons via text messages and launch monitors are now used in club fitting. Through all the high-tech waves of information and Internet blitzes for golf school packages comes one overriding question: "Is the student's game improving?" The team at Grand Cypress improved the student's game better than any golf school in the world. Knowledge is power, but communication and application of that knowledge are what ultimately make the difference in the student's development. The ability to communicate—a blessing I don't take for granted—makes me effective. However, it wasn't until I acquired knowledge of the golf swing that my foundation began to take form. Once I acquired the basic knowledge of the golf swing, the foundation was set in place. Then it was time to add the next critical building block—experience.

When young teachers come to me for advice, I paint a picture in their mind of what to expect. I say to them, "You are going to be forty-five minutes into a one-hour lesson and that student is still whiffing the ball. And when they do hit it, the ball rolls along the ground. You are going to panic and want to reach into your bag of tricks and start throwing too many things at them hoping something sticks." I tell the new teachers this because I am speaking from personal experience. The fundamentals of the setup are the foundation for any lesson. There are three compensations in golf most players make during setup: Grip, alignment or ball position. Make sure those three are correct along with posture and weight distribution and most students will eventually improve. Having the experience and patience to stand by and watch a student struggle can be difficult, but it is a critical component of the learning process. This ability to remain calm, patient and trust one's foundation while the student struggles is the key essential, personal quality that all great teachers possess. This trust takes a lifetime to develop because every lesson, like every day of life, is a little different.

In 1998, Dr. Mann and Fred Griffin published the book *Swing Like a Pro.* I believe it's the best instructional book for the golf swing. If SwingModel Video System is my blueprint for the golf swing, the book is my teaching Bible. The experience of teaching with the Grand Cypress staff made me a disciple of a teaching system. My Bible, teaching eye and discipleship became my foundation. Twenty years' experience gives me the confidence that no matter what is going wrong in the student's swing it is fixable. That is if the student has faith.

Christianity requires the same discipline as learning to play golf. By reading the Word of God, practicing God's Word in daily life, and believing His Word through faith, we develop a relationship with Him. Throughout my life I have been a creature of habit. Regimentation and a workable system are important concepts in every part of my life. However, when it came to my relationship with Jesus Christ, my routine had been reduced to a nightly prayer. I would spend countless hours watching my fellow working disciples teach every day to learn my trade but had no disciples of faith in my spiritual life to strengthen my faith or to worship with at church. I took the time daily to develop my work foundation but neglected my spiritual foundation by only worshipping at church on holidays and the occasional Sunday morning. My written foundation for teaching is *Swing Like a Pro*, which I consumed like nourishment to my golfing soul. My written foundation from God is the Bible, a book that collected dust and took up space on my office shelf. It took me forty years to discover that Christianity is not a solo journey. It can't be achieved alone. God wants us all to help each other using our God-given gifts. It takes the help of other people for one to grow in knowledge and faith, whether they are family members, coworkers, Bible study groups, close friends or disciples. Everyone needs disciples and close relationships in daily life to help get through difficult times and hold us accountable when we fall short in life.

After my divorce, I was lost as a man and Christian. I knew that I needed to get back into church worship. I thought about it, knew it would help me but each Sunday I chose to teach golf over going to worship. Eight months after my divorce, God brought the first of three women into my life, all for specific reasons. These three relationships provided the spiritual foundation and building blocks needed in my Christian faith and helped me move on with my life. Although there were some struggles and difficult times, all three relationships were necessary in my life and all three made me stronger as a man and in my faith.

My first relationship brought love back into my life. Our first date was at church and her influence brought regular church worship into my Sunday routine. Her influence brought me one step closer to God and was the first real step in my road back to living as a Christian man. Although our relationship did not last, I will always be grateful for her help and influence while I was at my lowest point. Soon afterward, I began another relationship with a woman who taught me the importance of reading scripture on a daily basis. I learned so much from this relationship about the Bible and about a man's responsibility to be the spiritual leader of the family. Because of her inspiration and the inspiration of my great-grandmother Dee Dee many years ago, I decided that I was going to start reading the Bible. In July of 2012, I began reading Genesis and on January 12, 2014, I completed Revelations. I finished reading the entire Bible on my forty-seventh birthday! This was the second critical step in the development of my spiritual foundation. By reading God's Word, I grew closer to Christ. This relationship made me realize that for me to write a book relating to Christianity, I must first know the Word of God. This initial reading of the Bible gave me a better understanding of God's Word and allowed me to better understand how I would use scripture in the writing of this book. It also inspired me to start attending Bible study on a weekly basis.

Filming golf tip at the Harbour Town
Golf Links, Hilton Head, S.C.

I moved into my current position in 2007. Ah, summers in Ohio and winters in Florida—the best of both worlds. In the fall of 2012, I took a giant leap of faith and moved my winter business back to a place I had once resided—Hilton Head, South Carolina. During the entire time I lived there, not once did I attend church worship on the island. God brought the third relationship into my life just at the right time—to lead me to the perfect place of worship, Low Country Community Church in neighboring Bluffton. I felt comfortable with my Ohio place of worship—Stonybrook United Methodist Church—but wanted to continue the consistency of worshipping in Hilton Head. This relationship was unique because we were both struggling personally when we met. God used both our struggles to help us through some very difficult times. I enjoyed our long talks about our faith, past mistakes and dreams. We're still close friends.

Dr. Jeff Cranston, pastor of my Bluffton church home, provided excellent biblical knowledge along with a moving weekly message, which stimulated my creativity for writing this book. God used three beautiful women to guide me to Sunday worship, inspire me to read the Bible cover to cover, and continue my momentum of Sunday worship at a place where I felt comfortable. All three of these spiritual disciples helped elevate my faith, giving me the confidence to begin this project. I had procrastinated for years. "One day I will write a book," I told myself. "When God gives me the platform, I'll start writing." I always thought my platform would be one of my students winning a PGA tournament or major championship. One day I mentioned my decision to write a book to Fred Griffin.

"Jon," he assured, "You will know when the time is right." He was correct. The right time came when I started putting God first in my life. That is the platform. *"Trust in the Lord forever, for the Lord God is an everlasting rock" (Isaiah 26:4).*

In the song *"Broken Roads,"* by Columbus, Ohio's own Rascal Flatts, people are referred to as *northern stars* guiding you to someone or something that God has planned for you. I certainly have lived my life on a broken road. Through it all, God brought disciples into my life to help build my teaching career and lead me back into my faith. Recently, I called Todd Meena, my friend and disciple in work and faith. We caught up on work, talked about college football and how each of our families was doing. I told Todd about my renewed faith, how I was attending Sunday worship regularly and about my Bible study classes. More than fifteen years ago, Todd mentioned to me that while playing on the European Tour he took the time to read the Bible cover to cover in one year. Like my great-grandmother

Dee Dee's comments had been before, Todd's were northern stars in my heart. They set a destination in my mind that guided me to fulfilling my goal. When I told Todd about my reading of the Bible, and completing it on my birthday, he confirmed my transformative accomplishment. "Wow, Jon," he said, "now that's what I call being reborn!" My foundation secured, I travel the road with confidence and humility as a teaching disciple.

"Go therefore and make disciples of all nations, baptizing them in the name of the Father and of the Son and of the Holy Spirit, teaching them to observe all that I have commanded you. And behold, I am with you always, to the end of the age" (Mathew 28:19–20).

CHAPTER 12

Surprise

But the angel said to her, "Do not be afraid, Mary; you have found favor with God. You will conceive and give birth to a son, and you are to call him Jesus. He will be great and will be called the Son of the Most High. The Lord God will give him the throne of his father David, and he will reign over Jacob's descendants forever; his kingdom will never end." (Luke 1:30–33)

The night that the angel Gabriel spoke these words to Mary her life changed forever. Mary was to be married to Joseph, a descendant of David. Her life was already set in motion, well-thought-out and ready to begin with her future husband. However, God had greater plans for both Mary and Joseph, plans that would change the course of human history. God favored Mary and gave her a gift—one He calls surprise.

Life-changing events often come by way of a messenger. So it was on a steamy summer day in 1995 as I worked the counter of the Grand Cypress Academy pro shop. I was twenty-eight and just out of the starting blocks as a professional golf instructor. The plan for my life was cemented with high goals that would eventually lead to my dream job of head instructor. Corporate life seemed awfully sweet. As a single young man, my personal life was equally enjoyable. My paycheck had grown substantially which afforded me a fairly comfortable lifestyle. For the first time, I felt in control of my life. Then the phone rang and our family's life changed forever.

"Grand Cypress Academy of Golf," I said, answering the phone.

"Jon," the familiar voice began, "my girlfriend's pregnant." It was my father delivering what would have been somewhat shocking news under ordinary circumstances. The fact that a fifty-one-year-old divorcee was about to become a new father made it even more of an unsettling revelation. The nervousness in Dad's voice was understandable. Still, his directness was typical of the man I knew who never minced words. Although I was speechless, my mind raced out of control. "My family is about to unravel," I thought as I slumped back into my chair. "What is everyone going to think of us now?" In life you take the good with the bad, the trials with the tribulations, but the initial shock of a life-altering event is something you remember. When God throws you a curveball and alters your well-laid plans, He speaks with authority letting you know He's in control. "This is My plan. Here is My gift to you. Here is My surprise!"

I remember where I was when President Richard Nixon was impeached, when the space shuttle blew up in the skies over Florida and when President Ronald Reagan was shot. It seems we never forget tragedies, famous and infamous world events or life-altering events. In addition to when they happened, we know exactly what we were doing and whom we were with during the occurrence. I remember every detail of that phone call from Dad. I selfishly wondered what my friends were going to think; after all, the sting of my parents' divorce after twenty-seven years of marriage was still fresh. I was still learning to cope with the fact that life is constantly changing, for better or worse. I selfishly wondered how the community of Black Mountain, the members of our church and my closest friends were going to respond to this news. My family had always seemed perfect to me as a child. How could this be happening to my family? I don't remember much more of the conversation with my father on the phone, except that I felt like I was in Bizzaro World.

The hit TV show *Seinfeld* was one of my all-time favorites. Jerry Seinfeld often used the term Bizzaro World to describe an upside-down situation. Dad's revelation certainly fit that description. The father seeking consultation from his offspring—eldest or other-wise—about an unplanned pregnancy is a bizarre conundrum. I told only a few of my closest friends and began to prepare for the inevitable. At twenty-eight, I should be considering fatherhood. Instead, I was about to become a big brother all over again!

On March 11, 1996, Shelby Lauryn Decker was born—my first and only sister. I wish I could say that I was at the hospital that day, waiting patiently to meet my new sibling, but I wasn't. I was in Florida, taking care of myself and wondering how I was going to cope with a new baby sister. I saw the pictures my father sent by mail and talked to the proud father as he said, "Jon, she's the most beautiful baby girl." Honestly, I felt removed from that experience. It also felt a little strange as I assessed our new family dynamic. That is, until I made the trip back to Black Mountain and I gathered that little bundle of joy in my arms. "She is so beautiful," I thought. "What a gift from God." I no longer cared how the members of our church felt, or what the locals or any of my closest friends thought. I had a baby sister and I knew that sometimes in life God's best gifts are those for which you never ask. Church members, locals and friends rallied around my family with a great amount of love and support, proving my fears baseless. For a while, I was angry with myself that I ever doubted them.

Indeed, the family dynamics were a bit strained as Shelby began to grow up. The stern disciplinarian I once knew, the man who would pull off his belt and wield it against his boys, turned into a teddy bear. As the eldest son, I have a very unique perspective of my father. I remember the well-chiseled, college athlete who served in the military after graduation. I remember a man in his mid-twenties who actively played all sports with his three boys. As a seven-year-old boy, I remember sitting on Dad's lap with my brother Michael as we helped him blow out the candles on the cake celebrating his thirtieth birthday. I saw this man in his forties cope with the harsh reality that his youngest son Brett had high-functioning autism. As an adult, I witnessed a middle-aged man mature in faith while becoming a devotee to his little, baby girl. My father, now wrapped around Shelby's little finger, had transformed into a comic-book figure. Sam Decker was now the mild-mannered new action figure MellowMan!

Dad and Shelby's mother had joint custody during Shelby's adolescence. Because I lived in Florida, Shelby and I were mostly pen pals. We would talk on the phone and I would get a photo in the mail every now and then, but very rarely did we spend quality time together. As Shelby got into her early teens, Dad had full custody and our visits became more frequent. Our relationship, although unusual and sometimes difficult to understand by others, started to really take root and evolve. All of the Decker men love Shelby and let her know it in our own, unique way.

Shelby Decker

Over the years, Shelby has been a blessing to our family. God's plans for our lives are not always simple, and as I have matured in my faith, I realize it is not always the plan that matters to God in His relationship with us; it is the journey. I love both my parents equally, but the ease with which I could converse with them varied depending upon the subject. One day Dad and I had a heart-to-heart during which he revealed details about the divorce. It helped me understand that divorce is not easy for anyone, especially the children involved. I also learned that my parents are not perfect and both have made mistakes. "Dad, do you love Shelby?" I asked. He turned his head sharply in my direction and looked at me with piercing eyes. "More than anything, Jon," he said, "like all my children."

"Well Dad," I said, "if you and Mom had not gotten a divorce, Shelby would have never come into existence." My father's eyes widened and for the first time, I think he truly understood that his divorce was necessary for him to receive his gift from God.

Shelby was our family's surprise from God, but in order for this surprise to come to fruition, there had to be some pain and suffering along the way. We as human beings make the mistake of trying to plan out our lives. Leave the details to God and trust that He will deliver His Plan on His time-table. God is more about the journey in our lives than the plan. Plans are easy to make, can be made with little thought, and changed without ever lifting a finger. In order to truly get close to God and have the relationship He craves in our lives, we have to stop wondering about the plans He has made for us and enjoy the journey no matter how difficult it may be at times. As Christians we reap the rewards from God when we put our faith in Him. James 1:12 states it best, ***"Blessed is the one who perseveres under trial because, having stood the test, that person will receive the crown of life that the Lord has promised to those who love him."***

Dad and Shelby

Years later, I had another surprise in my life, a moment that would bring me unexpected joy and change my life forever. During my twelve-year marriage, my wife and I were unable to have children. After years of trying, spending thousands of dollars going to fertility specialists, and saying a few prayers along the way, we came to the conclusion that children would not be a part of our marriage. One day after work in the spring of 2003, Fred Griffin asked me if I would be interested in being a mentor for one of his son's little league teammates. "Absolutely," I said and agreed to go to one of the practices to meet the young boy named Devin. Devin's mother had cancer and no support from his father or any other adult male in his life. He was being reared by his grandparents Betty and John while his mother Cindy was getting treatments for her cancer.

When I first met Devin, I thought he looked familiar and noticed that he was tall for his age, very strong and athletic. Fred had mentioned that he played golf and I thought to myself, "I can now give back to the game of golf and make a big impact in a young boy's life." At first, Devin was shy and reserved around me. I believe he had a difficult time relating to adult males since his father—who was supposed to be the most important male figure in his life—was not around. In time, though, we developed a wonderful relationship. We met once a week for a golf lesson and I attended most of his baseball games. Several times, my wife and I had Devin over to our house to swim in the pool. I taught Devin how to plant a tree, work around the house, and gave him advice that a father would give to a son. I wanted Devin to know that he could count on me, so every time we talked on the phone about meeting for a lesson, I always gave him the time and place we would meet and then followed up on my promise. We built a foundation for trust between us.

One December evening Devin's family came over for dinner. Afterward I planned to take Devin to the 2003 Tangerine Bowl at the Citrus Bowl Stadium in Orlando. Cindy was really struggling with the cancer, but this kind-hearted woman brought me a card thanking me for being a *father* to Devin, something he so desperately craved. As the tears filled my eyes, I realized God does answer our prayers in ways we could never imagine. Devin's grandmother always took photos of the two of us after every lesson or get-together. "Jon, you are not going to believe this," she said. "I was looking through Devin's old pictures and look, I found one of you and Devin when he was six years old." I looked at the photo in amazement! There I was at the academy handing Devin his official diploma for the completion of golf camp, a year before I became his official big brother. Devin's mom, smiling proudly, looked on as I shook her son's hand. God does have a plan, and through many trials and tribulations, Devin's path and my path had intersected. I knew at that moment Devin and I were meant to be and that God had given me a most welcomed surprise.

Who knew when this photo was taken, that I was to be Devin's mentor. Cindy was a proud mother!

Devin has a God given golf swing. My job is to provide guidance.

On Good Friday (March 25, 2005), Cindy passed away. I was honored when Devin asked me to sit beside him during the home-going service. He showed the poise and grace of someone assured that his mother was resting in heaven. I was there to comfort him, but his peaceful demeanor actually comforted me. He shows the same poise in his golf game. I have never seen Devin get upset on the golf course. As a child, I was a club thrower, cursed and threw pity parties when things didn't go my way on the course. Devin went through much more as a child than I could ever have imagined, yet God equipped him with maturity beyond his years. I have personally learned many life lessons by watching Devin and Shelby struggle during their childhoods. Both have shown real strength, the strength that comes from within when things don't go their way. My perspective as a child was totally different. My perspective was very jaded and somewhat idealistic. I thought families were supposed to be perfect. No family is perfect, no relationship is perfect and no round of golf is perfect. The concept of perfection is very much like an idealistic plan for one's life. It looks good on paper, seems right in our minds; however, in reality, it is unobtainable. God is now in the forefront for all the planning in my life.

After my divorce in 2011, I was forced to live a very nomadic lifestyle. I was working at the New Albany Country Club in Ohio during the summer months and at the Grand Cypress Academy of Golf in winter. To complicate matters, a declining housing market wreaked havoc on my situation. My ex-wife was still living in our home, so I had nowhere to live. Betty and Devin graciously provided housing for me during those winter months. Without their help, I would have never made it. It was great spending time with Devin, a senior in high school with college among his options. We had some very frank discussions of what he was going to face in college, the temptations, his work ethic and his college golf career. Upon graduation from high school, Devin received a golf scholarship to Jacksonville University. I was the proudest big brother on the planet. God used my personal sufferings to put me where I was needed, helping Devin. Betty graciously provided shelter for me when I needed it most, and through it all, God showered us all with His grace. I learned from this experience that pain, suffering and struggle are also surprises that shape God's plan.

The winter of 2014, I joined the StonyBrook United Methodist Church. During the six-week orientation for new members, I took classes every Sunday night to learn the history of the United Methodist Church, one dominated by John Wesley. As part of our everyday homework, we were to recite John Wesley's Covenant Prayer: "I am no longer my own, but yours. Put me to what you will, place me with whom you will. Put me to doing, put me to suffering. Let me be put to work for you or set aside for you, praised for you or criticized for you. Let me be full, let me be empty. Let me have all things, let me have nothing. I freely and fully surrender all things to your hope and service. And now, O glorious and blessed God, Creator, Redeemer, and Sustainer, you are mine, and I am yours. So be it. And the covenant, which I have made on earth, let it be made also in heaven. Amen."

The first couple of times I read "put me to suffering," I honestly did so in disbelief, saying to myself, "I have suffered enough the last five years to last a lifetime. I am the epitome of a mid-life crisis." One day after saying the prayer, I finally understood what this beautiful prayer meant. It is about our journey with God. It is about surrendering everything, and most importantly, it is about faith. Even in our darkest hours on this earth, if we trust in Jesus Christ, He will be with us. Knowing that the pain and suffering we are going through at times on this Earth leads us closer to Christ.

Shelby and Devin are similar in many ways. Both are poised beyond their years; both have a very strong Christian faith; and both have come from families that on the outside may seemed broken but on the inside are anything but. I feel fortunate to be a part of both their lives because I have learned from them both. As they enter adulthood, I look forward to their lives ahead. Shelby is my sister, yet in many of our personal discussions over family issues, I have been more like a father to her. I was to be a big brother to Devin yet in time I became his father figure as well. I have prayed thousands of times to God that one day I would be a father. I believed it was in my DNA and that I had the calling to be a father. God has a way of putting people where they are needed, as John Wesley so poetically described. God has put me where I am needed and by doing so blessed me with two gifts I never expected. I thank God for His gifts and look forward to where He leads me next. God hears our prayers and has seen our plans but what makes life exciting and what brings passion to my life is when God says, "Surprise, Jon, look what I have for you today!"

"For I know the plans I have for you, declares the Lord, plans for welfare and not for evil, to give you a future and a hope" *(Jeremiah 29:11).*

As Seen Through My Eyes

Luke Fisher, East Carolina University/
Minnesota Vikings, Tight End

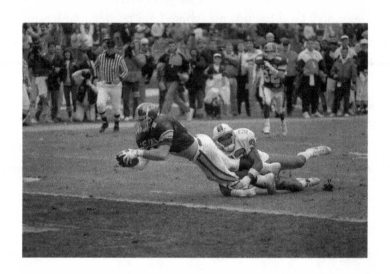

On January 1, 1992, electricity filled the air of Atlanta Fulton County Stadium. Our star quarterback, Jeff Blake, called the team to "huddle." It was late in the 4th quarter with less than two minutes to play, 3rd and 2 from the 22 yard line, and our season was on the line. Jeff called a play that our team had run numerous times, and I immediately knew my responsibility. As tight end, I was to run an option route. This play called for me to run downfield, engage the inside linebacker with a move, read his reaction, and then move right or left to the open field. As children, our plays were often drawn in the dirt. "Go deep" or "get open" were commanded with boyish enthusiasm, commonplace lingo between the quarterback and his receiver. Huddling near midfield against our bitter rivals, the North Carolina State Wolfpack, Jeff wasn't drawing in the dirt; he spoke to me with his eyes, like so many times before. That quick glance in my direction had worked all season in propelling our team toward an almost perfect season and on this day that "look" had resulted in eleven successful completions between the two of us. With precious time running out of the game, our herculean comeback would need one more catch to move the chains. Jeff's nonverbal communication said to me, "Luke, get open. I'm coming your way."

As I ran the first five yards, the inside linebacker dropped back. State was not going to get beat deep. After ten yards, I faked in toward the middle causing the linebacker to freeze. I countered by turning toward the sideline. Jeff did what he had done all year—put the ball right on the money with a perfect strike. It was then a sprint to the end zone. As I approached the goal line, I dove and stretched the ball over the chalk landing safely on pay dirt. I immediately rolled on my back and put both arms in the air as I was mobbed by my teammates. The sold out stadium went into bedlam! The 1992 Peach Bowl would go down as one of the greatest bowl comebacks in college football history. For the East Carolina Pirates, it was just another "can you top this moment" for a storybook season.

Later that spring, my unforgettable year continued as my childhood dream came true—I was drafted by the Minnesota Vikings in the eighth round. I arrived in Minnesota and met Brad Johnson. As rookies, Brad and I became great friends and decided to room together. Brad was a southern gentleman both humble and courteous on and off the field, but on the inside, he was highly motivated and a fierce competitor. My career would be cut short by injury after only two years. Brad would go on to win Super Bowl XXXVII as quarterback of the Tampa Bay Buccaneers. God has a way of bringing people together, and through Brad, I would later meet Jon Decker in Orlando.

My friendship with Jon has led to many rounds on the golf course where I struggled to learn the game. His patience with me has helped my game and made me realize that the power in golf comes from technique, not brute force. Jon and I also got together socially and enjoyed bachelorhood. In fact, I was with him the night he met his former wife. We have gone to ECU games together and often talk about our college days, family, and faith. I am proud to call Jon a friend and know that this book will reach that person lost in his or her personal journey. My senior year at ECU taught me that with a common goal and hard work, anything in life is possible, as long as you keep the faith and always "believe."

CHAPTER 13

Spirit

"If you believe, you will receive whatever you ask for in prayer" (Mathew 21:22).

Seldom does a high school student experience adrenaline overdrive. Mine was off the charts whenever I visited colleges of interest. Some of it might have been anxiety or excitement over the final decision of where I was going to live the next four years. Part of it surely was the pure joy of turning another page in my life. The transition from counting on Mom and Dad to steer me in the right direction to charting my own course was something of a rite of passage that I relished. My agenda included more than a few trips to Chapel Hill to visit the University of North Carolina. I also traveled to Furman University in Greenville, South Carolina. Later, our family traveled back down the mountain to South Carolina to visit Clemson University. As most football fans know, the Tigers have the fabled tradition of touching the desert rock before flooding the field, sending the home town fans into a frenzy. My grades were better than average. Of course, my real desire for college was to play golf and enjoy the college experience. In September of 1984, my junior year of high school, my family made the six-hour drive to Greenville, North Carolina, to visit East

Carolina University for a weekend that would set the course for my college journey.

I kicked off my weekend with a meeting with the Head Golf Coach Bob Helmick, followed by a tour of the practice facilities and dormitories. As I walked the campus on that beautiful autumn day, I became enchanted by the parade of gorgeous coeds out front of the student store. I filed that away as a place I had to revisit often if ECU made the final cut. It was suddenly on my radar! However, the defining moment for my decision came when our family attended the Pirates' home opener at Ficklen Memorial Stadium. Michael and I sat by ourselves in the nose bleed section, while our parents enjoyed a much better view of the field sitting with my aunt and uncle in their seats below. In the row directly in front of us sat a heavyset, middle-aged man along with his wife and mother. The family sat very quietly, almost with a nervous energy. Neither of them uttered a word for nearly twenty minutes. We all stood during the national anthem. Still no words were spoken. The crowd was at a fever pitch; the smell of fall permeated the air and the atmosphere sent me into a near-nirvana experience. College football on TV is one thing, attending a game is another, one of my most passion-filled events. Suddenly I heard the sound of a cannon blast and the Pirates came running out on the field. The stoic man in front of me rose from his seat and yelled, "Come on Pirates! Let's kick some ass!" I looked at my brother and we both started laughing. I said to Michael, "This is where I'm coming to college!" That weekend, I was overtaken by the spirit, the spirit of the Pirates!

My interest in East Carolina first developed because my aunt and uncle, Beth and Louie Eckstein, were both professors in economics there. Our family stayed at their home for the weekend which allowed us time to reunite with my cousins, Annie and Will. During my years at East Carolina, Aunt Beth would be like a second mother to me and my friends, always making us feel like we were home. During that weekend visit, I fell in love with Greenville and its spirit. There is nothing like a college town—a place where the entire community rallies around the home team through thick and thin. In Greenville, purple is the color of choice and on game day purple reigns. During my years (1985–90) at East Carolina, there was more thin than thick. We had our occasional high moments—beating in state rival North Carolina State twice at their home field, Carter Finley Stadium. Those are two high moments that come to mind—but most Saturdays ended in another frustrating loss. Losing never dampened the Pirate fans' enthusiasm or loyalty. I remember my final spring semester and attending our annual IFC banquet where all the fraternities came together, handed out awards, and listened to a guest speaker. That year new head football coach, Bill Lewis, was guest speaker. Coach Lewis was an amazing speaker, bringing passion and spirit to his speech. Toward the end of his speech, Coach Lewis made a statement that I will never forget. He said, "East Carolina University is on the verge of becoming a great football team, and the reason for this is our young quarterback Jeff Blake." I was astonished because at that time, Jeff Blake had very little playing experience for a team that was 6–5 the previous fall. In the spring of 1990, my time at East Carolina University ended, and I now had to face the real world, starting a new chapter in my life. But I knew that once I left Greenville, I would always follow my Pirates in every sport.

The fall of 1991 Coach Bill Lewis' prediction came true. Under his leadership and quarterback Jeff Blake's record-setting performance, East Carolina went 11–1, finished ninth in the nation and won the Peach Bowl. Every year, that game is replayed on ESPN as an *Instant Classic*. The season ended with the Pirates beating their bitter in-state rivals, the 12-ranked North Carolina State Wolfpack on New Year's Day in the Peach Bowl. It was a storybook season that captured the heart of the nation and put East Carolina on the map. More than 30,000 Pirate fans made the trip to Atlanta and watched East

Carolina rally from a 17-point deficit in the fourth quarter to win the game. The game-winning touchdown was a 22-yard strike from Blake to Luke Fisher. Suddenly the entire nation witnessed what I had experienced during my first trip to Greenville—the Pirates spirit!

Blake would go on to the NFL where he played for several teams including Cincinnati where he earned All-Pro honors. Fisher was drafted by the Minnesota Vikings and played two years in the league. His roommate while at Minnesota was none other than Brad Johnson, my old high school teammate from Charles D. Owen High School. I never knew Luke while attending East Carolina, but years later, we would meet through Brad Johnson in Orlando. That led to a great relationship between the two of us—one that continues today. Coach Lewis' prediction had come true for the East Carolina football program, and I was never prouder of my university and our passionate fan base!

I love being around passionate people, thus my attraction to East Carolina and Coach Lewis. Passionate people inspire others and are spirited individuals. But what is spirit and how does one obtain it? In today's media-influenced society, spirit is often confused with charisma or the *it* factor. The singer on *American Idol* with whom the nation falls in love, the basketball player who seems to always come through when the game is on the line and the golfer who seems to always make the clutch putt are examples of what spirit can be. However, spirit is much more than having the it factor or coming through in the clutch. I believe that spirit ultimately comes from deep within a person's heart in the form of a true belief in oneself. During the 1991 season, Coach Lewis and his staff came up with a slogan after a close loss in the opening game at Illinois. In the fourth quarter, East Carolina was down, but made a valiant comeback and actually recovered an onside kick to potentially win the game. The officials flagged East Carolina for excessive celebration, or showing too much spirit, dashing any comeback hopes that afternoon, and the

Pirates suffered their only loss of the season. The comeback showed great heart, determination, and above all, spirit.

On the eve of the next game against Memphis State, Coach Lewis wrote "I Believe" on a piece of paper and taped copies of it to every player's hotel room door. Memphis State was coming off a huge upset win over the nationally ranked USC Trojans in Los Angeles. "I Believe" became the team's mantra, and soon afterward, the fan base adopted it as well. Comeback wins over South Carolina, Syracuse and Virginia Tech became the norm. When the Pirates were down by 17 points in the fourth quarter in Atlanta, the fans all chanted, "We Believe!" The sound was deafening; the Pirate spirit that day overwhelming, and the result was a huge lift to an already inspired football team. Two words, "I Believe," inspired the impossible and showed the nation what spirit can achieve. I believe in this spirit so much that I now use it every summer while teaching junior golf camps.

Like most private clubs in America, the New Albany Country Club offers junior camps and clinics to introduce children to the game of golf. Our camps have become so popular because of our great teaching staff as well as the wonderful junior golfers in New Albany and the Columbus area. If there is any city in America that has the college spirit, it is Columbus, Ohio, home of the Ohio State University. The city bleeds scarlet and gray and is known for its passionate fan base. I love the home-team spirit of Columbus and wanted to bring that spirit to our junior camps, so I decided to add a Spirit Day to close the camp.

Paint it Purple! L to R Daley Juschka, Sarah
Klingerman and Harper Anderson

The first day of the camp, the kids are divided into two teams. As the week progresses, the teams compete for points until the final day of camp when the teaching staff plays with groups from each team in a fun filled scramble. I wanted to infuse spirit into the camp, so I told the camp participants, "On Friday, I will give extra points for all of you who wear purple." I always wear purple on Fridays, going back to my East Carolina Days of *Paint it Purple Fridays*. I was amazed as New Albany became a sea of purple. During the next camp, I said, "On Friday, wear your favorite team colors, hat or uniform." On Friday, all the kids came in various colors, hats, ribbons and uniforms. Of course, the scarlet and gray dominated the color scheme. Making the game fun is a must for effective teaching. Spirit Day is that and more.

Halloween Clinic. Arrgghh! Left: "Sweet"
Caroline Snyder/Center: Gwyneth Lee

As PGA golf professionals, we are faced with a major problem in today's society. Children are inundated with camps, activities, clubs and team sports. Golf may be a team sport in high school and college, but in the beginning, it can be lonely, require hours and hours of practice, and be very difficult to learn even for the most gifted athletes. If the kids are not having fun during camp, we lose them quickly to sports like soccer, lacrosse and dance. There is nothing wrong with any of these sports. In fact, I promote children playing multiple sports. However, I don't see many fifty-year-old men and women playing lacrosse or soccer. I believe that the spirit of team sports is just as vital in teaching junior golfers as learning the fundamentals of the golf swing. Golf for juniors has to be safe, fun and a wonderful learning experience.

2015 Spirit Award Winner Ryan Hurst

In 2011, I wanted to create a competitive way to promote spirit in our junior programs. I came up with the Spirit Award, a yearlong competition for all of our junior golfers. The criteria is based on ten areas of golf and voted on by all of our teaching staff. Each member of our staff nominates one child at the end of the summer. The nominations are announced during our year-end banquet, culminating with the highly anticipated Spirit Award winner. Past winners are allowed one nomination and one vote and are recognized at the banquet. The ten areas voted on are attendance, attitude, work ethic, history of the game, sportsmanship, rules and etiquette, improvement, dress code, desire and behavior. The winner's name is engraved on the Spirit Award plaque which features the East Carolina University Pirate in the center of the plaque. The winner also receives a Pee Dee the Pirate (East Carolina's mascot) head cover for their driver.

The juniors' enthusiasm was palpable as they really worked hard in an effort to claim the season-ending prize. As a result, the entire camp's spirit took a serious uptick. This award means a lot to me because it represents what I want from all my students—passion for the game of golf. My passion runs the gamut from golf to working out to watching college football to spending time with family and friends. I've always had a passion for children. I love the interaction with them and how it rejuvenates my spirit. However, none of these compare to the true spirit of my life now—the Holy Spirit.

My understanding of the Apostles Creed evolved as I matured in Christ. The words "I believe in the Holy Spirit, the Holy Catholic Church, the communion of Saints, the forgiveness of sins, the resurrection of the body and life everlasting" which had scant meaning to the child in church now stir the spirit within me. The term Holy Spirit was clarified during service at the StonyBrook United Methodist Church in 2013. One of our sermon series was taken from the book *The Wild Goose Chase* by Mark Batterson. This sermon series, directed by Pastor Mike Bowie, really shed light on what the Holy Spirit is and how it impacts one's life. Batterson writes, "Celtic Christians had a name for the Holy Spirit-An Geadh-Glas or the Wild Goose. The name hints of mystery. Much like a wild goose, the Spirit of God cannot be tracked or tamed. An element of danger, an air of unpredictability surround him."

My favorite illustration came when Pastor Mike described the Holy Spirit as a fountain with four bowls. The top bowl is the individual; the second, your family and friends; the third, community; and the bottom bowl is the world. The water is the Holy Spirit. Once it is poured into the top bowl, it begins to fill the individual with God's glory and love. It also solidifies the intimate relationship that God desires to have with you until you're consumed with the Holy Spirit. The Spirit then begins to overflow into the second bowl—family and friends. As the second bowl fills, the water overflows into the third bowl which is the community. Through this, the Holy Spirit overflows until God's Word and God's love are spread throughout the world. I have experienced most of this fountain and hope my experience in writing this book will spread God's Word unto the world.

The illustration of the Holy Spirit filling the four bowls shows how God does work in mysterious ways. I never imagined in my wildest dreams that I would write a book. Growing up, I wasn't a reader and only wrote in school for class assignments. Frankly, I was an athlete trying to just get by in school, never pushing myself academically. That all changed once I became a teaching professional. God started planting seeds in my mind. In time, the seeds formed into personal stories. Suddenly, I was having conversations with myself about these stories and how they could one day be put together into a book. The stories flooded my mind until it felt as if it were going to explode. Honestly, I was scared to start writing a single word as I began to rationalize with God. "I am not an author," I said. "Who would ever want to read my stories?" Procrastination became my middle name.

I suddenly started realizing that God's timeline was different than mine. His timeline is untamed. He has no fear. Fear comes from the enemy; yes, the enemy. I knew if I didn't start the writing process one day I would have to confess my fear to God: "I didn't believe in myself. I had no faith." For the first time, I realized what the Holy Spirit is. It is God Almighty living in my soul, having an intimate relationship with my heart and mind, punching the keys on my computer, making me feel safe, and telling me inside, "I am your rock, Jon, lean on me and start writing now!"

Once I began writing the flood gates were opened. The Holy Spirit consumed my every thought, while eating, teaching and even while having conversations with others. I felt as though I had a new best friend, even though God has always been with me. I was acknowledging His presence in all of my actions. I also realize that God craves intimacy with me and all his children, intimacy during quiet times. I was comforted during those lonely nights after my divorce. I often cried at night because I felt as though the world was letting me down. Now I felt safe. Writing became my therapy and my new connection to God. Before when I prayed, I felt as though I was having a one-way conversation. When I listened to God speak to me in my writing, I began to have a two-way dialogue, and the pieces started falling into place. I wanted to test my writing, so periodically, I would let my close friends read my chapters. I was surprised by the positive feedback. As always, my friends gave me the encouragement I desperately needed. The Holy Spirit had now spread from my mind unto my friends and family. Suddenly the second bowl was filling up.

I started using social media to promote my book. Facebook was a great way for me to keep friends, family and students up to date with my progress. The pastoral staff's approval of my writing was also a bonus. One day before Sunday service, I was talking with the youth coordinator, Ben Lilly, about working with the youth during their Sunday night meeting. I suggested to Ben that I would give the youth group a brief demonstration on putting and have them play a putting game, tic-tac-toe. Afterward, I would read them the chapter from my book titled "Want." As we were talking, Pastor Nikki walked by and said, "Jon, I loved reading your last chapter, keep writing. You are inspiring me!" The praise further lifted my spirits. I was going to church to learn the gospel, worship God and learn about His son Jesus Christ. Now my writing was inspiring the pastoral staff--the third bowl, my community, was starting to fill up!

On April 27, 2014, I went to speak with the youth group, knowing in my heart that this would be part of God's work to fill up the third bowl. The number of parents in attendance was humbling. I presented the golf information to the novice players, most of whom had never held a club in their hands before. The kids and parents enjoyed the game of tic-tac-toe. Afterward, I sat in front of them and prepared to read. I speak in front of groups on a daily basis and feel very comfortable most of the time. I will admit, though, I was extremely nervous because I was about to bare my soul to a group I had just recently met. This was the ultimate test for my writing.

I wanted the kids to hear "Want" because it addresses many teenage problems. "I want you to listen to what I have to say because these stories have been with me for years," I said. "I want you to take the next twenty minutes to really listen because these words are from God. This is what He is telling me to write through the Holy Spirit." I looked up and every eye was on me. You could have heard a pin drop.

My voice cracked as I read the first paragraph, yet I was composed. I felt the pitter patter of my heart and the rush of adrenaline as I began to perspire. Even though I was nervous, I was enjoying myself. Suddenly, I felt a calming spirit. I read the words with untamed passion and told myself, "Let the spirit go!" The teenagers laughed at the funny parts and when I looked up, I still had their attention. I felt like I was now in control of my emotions, until I got to the very end and started reading about the baptism of Jesus Christ by John the Baptist. Since reaffirming my faith, baptisms bring tears to my eyes because I have always wanted to be a father. I started to break down. I was no longer in control of my emotions and I began to cry. For two to three minutes, I cried uncontrollably and couldn't say a word. Through the deafening silence, I still felt at ease. I cried for many reasons, not the least of which is my love for Jesus Christ. I also cried for healing from my divorce and because I knew the Holy Spirit was with me, though I felt no shame. I finally composed myself to somehow finish my last sentence. I looked up with tears in my eyes, smiled and said, "That's all I got." The room erupted in laughter and applause, followed by a big hug from one of the teenagers, Bobby.

Mark Batterson was correct; the Holy Spirit is untamed. My dreams were to be a PGA Tour player, but God said, "Jon, I want you to teach golf to others." I dreamed of winning golf tournaments, holding the trophy, and standing on a platform creating personal fame and fortune—subsequently using that fame in helping others by promoting Christian faith. God answered, "Jon, I want you to write a book instead." I dreamed of being a father, the spiritual leader and head of a household. God said, "Jon, I want you to be a mentor and inspire juniors through the game of golf and through Christianity."

God's plan for me is still evolving as I now have a passion for writing, growing in my faith and promoting my Christian faith through golf and my book. I trust that the Holy Spirit will guide me through my life. The mistake many Christians make is they think that God is sitting on a throne looking down on them with a score-card and judging their every move. As a result, most people shy away from having the intimate, personal relationship God craves for all of us. I know that God is living inside of me through the Holy Spirit, and if I listen and write what I hear inside, I will live an abundant, healthy, exciting, untamed life. My motto for my relationship with God and his son Jesus Christ is very simple: "The goose is loose; let the Holy Spirit fill my heart, guide my mind and overtake my dreams in this life, leading me into my everlasting life to come."

CHAPTER 14

Nine Eleven

"Remember the words of the Lord Jesus, how he said, It is more blessed to give than to receive" (Acts 20:35).

The somber mood swept over the room like fog off the ocean on that October day in 2001. I sat in the staff meeting at the Grand Cypress Academy of Golf with growing anticipation of what was sure to be an unfavorable forecast of the academy's future. The entire staff, sales team, instructors, administrative staff and outside-range staff sat quietly as we went over the sales reports and projected business forecasts for the remainder of 2001 and the spring of 2002. All through the late 1990s the golf school business had thrived. The stock market roared, people traveled unfettered by fear or finance, and the corporate golf school business was on fire! The majority of this business for Florida stemmed from the northeastern part of the United States, most notably New York City. Brenda Pfeifer, the academy's sales manager, sat in front of the meeting and read the numbers for the recent cancellations and lost business. "Today," she began, "Lehman Brothers cancelled their spring clinic. Numerous people who were scheduled to come to the clinic died in the World Trade Center. Lehman Brothers has a freeze on all corporate events."

"The image of that airplane turning into the World Trade Center is a picture in my mind that I will never forget," said Academy Director Fred Griffin. Fred is surely not alone, September of 2001— the day the world stood still, the day known worldwide as *Nine Eleven*—is forever etched in the memories of all who lived through it.

On September 10, 2001, I was in the middle of a long day of teaching golf in Arizona. Ford was hosting an instructional golf clinic near Phoenix for their top sales people and had hired many of the Grand Cypress instructors for their private golf school. After three days of teaching in the blazing desert heat, I was looking forward to returning home to Orlando. The event coordinator noted our travel preferences. "You have two choices, Jon," she said, "you can take the a.m. flight tomorrow or the red-eye tonight."

"I'll take the red-eye tonight," I said. My fellow instructors all elected to take the morning flights. I sat at the bar at the Boulders Resort waiting on my town car to drive me to the airport. I enjoyed a drink and watched the season-opening Monday Night Football game between the Denver Broncos and the New York Giants. The peaceful desert made for a very relaxed ride toward the Phoenix Sky Harbor International Airport. I arrived at my gate well ahead of time and sat down to watch the remainder of the football game. Suddenly, the airport intercom came on and announced that our flight had been delayed by one hour; our plane was ready but the flight attendants had not yet arrived in Phoenix. They were on another airplane in transit. "Oh well, at least I get to finish watching the game," I thought to myself.

As I boarded the plane, I looked around and thought, "This is awesome, open seating!" The plane was only half-full, so I knew I would be able to stretch out and grab a few winks. After take-off, I asked the flight attendant if I was going to make my connection to Orlando. "I don't know, sir," she said. "It is going to be very close, but if you do miss your connection, there are plenty of other flights to Orlando." Knowing the situation was out of my hands, I rested my head on a pillow. The next thing I heard was the sound of wheels hitting the ground in Atlanta. The Hartsfield-Jackson Atlanta International Airport is massive, so the odds of making it to the gate on time—forget about my bags and clubs making it—seemed very remote. As I hurriedly exited the plane, I asked the lady giving out connection information, "My connection is to Orlando. What is my gate number?"

"You're in luck, sir, your connection is at the next gate," she said. I couldn't believe my good fortune. In one of the largest airports in the world, my connection was a mere fifty feet away! I handed over my boarding pass, smiled and calmly boarded the plane, the cabin door immediately closing behind me. I was the last one to board and felt the sting of the other passengers' eyes impatiently staring at me.

"I was the last one on the plane," I said to the flight attendant. "My flight was delayed out of Phoenix. Do you think my luggage and golf clubs will make it?"

"It will be close, but most likely they didn't have time to transfer them over," she said.

"Oh well," I said, "just glad to be going home." On the morning of September 11, 2001, I safely landed in Orlando, eagerly walked off the plane and headed toward baggage claim. As I rode the escalator down to the baggage claim area, I heard the familiar sound of the bells and horns ringing at baggage claim. Seconds later, the baggage carousel motored up. I was still high above on the escalator looking down when a single door slowly opened and a golf bag was set out by one of the airline employees. I recognized the travel cover. It was my bag! A few seconds later, my luggage appeared on the carousel. I thought, "Huh, last bag on, first bag off." This entire sequence of events happened before I reached the bottom of the escalator.

At the bottom of the escalator was a town car driver with *Decker* written on a sign. I couldn't believe the convenience. I remarked to the town car driver, "Today is my lucky day. I will never forget this flight for the rest of my life." It was great to be home. I was ready to see my wife and my dog Rokky. I also looked forward to some much-needed rest. As soon as I walked through the front door of my home, my wife greeted me with the horrific news that a plane had crashed into the North Tower of the World Trade Center. My first thought was of a private plane whose pilot had simply lost control, had a heart attack or possibly engine failure. I didn't have a cell phone, so my wife had no idea that I was safely on the ground, and she was visibly upset. I sat in front of the television and watched on live television as the second commercial airline flew into the South Tower. Suddenly, the reality of the situation began to hit me. America was under attack! How could this be happening?

September 11, 2001, would indeed be a travel day I would never forget, but for all the wrong reasons. This day had a profound impact on the world while stirring emotions of fear, anxiety and helplessness into the hearts and minds of the people of this great country. America was hijacked and attacked on native soil by terrorists using one of the greatest forms of transportation in the world was unfathomable. Commercial airplanes, with defenseless people on board, were used as human missiles in a way not even a Hollywood studio could have imagined. America was under fire. New York City was Ground Zero. The Pentagon was a war zone, and a reclaimed strip mine in Stonycreek Township, Pennsylvania became a cemetery.

Nine Eleven not only impacted the world's economy, it directly affected the way people travel, the way they thought about traveling and brought a thriving economy to a screeching halt. Closer to home, Orlando immediately felt the effects of Nine Eleven. All airline travel was shut down. In fact, my work colleagues from Grand Cypress were stuck for a week in Arizona with no way home. Rental cars were not available; planes were grounded, and the thought of going to a golf school or giving a golf lesson became a matter of little or no import. September 11, 2001, impacted the lives of every human being on this planet, in ways that are still being experienced today.

As we sat in the sales meeting, one thing became very apparent. In order to survive, we were going to have to adapt. After Nine Eleven, corporate golf schools immediately went on the decline as businesses looked for ways to cut expenses. Individual golf schools and private lessons would now be our staple. Being creative, learning to reach our customers individually via e-mail and offering lesson packages became the norm. Gone were the days of showing up to work with a full book of lessons. It was time to scratch and claw for business. Tourism, leisure activities, hotels, theme parks, resorts and travel were so affected in the state of Florida by Nine Eleven that thousands of Floridians lost their jobs and many leisure businesses were forced to shut down. I remember being so upset after Nine Eleven, and personally telling myself, "There is nothing I can do to change what happened, but I am not going to let what just happened stop me from succeeding as a teaching professional." I was determined to turn this terrible situation into some form of positive growth, so I began to do what seemed to come naturally. I began to write.

After Nine Eleven, I started collecting e-mails from my students and began writing golf tips. I noticed that my students liked the extra effort and with that, came repeat business. To help promote business, I decided to contact my local newspaper—the *West Orange Times.* To my pleasant surprise, they graciously agreed to publish my tips. Shortly after that, my tips were featured regularly in my hometown and in a newspaper in Michigan. I followed up lessons with phone calls which helped in developing a following. The resort produced video tips which were played in the hotel and villa rooms, and our sales meetings turned more into brainstorming sessions. I have to admit that I became excited about the new way of marketing and creating business for the resort. In the past, Grand Cypress used its close proximity to Disney World and name recognition as its primary marketing tools. Persistence and creating a business model in step with the changing time were now a priority. From my perspective, it had to be a business model that fit perfectly with my personality and the way I have tried to tackle all my obstacles in life. Galatians 6:9 states it best, *"Let us not become weary in doing good, for at the proper time we will reap a harvest if we do not give up."*

Golfers need to 'practice their play' to improve

CHIP SHOTS

by Jon Decker

Several years ago I noticed Ted Tryba, a two time winner on the PGA Tour, standing beside the Academy of Golf par 4 practice green hitting drivers back down the fairway towards the par 4 tee box.

The academy's par-4 is a 411-yard dogleg right hole from tee to green and is a very demanding driving hole. I thought this was strange that Ted was playing the hole backwards and asked, "what are you doing"?

He said, "I am playing Augusta in two weeks and I am practicing my tee shot for (hole No. 13)."

Now if you are not familiar with Augusta National 13th hole it is a par-5 dogleg left hole. What Ted was doing was "practicing his play."

Jack Nicklaus designed the Academy of Golf with the three practice holes so that the game could be taught, practiced or played.

The great thing about these holes is that if you hit a poor shot there is no problem in hitting another shot. If you don't have a practice hole then try some of my favorite ways to "practice your play."

1. Hit two balls and play the worst ball. This game promotes scrambling and working on trouble shots.

I would not recommend doing this on a busy day at the course — this is great for the practice holes.

2. Play pullbacks. Putt against a friend and every time you miss a putt pull the putt back 1 club length. This game is great for working on short putts.

3. Practice your pre-shot routine.

Remember to always pick a target and try to visualize your shot.

4. Play the golf course on the driving range. Pretend the first hole is 400 yards. Hit your drive and estimate how far it went. Let's say it went 250 yards. What club do you hit 150 yards into the wind?

Now pick that club and hit it. Remember to play all mis-hits but no putts. This game promotes shot making.

5. Work on uneven lies. This is one of the least practiced areas in golf. Remember most shots in golf are not on a tee or flat ground.

6. Hit fairway bunker shots. Most people practice from the greenside but neglect the longer shots.

7. Play a hole with only one club. This promotes total shot making. I'm always interested in what club people will choose.

8. Play different tees. If normally the gold tees are what you play move up and try the white tees or vice versa. This makes you think on your feet about club selection and scoring shots.

I hope you are able to enjoy a few more rounds of golf before the fall turns to winter.

After Nine Eleven my golf tips were featured in *(The West Orange Times, Black Mountain News and the Tri-County Times)*

Like most businesses, tourism and leisure activities are directly related to the economy. I have always said, "Golf lessons are a leading indicator for the economy." Simply put, when I am busy teaching, the economy is doing well. Six years later, the second major setback for the world's economy began in the form of the housing decline. Once again people stopped traveling, golf communities became ghost towns, and the PGA golf professional was forced to find creative ways to increase rounds, lessons, and subsequently, revenue. I owned a large lakefront dream home outside Orlando and a new condominium in Ohio. When the housing market began its historic crash in 2007, it wreaked havoc on my real estate investments. My once large and growing pool of home equity plummeted into an ocean of debt. The Florida housing market was paralyzed as For Sale signs littered the streets of every neighborhood in America and the term recession became a household word. Once again, while the stock markets were struggling to correct themselves, people stopped playing golf.

As wonderful as the game of golf is, it has inherent problems. The cost of maintaining a golf course alone is astronomical. Today's millennial generation wants instant gratification. Five hours on a Saturday afternoon are difficult to justify when there is youth soccer in the morning. Golf is a very expensive sport. The cost of clubs, green fees, equipment, travel, golf attire and golf balls make a leisure sport more like having another child. And if you want to join the most exclusive country club, get ready to spend some serious cash. Despite the expense associated with golf, the biggest reason for the decline of the game of golf is probably the fact that it is a very difficult game to learn and play.

Club manufacturers have made the equipment and golf balls as user friendly as possible. Golf can be extremely frustrating, and no one wants to play poorly. I have empathy for the new player because I, too, felt those same struggles, insecurities and fears of learning the game. I eventually learned to excel at the game through pure persistence. Most people try the game, get frustrated, and then want to try another sport. Quality instruction is the most integral part of learning and growing the game of golf whether it is teaching the proper swing fundamentals, teaching the rules and etiquette, motivating students to improve, or simply empathizing with a struggling player. Playing golf is fun when you play well. If you are struggling at this great game or want to learn it for the first time, do yourself a favor and seek the guidance of a PGA golf professional. Golf and life are so similar as both provide joys and struggles. Struggling golfers are very much like struggling people. They need guidance. In my own journey in faith, I can think of no better place for guidance for the struggling person than the church.

After September 11, 2001, church worship increased dramatically in this country as people prayed for the victims, their families and for the relief efforts. In addition, church donations increased. So did military enlistment, volunteerism, blood and philanthropic donations. Sometimes God's plan involves shock to bring His children home. Unfortunately, it sometimes takes a tragedy to get people back into prayer or church worship. I have always prayed but not always gone to church. Like all Americans, I felt heartache and sorrow for the victims of Nine Eleven and prayed for the victims' families, but at that time in my life, church worship was not part of my weekly routine. I do not understand why terrible things happen to good people. I just know that they do. It is part of the Christian journey. *"But he said to me, "My grace is sufficient for you, for my power is made perfect in weakness. Therefore I will boast all the more gladly about my weaknesses, so that Christ's power may rest on me. That is why, for Christ's sake, I delight in weaknesses, in insults, in hardships, in persecutions, in difficulties. For when I am weak, then I am strong" (2 Corinthians 12:9–10).*

While the economy of this troubled world was declining, the business of church worship and church donations were steadily increasing. Americans attended church worship in record numbers after Nine Eleven as people went to God, not their 401K's and bank statements, to provide comfort from the world's struggle with sin and evil. For the moment, church worship was at the forefront of many Americans' minds. Although I have always been a Christian and was raised in the United Methodist Church, I backslid as a young, working man and got away from my roots of regular church service until the fall of 2011. I had to lose my marriage, sell my dream home and my condo before I got shocked back into a regular worship routine. God used these heartaches to bring me back to Him and lead me to a better place in my life—a place where I put God first. Faith in God is now the most important aspect of my life, and regular church worship is part of that faith. Although I often fall short, I have learned some difficult but necessary lessons and have committed to always put God first in my life.

My commitment to join the Stonybrook United Methodist Church was the first time in my life where I made a commitment to worship and serve God with my own free will. Before, my parents made that decision for me. I took my new member classes seriously, volunteered to usher and greet on Sunday mornings, provided a golf clinic to the Methodist Youth, and read my chapter "Want" to the youth group and their parents. I also had to make a financial commitment to the church in the form of tithing.

On November 10, 2013, Dwight Montgomery, the leadership board chair for the Stonybrook United Methodist Church, spoke about money and the act of tithing. Tithing is a commitment to give a portion of your income toward the church. Dwight said something that really made an impact on the way I thought about giving money to the church when he said, "It is not your money. It is God's money. We are just stewards of God's money." I had never thought of money in that manner, but Dwight was correct. Every penny I have ever worked for was earned because of the gifts God gave me. The United Methodist Church, like many others, recommends giving 10 percent of your annual income to the church. When Dwight made that statement, it really impacted me, and a very large lump began to grow in my throat. I realized that for me to give my 10 percent, I must change my lifestyle and my spending habits. I knew what I was currently giving was not even close to 10 percent, and for me to budget and work up to that number, it was going to take time, planning, and plenty of prayer. *"Now this I say, he who sows sparingly will also reap sparingly, and he who sows bountifully will also reap bountifully. Each one must do just as he has purposed in his heart, not grudgingly or under compulsion, for God loves a cheerful giver" (2 Corinthians 9:7).*

The fact that I am writing a book still amazes me. I know that the words are not coming from my mind and heart, but through the Holy Spirit. I want this book to glorify God not Jon Decker. I want it to inspire people in more ways than playing golf. I want it to inspire a troubled soul to find its own Stonybrook or a child of God heading down the wrong path to change to a better course in life. God is using me, in ways I never imagined, to spread His Word. I now recognize that this book is part of my journey, a journey that God has prepared for my life. I feel as though I am not an author but a messenger of God's Word. Simply put, this is ultimately what being a Christian is all about—the glorification of God, spreading His Word, and giving to others. I want to give to others in the business of selling my book. By the examples set by the church, I want to tithe 10 percent of every book sold to go toward charities close to my heart. Ten percent of the profits of every book sold will be equally divided and spread to these worthy organizations—organizations that have touched my life in some way. While promoting this book at a particular venue, I want 10 percent of all personal profits raised at the venue to go directly to its charity of choice. Ten percent of all personal profits for books sold otherwise will be divided equally between the following organizations close to my heart:

- The First Tee (promotes the game of golf to the youth of America)
- United Methodist Youth Group
- Local Food Bank (provides food to those in need)
- Autism Speaks (research and education for autism)
- Nathan B. Carse Memorial (scholarship fund)
- Tuesday's Children (funds go to the children from Nine Eleven and other disasters)

The Twin Towers have now been replaced by the Freedom Tower, a symbol of America's resolve and resiliency to rebuild what evil intentions tried to take away. Days after Nine Eleven, I was strung out with mixed emotions watching the relief efforts take place. On the one hand, I felt blessed to know that the plane I was traveling on was not part of the terrorist activity. Yet I could not help but feel a sense of guilt because my flight returned home safely while four other flights ended in tragedy. After Nine Eleven, I made a promise to myself to somehow use that horrific day, in some small positive way, to better the lives of others. I had no idea that it would result in me telling a story in the introduction of this chapter. As time passed and the reality of Nine Eleven became more apparent, I knew that this story would indeed be part of my book. America will never forget the victims and the brave men and women who risked their lives to help save others. To you, the reader, I say thank you for purchasing this book. Know that by doing so a percentage of the money will go to the victims' families of the tragedy known throughout the world as Nine Eleven.

CHAPTER 15

Want

"The LORD is my shepherd; I shall not want. He maketh me to lie down in green pastures: he leadeth me beside the still waters" (Psalm 23:1–2).

After a long day of teaching golf and following college basketball's *March Madness*, I began watching the television show *60 Minutes*. It was March 20, 2005, and the action on the court had me firmly in its grip for much of the day. I hadn't planned on watching the news documentary that Sunday evening but found myself engaged in the storylines as they unfolded. Little did I know that I was about to learn a life lesson of profound and lasting impact. One story in particular changed both the way I view my life and how I teach the game of golf. The episode narrated by Bob Simon was titled "The Sea Gypsies" and highlighted a small group of nomads referred to as the "Sea Gypsies of the Andaman Sea." They call themselves the Mokens. Untouched by civilization, the Mokens live on a small island several hours by motor boat off the coast of Thailand. On December 26, 2004, a tsunami devastated Thailand, killing more than 175,000 people. It also totally destroyed the Mokens' primitive dwellings. Miraculously, all of the Mokens survived the natural disaster—a fact that still amazes scientists. Mokens have their own language. So untouched by civilization are they that they exist minus modern conveniences. Imagine an existence consisting of fishing for your breakfast and dinner. No intrusion by the outside world, just fellow Mokens who share the same interests and lifestyle. Primitive, yes, but also a simplistic, peaceful existence bound by togetherness in purpose. Dr. Narumon Hinshiranan, a Moken anthropologist, served as interpreter for the *60 Minutes* piece, shedding light on the mysteries of this archaic civilization. At that very moment, my life changed forever. Dr. Hinshiranan explained that the entire Moken language translates to the English language—the entire language except for one simple word. That untranslatable word is *want*.

I was inspired by the Moken story as I listened to Dr. Hinshiranan describe the Moken society. At low tide, they fish for sea cucumbers and at high tide shellfish. The search for food consumes their daily lives, and every night, the entire Moken community sits around a fire and sings to the sea gods. They sing about the *great wave* that cleanses the land. The Mokens knew the signs of the great wave, and by paying attention to these signs, they all survived with the devastating wave. The signs appear simple enough: First, the water recedes rapidly; then there is a small wave; then the devastation begins. Mokens refer to the tidal wave as "the wave that eats people." The Mokens didn't realize that the water was receding because of an earthquake thousands of miles away. Predestination and nature rendered that kind of knowledge totally unnecessary. They survived because for generations the devastation was foretold. The Mokens didn't need a Richter scale or tsunami warning system to forewarn them of an impending disaster. The first sign of trouble came by way of an insect—the cicada. The cicadas that inhabit the island normally produce a loud, constant noise. However, on December 26, 2004, the cicadas suddenly went silent. The elephants on the mainland all started lumbering toward higher ground, well before the devastation began. The insects knew the signs, the animals knew of the danger, and the entire Moken society survived while many on the mainland perished.

God equips every living being with instincts, gut feelings or intuition. Some of it is lifesaving information passed from parent to child. According to Charles Darwin only the strong survive. The insects and elephants use instincts to evolve and to survive. The Mokens use community gatherings and song to pass down vital information from generation to generation. Without it, the entire Moken society would likely have perished long ago. When the cicadas stopped making their noise, the elder fisherman of the village started yelling to his daughter and her young friends to run for higher ground. They thought their father was delusional from alcohol. But when the water receded, they knew exactly what to do. The impact of this story in my life was not the inspirational fact that all the Mokens survived. It was much more than that. What impacted my life is the fact that the Mokens had no use for the word want. In fact, Dr. Hinshiranan tried to explain the word want to the Mokens, and they simply did not understand her. So much for the fable about a poor soul being stranded on a deserted island and finding a genie in a bottle. The Mokens wouldn't know how to reply when asked by the genie, "What are your three wishes or wants?" When I heard this part of the story, suddenly my life seemed very shallow, and my problems were immediately put into perspective. What would America be like if the word want was nonexistent, as it is for the Mokens?

When I think of the word want, my favorite comedy, *Caddy Shack*, comes to mind. In one scene, the affluent Judge Smells and his entitled grandson, Spalding, are walking into the halfway house for lunch after nine holes of golf. Most golf courses have a halfway house, a place where players grab a quick snack between nines. In this famous scene, Spalding is listing all the food items he wants for lunch. Spalding says, "I want a hamburger. No, I want a cheese-burger. I want a hotdog. I want a milkshake. I want potato chips."

Judge Smells grabs Spalding's arm, spins him to the side, and barks back, "You'll get nothing and like it!" I die laughing every time I think of it. Often my friends and I use the Spalding line when ordering food. The classic scene, although over the top, represents the attitude that many young Americans have today. Their sense of entitlement knows no bounds.

Today's teens are consumed with playing video games, text messaging friends, posting selfies on social media and gobbling up fast food cuisine. This behavior describes not only the youth of America but also many adults. Gone are the days of growing food in a home garden, talking face to face with a friend or sitting around the table as a family after dinner and playing a board game. I have witnessed, on numerous occasions, teenagers eating out with each other while texting with other friends who are not even in the same room. Mankind has always wanted or coveted money, fame and fortune. However, now society wants more than material possessions. We want to live or scrutinize the lives of others. Whether we tweet our every move, post a selfie, or watch a reality TV show, society feels the need to spin our lives into something that may not actually be; or we want to watch other people live their lives to make ourselves feel better about our current situation. We have no problem listing our wants but plenty of problems working for them. The Bible states it best:

> *But understand this, that in the last days there will come times of difficulty. For people will be lovers of self, lovers of money, proud, arrogant, abusive, disobedient to their parents, ungrateful, unholy, heartless, unappeasable, slanderous, without self-control, brutal, not loving good, treacherous, reckless, swollen with*

conceit, lovers of pleasure rather than lovers of God, having the appearance of godliness, but denying its power. Avoid such people. (2 Timothy 3:1–7)

I'm not oblivious to these wants or desires. I fell into that very trap when building my beautiful, lakefront, dream home in Orlando in 2003. The additions of a massive swimming pool and numerous upgrades, too many to name, were everything my marriage wanted but not what my marriage needed. The downturn in the housing economy taught me a very difficult but necessary lesson: Being a slave to one's home is not the purpose of shelter. Living within my means, returning to church worship, reading the Bible, and returning to my roots as a child of God are now the wants of my life.

I'm so thankful for what God has provided me, especially loving parents and supportive family. I was fortunate to have all the necessities of life growing up to not only survive but to flourish. I have been blessed in so many ways, especially my childhood, one that was nothing like the Moken life. Yet even while my father's career was flourishing, my parents required my brothers and me to contribute to our household. Mom and Dad were also great at developing our self-esteem. "Jon, you could be the President of the United States of America one day," I remember Mom saying matter-of-factly. I don't know if she actually believed that, but she made me feel as though I could accomplish it. As a teaching professional, I try to take the lessons learned from my parents to encourage my students when they are struggling at this very difficult game. My parents never set limits on their children. They believed in setting goals, being accountable for our actions, and meeting expectations. We had a list of chores and were expected to complete our chores. Afterward, we were rewarded with a weekly allowance—instrumental in our young lives because it built self-esteem and taught us the value of working.

Some kids are blessed with talent,
some kids are blessed with a strong
desire to succeed and some kids
are blessed with both. Fletcher
Wunderlich is blessed with both. 3rd
Place US Kids World Championship

While working with junior golfers, I ask them a simple question, "How many of you want to be a PGA Tour player?" Usually about half the kids will raise their hands. My follow-up to that is "Great, now let's talk about the work needed to reach that lofty goal." My desire is to have all my juniors set their goals high but make them accountable with hard work to reach their goals. I also emphasize that their goals do not have to be golf-related because I realize not all children want to excel at golf. My personal goal as a teacher is to have all my juniors learn in a safe environment, have fun and learn the fundamentals. That includes full swing and short game in addition to the rules and etiquette of golf. I have them write down their goals and objectives. Goals are long term while objectives are much different in that they are more easily attainable and measured by time. For example, my goal as a child was to play on the PGA Tour and break Jack Nicklaus's record of 18 major championships. I had the same goal as Tiger Woods long before his name became recognizable worldwide. One of my objectives as an eighth-grader during the summer was to break 90 by the end of August—one I accomplished.

I have no problem admitting that I failed with my lofty goal as a teenager. I remember telling my father, "I want to break Jack Nicklaus's record of 18 majors." Although I failed at my goal, it drove me to become the best player possible with the talent that God gave me—talent, by the way, for which I am extremely thankful—and led me onto a path of teaching golf to thousands. My lofty goal leads me in my life and career. It also became a cornerstone for this book. All that I have achieved professionally started with one simple childhood goal. Dad could have said, "Jon, there is no way you will ever reach that goal. Why don't you just try and make the high school golf team." If my father had told me that, I would have been devastated. He would have limited my dream, and who knows where I would now be as a teaching professional. My dreams have always been big—just as big as Tiger's. I was just blessed with different talents than him.

Bob Rotella, one of the most respected sports psychologists in the world, describes it beautifully in his book *Golf is not a Game of Perfect*: "I am not a shrink; I am an *enlarger*." My parents are enlargers. My parents told me as a child, "Jon, you can be President of the United States or you can play on the PGA Tour. You can do anything you put your mind to." I still remember those words of confidence. Many children are held back by their parents' discouraging words. "Johnny, your grades are never going to be good enough for college" or "Susie, your voice is not good enough to try out for *American Idol*." Those kind of evaluations don't exactly instill confidence, so please don't parent your child as a shrink; parent them as an enlarger. Words do impact people, so choose yours wisely. Proverbs 16:24 says it best, ***"Gracious words are like a honeycomb, sweetness to the soul and health to the body."***

Positive reinforcement is essential for teaching golf. I remember during one lesson a lady telling me, "Jon, you are the most positive person I have ever met." After the lesson, we went out onto the golf course for some playing instruction. On the second hole, she made a mighty swing and hit the ball, rolling it about a foot off the tee. She looked at me and said, "Now Jon, you can't possibly say anything positive about that shot." I replied without hesitation, "I love the way you are dressed today!" We both laughed. Sometimes a compliment goes a long way. The book, *I Declare,* by Joel Osteen has also impacted my life. Although I'm positive while teaching others, life's struggles, including a divorce and the housing market crash turned my positive thoughts into negative self-talk. I became a negative Nellie. There is an old saying, "An idle mind is the devil's playground." Through Joel Osteen's book, I learned to turn my negative thoughts and words into positive declarations. Suddenly, I was able to recover my positive attitude and personality.

I view the word work in a positive light, while want has negative connotations in many cases. I ask my students to replace want with work. For example, "I want to hit my driver 25 yards farther" becomes "I will work on my swing technique and my exercises to get stronger to gain 25 more yards." By exchanging work for want, a golfer can improve, a relationship can be repaired, and a child can earn a scholarship to college. Words provide power and can affect a person's self-esteem, comfort a broken heart, and provide symbolism and structure to a poem or novel. There is no greater example of this than the Bible.

The Bible often uses water to symbolize cleansing or awakening. In Genesis, God cleansed the earth by forty days and forty nights of rain, which flooded the entire earth. This massive flood cleansed the sin and evil that inhabited the earth and allowed Noah and his ark, his family and the animals to survive. It was followed by a covenant between God and the earth: ***"I have set my bow in the clouds,*** *and it shall be a sign between me and the earth"* (Genesis 9:13). Every time I see a rainbow, I think of God's covenant.

In the Gospel of Mathew, John the Baptist baptized Jesus in the Jordan River. *"And when Jesus had been baptized, just as he came up from the water, suddenly the heavens were opened to him and he saw the Spirit of God descending like a dove and alighting on him. And a voice from heaven said, "This is my Son, the Beloved, with whom I am well pleased" (Mathew 3:16–17).* The baptism of Jesus with water opened up the heavens and the voice of God was heard. Often when I witness a baptism today, I think of Jesus Christ and John the Baptist and instinctively look upward.

Revelations 22:1–2 talks about the River of Life. *"Then the angel showed me the river of the water of life, bright as crystal, flowing from the throne of God and of the Lamb through the middle of the street of the city."* When I think of Revelations, I am reminded of the Mokens, who learned their future from their forefathers and passed this information on to the next generation. Because the Mokens believed their forefathers' stories, all of them survived. As Christians, the book of Revelations foretells the return of Jesus Christ to the earth and talks about the Kingdom of God in heaven—a place with no night. *"There will be no more night; they need no light or lamp or sun, for the Lord God will be their light, and they will reign forever and ever" (Revelations 22:5).*

Christians should learn from the Mokens by listening to the words from our forefathers in the Bible, for they are the signs of what is to come. We should also worship with celebrations of song, foretelling Jesus' triumphant return. If we listen to these words, like the Mokens, we will survive this life, preparing for an everlasting life—where, like the Mokens, we will live under God's glory and never again want!

CHAPTER 16

Uncle Bill

Bill Decker

"For I was hungry and you gave me food, I was thirsty and you gave me drink, I was a stranger and you welcomed me, I was naked and you clothed me, I was sick and you visited me, I was in prison and you came to me" (Mathew 25:35–36).

In March of 2006, I discovered that God is the ultimate travel agent, trip advisor, and life planner. The revelation came to me after a very long day of lessons at the Grand Cypress Academy of Golf. It was a time of transition as my life journey evolved through another unexpected phone call. "Jon," said Director of Instruction Fred Griffin as I left the lesson tee, "I got a call from New York today from Tom Barnard. Tom is part of a search committee to find a new director of instruction at New Albany Country Club near Columbus, Ohio. I recommended you. Here's his number. Give him a call if you're interested."

"Thanks, Fred," I said. "I am interested." That afternoon would be the first step in my move to New Albany, Ohio, and a state 1,200 miles away that I had briefly visited as a child. At least that's what I thought. It wasn't until nearly thirty years later that I realized how God's plan for me to move to Ohio had been unfolding. I just didn't know it at the time. His plan for me was to go to Florida to receive my education and experience in teaching golf at Grand Cypress. He knew my travels to Florida would be critical to both my development as a teacher and as a player on the mini tours, that my time in the sunshine state would be essential for developing work relationships, meeting my future wife, and developing many lifelong friendships. God has a plan for each life, and from the outside looking in, one would think my plan to move north all started with a phone number on a piece of paper and a boss' recommendation. God's plan, however, was much more involved than that and it began long before my residence in Florida. God's plan for my career move north started when our family took a summer trip to Ohio to visit relatives, experience the Midwest and farm life. Yes, communing with farm animals was part of God's plan for my career, and it played out the summer of 1980 during a visit with Uncle Bill.

My parents were not only road warriors, but they understood the value of exposing their children to the world beyond
Black Mountain, North Carolina. Summer vacation took us to the
beaches of Carolina, an excursion to the northeast where we visited
Washington D.C. en route to New York City, Cape Cod and Hershey,
Pennsylvania. As a high school graduation gift, Dad and I returned to
New York City for a guys' weekend. That was great but totally different from our trip to Ohio some years earlier. Anticipation had been
at a fever pitch as we prepared for our trip to Ohio and a visit with
Dad's favorite uncle—one Bill Decker. Before retiring as a general
contractor, Uncle Bill oversaw the construction of office buildings
and other commercial real estate throughout Ohio. However, his real
area of expertise was building family restaurants like Olive Garden
and Bob Evans. As a friend of the Evans family, Uncle Bill built more
than fifty of their restaurants nationwide. He and his wife Vanieta
have a daughter named Janelle, my second cousin. Several years older
than I and a real beauty, Janelle had just turned seventeen when we
arrived in Ohio. She drove a sporty red Chevy Monza and allowed
my brothers and me to ride with her. Having a beautiful girl drive
us around in a cool sports car was the stuff of dreams back then. We
had to be the envy of every boy in their tiny hometown of Gahanna,
a suburb east of Columbus. The trip is etched in my memory for
many reasons; not the least of which is those car rides. In fact, I
think of Uncle Bill every time someone mentions Columbus or the
state of Ohio. During our spring break vacation, Uncle Bill took our
family to his farm which sits on eighty-five acres east of Gahanna.
The family started a business—Three D Farms—and bred Arabian
horses for show. Arabians are huge horses blessed with great power
and strength. Their beauty left me awestruck! The vacation was also

memorable because I got to meet new members of my extended family, members of the massive Decker family tree.

Uncle Bill was born on September 25, 1928, and is one of sixteen children, including his older brother Clifford Decker, my grandfather. Bill is the youngest son of Max and Cora Lee Decker. The couple had eight boys and eight girls, all living in a small farmhouse. The family worked by day with little to no education and slept three to four children to a single bed. The family farm was located in Valdese, North Carolina, where they grew peanuts and cotton commercially plus food for the family. When the Decker children were old enough to walk, they began working, carrying water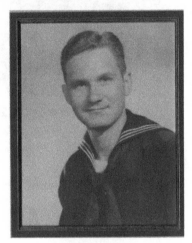

Clifford Decker

out to the fields for the older children. The men farmed the land while the women were more domestically inclined—cooking and cleaning. Bill received a ninth-grade education while most of the older children went without any formal education, only learning to read in Sunday school. Many nights, Cora Lee would sit by the fire struggling to read the Bible to her children. Although there was a lack of material possessions, the children never went hungry. The Decker story was so inspiring that they were featured in *Life Magazine* with a picture of the entire family and a caption that read, "If you can beat this we will pay you $10.00," a small fortune during the Depression.

$10.00 For A Picture To Beat This

The above picture (photo by Greene) first appeared in Miss Beatrice Cobb's Morganton *News-Herald* a week ago and has been published in several other papers since. It shows the Decker family of Icard township, Burke County—Mr. and Mrs. Max and their 16 children. All of the children, including one set of twins, have been born in the home where the parents now live. Four of the daughters are married but none of the sons are. When they all gathered at the home the other day, the in-laws were not included in the photograph.

Bernice, the little girl out in front, is 5 years old. Miss Bessie, the oldest of the children, is 30. Mr. and Mrs. Decker are shown at the left of the picture.

It's an interesting picture, and we congratulate Mr. and Mrs. Decker on their splendid family. At the same time, we believe that some wide-awake photographer—amateur or professional—can send us a picture of a family in North Carolina which is larger than that of the Deckers. We will pay ten dollars for such a picture, providing it is good enough so that a cut can be made from it.

Courtesy of *The Morganton News Herald*

After receiving my recommendation from Fred Griffin and several phone calls, the interview process with the New Albany Country Club began. That's when I began to research the Columbus area online. I didn't know the exact location of New Albany; nor did I know exactly where Uncle Bill's house and farm were located in relation to the New Albany Country Club. One day I was talking about the possible move to Ohio and the interview process with my father, and he decided to give Uncle Bill a call. The last time I had seen Uncle Bill was when my grandfather Clifford Decker passed away in March of 2000, and Uncle Bill flew down to North Carolina for the funeral. I hadn't seen Vanieta or Janelle since our summer trip in 1980. When my father called Uncle Bill, Vanieta answered the phone. "Jon is interviewing for the director of instruction position at the New Albany Country Club near Columbus. Do you know where the club is located?" Dad asked.

"Know where it is located," said an excited Vanieta. "We are Charter Members of the club!" She further explained that the club was located just a few miles from their home in Gahanna. Dad delivered the good news, which presented me with proof positive that God's plan for me was unfolding right before my eyes.

In February of 2007, I was offered the position of director of instruction for the New Albany Country Club. At the time, I was still married and worked out an agreement to spend my summers in Ohio teaching the New Albany membership and during the winters I would come back to Florida and teach at the Grand Cypress Academy of Golf. The idea was to have the best of both worlds, which meant I needed a summer home. We used the equity in our Florida home to purchase a condo in Ohio. We took advantage of a booming housing market early in 2007 as the proud owners of two appreciating assets—a beautiful lakefront home in Florida and a brand new condo with a creek and wooded lot in Ohio. I felt like a real estate tycoon. We had plenty of equity and the bank had no problem loaning us the money. In April of 2007, I moved to Ohio alone while my wife stayed in Florida working at her job.

In order to make the move, I would need to spend several weeks with Uncle Bill and Vanieta because the condo was still under construction when I arrived. It was time well spent as we really reconnected, even reminiscing about our family's trip to Ohio so many years earlier. I also went out to the family farm again to see all the horses and the new home that Janelle had built on the farm with her husband and three kids. It was a special time spent with my extended family. The highlight might have been Uncle Bill's stories from his childhood as one of the sixteen children. I learned about my Uncle Troy's experience on D-Day, how half the sixteen were drafted into military service and returned home safely. Sadly, Bill's stories included a tragedy involving his older brother Valco, who, as a fifteen-year-old, drowned swimming in the river. Enjoying my family's hospitality also afforded me the opportunity to familiarize myself with New Albany. I thought to myself, "What a great gift from God, having family located exactly where I needed them during a life-changing transition." Isaiah 58:11 states it best, *"The Lord will guide you always; he will satisfy your needs in a sun-scorched land and will strengthen your frame. You will be like a well-watered garden, like a spring whose waters never fail."*

My time in Ohio that first season was a blur: a new job, meeting new members, learning my way around town, and living 1,200 miles from my wife and home in Florida. Bill and Vanieta helped with my transition north, but I was eager to move into my new condo and have my own space. In June, the condo was complete and the new furniture was being delivered. I was now back on my own and ready to move forward with my life. In November, I turned off the water, locked the doors of the condo, and moved back south to Orlando for the winter months. This back-and-forth movement occurred until January of 2011, when my divorce papers were filed. The divorce was only the beginning of my troubles. The bottom had dropped out of the housing market and my two appreciating assets were now two depreciating assets. Personally, I started to reach lows in my life that I had never experienced. My life seemed to be spiraling out of control.

The family also received devastating news in the summer of 2010. Vanieta had pancreatic cancer. The cancer struck quick and by August of 2010, Vanieta was on her death bed. Hospice was called in, and I went to her home for a final visit. I walked into her bedroom by myself, closed the door and sat down by her bed. We talked for several minutes, but I could tell she was tired. Before I left the room Vanieta spoke these last words to me, "Jon, you have been a breath of fresh air for this family. Promise me you will take care of Bill. He is going to need you."

"I promise you I will," I said with conviction. I gently kissed her on the cheek and said good-bye. It was the last time I saw her alive.

After my divorce, I put both the home and the condo up for sale. Several months later, the condo sold. However, unloading a big home—even one on a lake—in a depressed Florida housing market would take some time. Uncle Bill bravely dealt with living alone for the first time, missing terribly his life partner of fifty-five years. Uncle Bill was lonely and welcomed me with open arms. I was struggling financially, paying for a house in Florida which I no longer lived in and was now going to live with a man twice my age. God was once again guiding me in ways that I could have never imagined. I listened to God's guidance in my heart, knowing that moving in with Uncle Bill would benefit both of us. God was putting me where I was needed most.

Despite our age difference, we shared one constant: We both woke up early and enjoyed the morning hours. Since my divorce, my new routine is to wake up, drink my coffee, and read my devotionals and the Bible. I thought at this point in my life I would be raising children and hurrying off to work. I made up my mind to make the best of my new situation by strengthening my faith. Bill would usually wake up after me, pour a cup of coffee, then engage me in conversation. My mornings are filled with family history and invaluable life lessons. I cherish these times as I've learned about his childhood, the Depression, living on a farm, my great-grandparents and my numerous great-aunts and uncles. By talking with Uncle Bill every day, I learned so much of how I think as a man. It has also influenced my taste for certain foods, and I have a much better understanding of my heritage.

Perhaps my favorite story of Uncle Bill's involves the caring and sharing of a large family during hard times. Uncle Bill told me that when one of his siblings got a piece of candy, they would pass it around to share. It nearly brought tears trying to imagine sharing one piece of candy with that many mouths. It was this simple act of kindness that has impacted me the most while spending time with Uncle Bill. Sharing is one of the greatest expressions of love. It is what Uncle Bill expressed by allowing me to stay in his home during the most difficult time of my life. I will never forget it. *"Do not neglect to do good and to share what you have, for such sacrifices are pleasing to God" (Hebrews 13:16).*

Several months after Bill and I started living together, I noticed something strange about our conversations. Uncle Bill was repeating his questions to me. I chalked it up to old age and the early hour, but Janelle shared the news to me that Uncle Bill had been diagnosed with Alzheimer's. This disease tested my patience much more than teaching a golf lesson. It also tested my resolve. During the mid-1990s, I had the pleasure of playing golf with actor Bill Murray while working at Grand Cypress. It was after the hit movie *Ground Hog Day* came out. In the movie, Murray plays TV weatherman Phil Connors and is stuck in the day of February 2nd, otherwise known as Ground Hog Day. Each day, he has the same conversations with the same people; life never changes for him; he tries to kill himself but wakes up in the same day every day. I remember my conversations with Bill Murray about *Ground Hog Day* while we were putting on the practice green before our round. "I really enjoyed watching *Ground Hog Day*, Bill," I said. His response surprised me, not because it lacked wit but because it was very insightful for a funny man. "It changed your life, didn't it Jon?" he said.

L to R Ben Krisopelt, Harold Wyatt, Eric Eshleman, Bill Murray, Joey Hidock, Jon Decker and Carl Alexander

Living with someone who has Alzheimer's is like the movie *Ground Hog Day*. The movie reminded me of what my life had become; a repeat conversation with someone who didn't remember our most recent dialogue, as if it had never happened. Surprisingly, the movie did change my life in a way. I decided to treat each conversation one at a time and ignore the repetition. By not interrupting Uncle Bill, he was able to maintain his dignity. After all, in Uncle Bill's mind the conversation was fresh, similar to how the residents of Punxsutawney, Pennsylvania, felt in *Ground Hogs Day*. When Phil Connors let go and lived with the town's people one conversation at a time, one Ground Hog Day at a time, he matured as a person and fell in love. Eventually normal life was restored.

The movie had a wonderful message, and Murray's comment produced an unexpected life lesson for me. During the round with the famous actor, I was in awe of the fact that I was playing golf with a Hollywood movie star, when in reality God was using this experience to prepare me. In retrospect, it was part of God's complex plan for my eventual move to Ohio in that it became a way for me to deal, in my own mind, with a disease that was robbing my Uncle Bill of his.

Through this transition of living with Uncle Bill, I have matured as a man and learned more about my family heritage. More importantly, I've gained an older sibling. Janelle is like a big sister to me and I a little brother to her—a first for both of us. Together we have learned to help Uncle Bill adjust to the latter days of his life. We've also shared the experience of divorce, ironically a life-changing event we went through at virtually the same time. We were able to console each other through conversation during a very difficult time.

Living with Uncle Bill has also helped me grow in my spiritual faith, for many reasons. One day while driving along Clotts Road en route to Uncle Bill's, I noticed radio station 104.9 The River. Thinking it was a country-western or rock-and-roll station, I tuned in. The Christian music format was a welcome surprise. Soon I was hooked on music that filled my soul with joy at a time when I needed it most. *"For you make me glad by your deeds, Lord; I sing for Joy at what your hands have done. How great are your works, Lord, how profound your thoughts!" (Psalm 92:4–5).*

Living with Uncle Bill also has helped me develop spiritually as I have been challenged with aiding him in increasing his faith. Imagine learning of God and the life of Jesus Christ during your lifetime and having a disease rob you of that vital spiritual knowledge. When I first arrived in Ohio, Uncle Bill would watch church service every Sunday morning on television. As the Alzheimer's began robbing him of his memories, I noticed he stopped watching on Sunday mornings. It is my personal goal while living with Uncle Bill to make sure he is prayed for and accepts Jesus Christ as his Lord and Savior. We've had many talks about God, His son Jesus Christ, and heaven. Ultimately, with religion comes one basic principle: You must take a leap of faith. Sometimes it's difficult for many people in sound mind and body. Imagine trying to take a leap of faith when you can't remember a conversation you had only ten minutes ago.

Uncle Bill and I have also had many fond moments. Monday night is our date night, and I always take him out to dinner at O'Charley's, where he loves the rolls. "They've got good beer at O'Charley's," he always says of the Bud Light! One night, Uncle Bill was struggling with his memory. He had spent several days in the emergency room with some blood issues and gout. Since his discharge from the hospital, his memory had diminished to the point where I didn't understand what he was saying. After dinner one Monday night at O'Charley's, I went to get the car while he waited for me to drive up to the front door. I was tired, frustrated, and honestly, losing my patience as I walked to the car. I pointed to the heavens and declared, "This one's for you, Vanieta." As I pulled the car around, out walked Uncle Bill accompanied by a strange lady. She held him by the arm and helped him into the car. "Uncle Bill always picks up the pretty women," I said, which drew a hearty laugh from the lady.

"I can't believe I saw Bill in the waiting area," she said. "I haven't seen him since Vanieta died. You're not going to believe this but yesterday I deleted Vanieta's number from my cell phone. And today I see Bill for the first time in over three years. What a small world." I smiled because I knew Vanieta was giving me a sign, one that brought encouragement during a very long day.

The Bible states that when we do good works on this earth, our treasures are stored in heaven. Although I lost a beautiful lakefront home and a brand new condominium, these were not the treasures God purposed for my lifetime. God used my poor real estate decisions, a divorce, and a decline in the housing market to put me where He and Vanieta needed me most, Gahanna, Ohio, with Uncle Bill. God's plan for Ohio has been unfolding for almost thirty years. I look at Uncle Bill's generosity to me and I'm thankful. It demonstrates God's grace and Uncle Bill's kindness. Treasures will be stored in heaven for Uncle Bill. And who knows? Maybe a few for me one day, comforting thoughts when realizing at one point in my life I had lost all my earthly treasures.

Time tags us all, and there are no guarantees in life. I might die tomorrow and never see the age of eighty-eight, Uncle Bill's current milestone. I might never father a child or be the head of a household. Life is not always fair, but God *is* always fair. During my lifetime, I have much more for which to be thankful than to complain about. Each day I remind Uncle Bill that he has a roof over his head, money in the bank and food in his stomach. And on Monday nights, a tall, cold, draft Bud Light! God answered my prayers in May of 2014 when our Florida home finally sold. God's grace is sprinkled into our lives daily one spoonful at a time. The day will come when Uncle Bill will return to his heavenly home among his wife and family—a family that lived together under one roof, sharing the workload, worshipping together, and every now and then, sharing a piece of candy. Uncle Bill is correct about one thing: "There is no such thing as a bad piece of candy."

In memory of Paula Christine Wright

Courtesy Charles D.
Owen High School

July 13, 1964–March 23, 2014

My Dream is dedicated to Paula Christine Wright. In April of 2013, I shared with you this chapter. I enjoyed our brief time together that day and know that you are at peace. At Charles D. Owen, you were a queen; now you are an angel. Rest in peace and enjoy your everlasting life!

CHAPTER 17

My Dream

"For God speaks again and again, though people do not recognize it. He speaks in dreams, in vision of the night, when deep sleep falls on people as they lie in their beds" (Job 33:14–15).

I have a dream that one day this nation will rise up and live out the true meaning of its creed: "We hold these truths to be self-evident; that all men are created equal." I have a dream that one day on the red hills of Georgia the sons of former slaves and the sons of former slave owners will be able to sit down together at the table of brotherhood. I have a dream that one day even the state of Mississippi, a state sweltering with the heat of injustice, sweltering with the heat of oppression, will be transformed into an oasis of freedom and justice. I have a dream that my four little children will one day live in a nation where they will not be judged by the color of their skin but by the content of their character. I have a dream today. (Dr. Martin Luther King Jr.)

On August 28, 1963, civil rights activist, Dr. Martin Luther King Jr., gave his impassioned speech, "I Have a Dream." In front of the Lincoln Memorial in Washington D.C., more than 250,000 people witnessed Dr. King call for an end to racism in this country. It is arguably one of the most famous speeches in United States' history and certainly at the top of the list in regard to civil rights. I have listened to the speech and read the text, so I understand the importance of his dream for America. Dr. King was called to lead, and he was certainly led by his dream. In many cases, dreams do lead individuals to greatness; but all too often, dreams are crushed by individuals, circumstances in life or poor decisions. I, too, have had a dream— one which had a profound impact on my life. This experience is arguably the most important event of my life because it came directly from God.

During my sophomore year at Owen High, I had a dream that has endured over thirty years. In fact, not a day goes by that the dream doesn't creep into my recall. It has shaped who I am as a man and how I view life. Its importance has inspired me to share it with the world. Normally, I am not one to recall my dreams. I have ordinary dreams like most people. When I was going through my divorce, I had several nightmarish dreams of being confined in an elevator, no specifics, just the kind of dream that your average psychologist could interpret. I would wake up, realize it was a bad dream and after some time, the anxiety would disappear. The dream I had in high school was much different. That evening I lay in bed struggling from the effects of bronchitis. I finally fell asleep accepting the fact that I was in for a long restless night. Sometime in the early morning, my dream began.

Ironically, I was consciously dreaming, very aware of being in a trance-like state. In my dream, I watched from on high (suspended perhaps one hundred feet in the air) as my brother Michael and I engaged in a fist fight with deadly intentions. It was like one of those old, black-and-white movies with the two of us going at it in the front yard of our Black Mountain, North Carolina home. I asked myself, "Why are we fighting?" All of a sudden, evil voices rang out, "Kill him!" The clouds above our house grew darker, and the voices frightened me as they grew louder. I said, "No, I don't want to kill my brother!" Suddenly from the left, I heard another chorus of voices—angelic in tone. The angels sang to me, but not in English. They appeared to be singing in Latin, French and Italian, but it is possible that they were speaking to me in tongues. The voices wafted beautifully through the air. "Wow!" I thought, "English is not their native language." I yelled, "What are you saying? I don't understand!" At that moment, I saw pictures of men and women from what I perceived to be the Civil War era. I saw young boys in uniform, men with thick beards and mustaches, and I saw my great-grandmother. I yelled, "Dee Dee!" She didn't answer. I saw my Uncle Barney and Aunt Toots. I yelled their names, too, but to no avail. I recognized some, but most of the people were just faces, as if I were looking at a yearbook from a high school I never attended. I saw the buttons on the soldiers' uniforms to the houndstooth wool on their jackets. Most of the soldiers were mere boys at war. The black-and-white pictures and the dream itself were in stark contrast to my everyday life.

Suddenly, in a low base tone, a voice rumbled from a distance out of the right: "Abraham, Isaac and Jacob." Like a thunder clap, the voice reverberated: "I am who I am. I am the Alpha and I am the Omega. I am the beginning and I am the end." Clearly, it was the voice of God. It is important that the voice of God came from my right side. It means that I was to God's left side, verifying the scriptures which state that Jesus sits to the right hand of his Father. The entire sequence of God's voice was like listening to music on the radio as the audio increases from barely audible to booming loud in a matter of seconds. Shortly after that, I heard an angel say, "This light was sent to you by." Then I saw a picture of a man from the Civil

War. Suddenly the dream was in vivid color—the clouds separated, revealing a brilliant, blue sky with a light unlike anything I'd ever seen shooting directly at me. Like a rush, this light came shooting toward my chest and up to my face; it looked like fire and sounded like the wind. It was now front and center-symbolically the center of my life, I believe. I recognized who it was immediately. As the tears filled the wells of my eyes, I raised my arms in the air and cried, "Jesus, please take me."

"It is not your time," Jesus said. "You have much work to do." I looked at His face but could not see Him for His face was blurred. For more than thirty years, I wondered why I couldn't see His face.

I could see only my eyes, like a reflection. I began receiving information about my reflection while dreaming. We are all born with qualities that are in Jesus' form; some are talents, stature, facial features, personality and abilities. I was digesting all of this while the dream was taking place. In my mind, I was commanded to look down. My eyes moved down from His face where I could vividly see His white robe. The body of Jesus was clearly visible, and I looked down at His bare feet. I could see His toes sticking out from underneath the flowing white robe. As I looked back upward, I gazed at His arms. His palms were turned toward the floor. He suddenly opened His palms toward me and a blaze of light emanated from them. I could feel my soul lifting from my chest.

I cried uncontrollably like a child. Again, Jesus told me, "It's not your time." I felt my soul rise from my body and float over my bed. It made me realize how heavy our physical bodies actually are and why we need sleep in order to carry around all that weight—the weight of the world. My soul was light as a feather and I could fly but only momentarily, then my soul returned to my body. The tears continued to flow as I awakened from the revelatory sleep. I lay on my back with my arms extended in the air. Realizing I was completely healed from my illness, I ran up the steps and told my parents about my *amazing experience*. They were in shock and suggested I go to my preacher for interpretation of the dream. So I set up a meeting that day with our pastor at Black Mountain United Methodist Church. I told him about my dream. From his reaction, it was clear he didn't believe me.

As my teenage years raced by, I totally dismissed the dream. "Why would God give me a gift like that? I'm not a preacher. Who would ever believe me anyway?" My guilt grew with each passing year because I believed I was supposed to use this dream to help others, yet I refrained from repeating the story. I did tell a few others, but for the most part, I stored the experience deep in my memory banks. In the summer of 2012, I began attending Stonybrook United Methodist Church in Gahanna, Ohio, on a regular basis. One Sunday, Pastor Mike Bowie said, "God asks ordinary men to do extraordinary things." All of a sudden it hit me! I went home and grabbed my Bible. It had been years since I had opened my Bible. The scripture in John 3:16 has always been my favorite one, so I turned to it and read. Ironically, never before had I read past John 3:16. This time, however, I continued reading through John 17–21. That's when the dream began to make sense.

> *"Indeed, God did not send the Son into the world to condemn the world, but in order that the world might be saved through him. Those who believe in him are not condemned; but those who do not believe are condemned already, because they have not believed in the name of the only Son of God. And this is the judgment, that the light has come into the world, and people loved darkness rather than light because their deeds were evil. For all who do evil hate the light and do not come to the*

light, so that their deeds may not be exposed. But those who do what is true come to the light, so that it may be clearly seen that their deeds have been done in God." (John 17–21)

For years I didn't understand the angel's open-ended statement: "This light was sent to you by" or what the angels meant by "light." After reading the Gospel of John, I began to understand the importance of the word light in the Bible. The next Sunday, I saw Pastor Mike at worship service and asked if we could set up a meeting. After several failed attempts to meet due to schedule conflicts on both our parts, we finally met in his office on August 1, 2012. During the meeting, I revealed my dream to Pastor Mike and I read John 3:16–21.

"I've got goose bumps," he said.

"Why?" I asked.

"Look at this, Jon," said Pastor Mike, opening his desk drawer and withdrawing his daily devotional. "The Methodist Church provides me with a daily devotional and journal," he said. "Look what it says I am to read today August 1, 2012." There in his journal written in bold type was John 3:16. "I believe you, Jon," said Pastor Mike. For the first time, I felt validation from someone other than my parents that my experience was real. I also knew that if our meeting had gone according to our original planned date in July not August 1st, Pastor Mike's devotional would not have read John 3:16.

I asked Pastor Mike about the circumstances surrounding the dream. "I was sick," I said, "did I die?"

"No," Pastor Mike said. "The reason is, Jon, you were not able to see Jesus' face." He explained that we can only see Jesus' face when we die. But He said, *"You cannot see my face, for no man can see me and live" (Exodus 33:20)*. Pastor Mike also explained that the word light described by the angel is the Holy Spirit. He said that the light will be with me until the day I die. He said, "The dream represented good versus evil." I chose good by accepting the Holy Spirit. "Since you were in the presence of Christ, you were healed from your sickness." I told Pastor Mike that I knew I needed to share my experience with others. I also knew that it was time for me to start writing my book for I had the validation to begin the process.

Writing this chapter has impacted me in so many positive ways. It was the very first chapter I wrote for this book in the early spring of 2013. It has validated an experience that I'm certain happened in my life. It has taught me to go to scripture to learn about my experience or when I need answers to life's questions. I have also learned that everything that happened to me in my dream or vision is validated in the Bible. It is as comforting as an old, well-worn blanket. It renders others' doubt meaningless. God uses dreams to communicate with His children. He wants us to take the time to research, ask questions and seek guidance to understand our dreams. God wants an intimate relationship with all of His children. It is His desire for us to seek Him through prayer, faith and scripture on a regular basis.

Perhaps the most profound impact the dream has had on my life is that I no longer fear death. I certainly don't want to die anytime soon. I love life and wouldn't want to die horrifically. However, I don't fear death itself. The reason is so simple and was spoken to me directly by Jesus Christ in the statement: "Your time has not yet come." I know my time will come someday. I'm aware that my days on earth are limited and that time is a precious commodity. The simple fact that God knows the second I am to leave this earth allows me to relinquish the fear of death. God knows my path, journey and destination. I have the free will to trust Him or the free will to resist His plan and find my own way. The latter would surely cause me to flounder. The feeling of love I felt when I was in the presence of Jesus Christ can't be measured in human terms. It filled my heart. No amount of money or fame could replace it. Jesus Christ made me feel as though I was the most important person in the world. He feels the same way toward you and all His children. I plan to make the most of my life and enjoy the journey. However, I long for heaven and my everlasting life to come because of my dream and faith that Jesus Christ is my Lord and Savior. Even if I live to be one hundred years old, that time on this earth is but a second to God. *"But do not overlook this one fact, beloved, that with the Lord one day is as a thousand years, and a thousand years as one day" (2 Peter 3:8).*

Life can be led by dreams, inspiring ordinary men to do extraordinary things. Dr. Martin Luther King Jr. was one such individual. Not only did his dreams lead him through words that inspired people to look at the world differently during a very troubling time, they led him to his ultimate destination in a prophetic and poetic final speech delivered on April 3, 1968. "I've Been to the Mountaintop" came one day before his death in Memphis, Tennessee. The last paragraph of his speech not only foretold of his death but revealed the inner strength he possessed during one of our nation's darkest hours. Dr. King closed this final speech by saying, "Like everyone, I would like to live a long life. Longevity has its place. But I'm not concerned about that now. I just want to do God's will. And He's allowed me to go up to the mountain. And I've looked over. And I've seen the Promised Land. I may not get there with you. But I want you to know tonight, that we, as a people, will get to the Promised Land! And so I'm happy, tonight. I'm not worried about anything. I'm not fearing any man! Mine eyes have seen the glory of the coming of the Lord!"

No fear. No worry. His will be done. Thank God for my dream.

CHAPTER 18

Snap Shots

"For our citizenship is in heaven, from which we also eagerly wait for the Savior, the Lord Jesus Christ, who will transform our lowly body that it maybe conformed to His glorious body." (Philippians 3:20–21).

I have always been intrigued by the afterlife. In fact, during the past couple of years, I've spent countless hours on YouTube researching personal experiences with life after death. I particularly relish stories of those who have had similar experiences as mine. Sid Roth's show *The Supernatural* has helped me understand how God communicates to and through His children. Every interviewee on the show has had amazing encounters, surreal experiences that border on the unbelievable. Yet all of them express the startling similarities of their experience. They feel their spirit leave their body, see their body from above, see a beautiful light, and experience no pain, only love and joy as their life flashes before their eyes. My experience during my dream was similar as well. I saw a beautiful light, not blinding but inviting. I felt unbelievable love, so much love that I began to cry; and I saw snapshots of family members who had passed and people

I had never met. Remember, my experience was only a dream. The amazing thing about the snapshots is the fact that they were brief, moving very quickly in front of me like a deck of playing cards deftly dealt by a Las Vegas dealer. I asked myself, "Do I know that person?" Intermingled among the unknown were family members like Dee Dee, my Aunt Toots and Uncle Barney. I yelled their names as their snapshots whizzed by. God has brought many people into my life, some famous by worldly terms and many regular people, yet they made a big impact on my life. This chapter is about those people, those fleeting moments in time where God says to me, "Savor this moment, Jon. Your life is passing you by. Stand still, smile and say, 'Cheese.' You never know when the snapshot taken at this moment will pass before your eyes again before you return to your everlasting home."

Like personal relationships, some stories in this chapter are very brief while others need more space to develop. All of these stories and these men and women have impacted my life. I am certain that when I die, their smiling faces will pass before my eyes again.

Coach V

As a scrawny eighth-grader in 1981, I walked down the hall toward Coach White's physical education classroom. "Jon," said Coach White, "the school is participating in the Muscular Dystrophy Shoot-A-Thon. First prize for the state of North Carolina is a trip to Raleigh to attend the Wake Forest, North Carolina State basketball game. The winner also gets to sit on the bench during the game with Coach Jim Valvano." If I could describe myself in one word, that word would be persistent. I quickly made up my mind that I was going to win that competition!

Guidelines for the basketball Shoot-A-Thon were simple: Each competitor would solicit sponsors to donate money for each shot made during a three-minute time frame. I have never worked harder for anything in my life. My determination meter was off the charts as I went door to door to every home in Black Mountain, or so it seemed. The day of the competition I was so nervous that I missed several shots, but in the end, I made sixty-six baskets from close range. Afterward I cried because during my practice sessions, I had made more than seventy shots several times. With no assistance from anyone, I raised $806 for Muscular Dystrophy, surpassing all my classmates at Black Mountain Middle School.

Shootout Winners

Jon Decker, (left) Sandy Wooby and John Daniel were the leading winners of the Easter Seals "Basketball Shootout" competition which raised more than $12,000 in Western North Carolina to fight birth defects. Decker was regional winner. Miss Wooby placed first at Pisgah Elementary School and Daniel was first at Weaverville Middle School. Superior Sports Co. of Asheville also sponsored the competition. (Staff photo by Ewart Ball)

Courtesy the Asheville Citizen Times

A week later, Coach White gave me the news. I came in second place in the entire state of North Carolina. A youth from the Raleigh area raised more than two thousand dollars. Although I gave it my best effort, I fell way short. I was devastated! Consolation came in the fact that I had the highest total for Western North Carolina. I was featured in the *Asheville Citizen-Times* and received an invitation from the Western Carolina University basketball team to sit on the bench during one of their games. I had the pleasure of meeting all the players and during halftime was presented an autographed leather basketball at half court. After the game, I got my picture taken with Western Carolina basketball coach Steve Cottrell and player Ronnie Carr. Carr hit the first three-point basket in NCAA history. I was also invited to Charlotte and featured on live television during the Jerry Lewis Telethon. But the prize I wanted and worked for was a seat on the bench with Jim Valvano while he coached against my father's alma mater, Wake Forest University.

Later that spring, Coach White knocked on the door of our classroom. As he entered the room, he was carrying a rather large box and announced to my homeroom teacher, Ms. MacIntosh, "This package came for Jon Decker in the mail." Surprised, I opened the box as all my classmates huddled around me. Inside the box was an autographed basketball from the 1981 N.C. State Wolfpack basketball team. The first autograph I saw on the basketball was that of Jim Valvano. It read, "Coach V." The other signatures included Thurl Bailey, Sidney Lowe and Terry Gannon. Two years later, Coach V and those three players led the Wolfpack to an upset victory over the University of Houston in the NCAA national championship game. Those autographed balls are still among my most cherished memorabilia.

On April 28, 1993, Jim Valvano died of cancer. He was forty-seven years old. Several months before his death, he spoke at the ESPY Awards. I remember crying as I watched him speak, and I will never forget one part of the speech, "God asks ordinary men to do extraordinary things." Years later, while sitting in the Stonybrook United Methodist Church, Pastor Mike Bowie expressed the very same sentiment to the congregation. "God asks ordinary men to do extraordinary things," he said. At that moment, I felt the presence of God speaking to me to set up a meeting with Pastor Mike and share my dream. At that moment, God spoke to me, and I knew that it was time to write this book. God used Coach V's dying message to the world to motivate me to reach beyond my comfort zone and put my feelings and God's Word in story form. Thank you, Coach V!

As Seen through My Eyes

Brad Daugherty, *ESPN* analyst

Courtesy of Charles D. Owen High School

Growing up in the Swannanoa Valley was a special time in my life. Jon's book brings back great memories of a time I will never forget and people, such as Coach Bill Burrows and Coach Bruce Arrowood, who shaped me as the man I am today.

Courtesy Charles D. Owen High School

In the fall of 1981, I was an eager freshman at Charles D. Owen High School who enjoyed most of my classes, even Algebra I with Mr. Sapp. As in most of my classes, Mr. Sapp's class had alphabetical seating. As I sat in Mr. Sapp's classroom the first day of school, I looked around at many familiar faces, including those whose last names began with a *D*. Suddenly, I noticed who was sitting to my right—none other than the most famous face in the Swannanoa Valley, six-foot-eleven basketball star Brad Daugherty! I was totally in awe of Brad, one of the most highly recruited basketball players in the country. Every day of class, he had a stack of letters a foot high from college coaches courting him. I remember North Carolina's Dean Smith coming to Owen's packed gymnasium to watch the senior center play. I played on the JV team and got to watch our varsity team win every regular-season game that year except one. The team breezed through the state playoffs and made it to the finals of the State Tournament in the Greensboro Coliseum, where they lost a close game to Warren County High. Warren County was led by David Henderson, who went on to play for the Duke Blue Devils the following year.

After the season, Brad narrowed his teams to the University of North Carolina and the University of Maryland. One day Principal Lyle excitedly announced over the public address system, "I am proud to announce that Brad Daugherty has just signed with the University of North Carolina. He is going to be a Tar Heel!" The entire school erupted in shouts of joy. Brad went on to become an All-American at UNC playing with Michael Jordan, Kenny Smith and Sam Perkins. After college, Brad was the number one pick in the 1986 draft by the Cleveland Cavaliers, a draft made infamous for the tragic drug overdose and premature death of the number two pick, Len Bias. I was disappointed because one of my favorite teams, the Philadelphia 76ers, had the first pick and traded it just before the draft. I remember talking with Brad about going to Philadelphia. He was excited because of the 76ers' star players, Julius "Dr. J" Erving and Charles Barkley. Charles would later say that it was a "big mistake by Philadelphia not drafting Brad." Brad played his entire career in Cleveland, and on March 1, 1997, the Cavaliers retired Brad's jersey (No. 43).

Owen's Daugherty Picks Smith, UNC

By JIM HAMER
Sports Editor

Brad Daugherty realized a boyhood dream this morning when he made his final decision to attend the University of North Carolina and play his college basketball for Coach Dean Smith's Tar Heels.

The 6-foot-11½, 222-pound senior center for Charles D. Owen High School in Swannanoa made his choice Tuesday after narrowing a list of 174 colleges down to North Carolina and Maryland.

Daughtery, who turned 16 years old Oct. 19, made his verbal commitment after a weekend visit to Chapel Hill. The decision came two weeks before his Owen Warhorses' basketball team opens its regular season at Clyde A. Erwin High School Nov. 24.

As a junior, the son of Mr. and Mrs. Roy Daugherty teamed with five Owen seniors to lead the Warhorses to a 23-1 record in 1980-81 under Coach Bill Burrows.

Daugherty averaged 17 points per game, 13 rebounds, eight blocked shots and seven assists, according to Burrows.

OWEN'S BRAD DAUGHERTY

Courtesy Charles D. Owen High School

During algebra class I attempted to persuade Brad to sign with Wake Forest University, which always elicited a huge laugh from Brad because my father had talked to him, as well. Life has a way of working out, and as it turned out, UNC was an excellent choice. Brad loves to hunt and fish and the great outdoors. As a freshman in college, I worked at Brad's basketball camp and played in an alumni basketball game during Brad Daugherty Day in Black Mountain. The gymnasium was packed that day as seemingly the entire town of Black Mountain honored their hometown hero. Sitting in the stands for that game was Brad Johnson, a man who would take Black Mountain to another level of fame years later as the quarterback of the Tampa Bay Buccaneers.

What made Brad Daugherty interesting to me was that his true passion in life was not basketball but stock car racing. In the mid-

1980s, very few minorities followed stock car racing, especially in the mountains of North Carolina. The reason Brad wore the number 43 at Owen and in Cleveland was because his hero, NASCAR legend Richard Petty, drove the famous car emblazoned with the red-and-blue number 43. Brad wore the number 42 jersey while playing for the Tar Heels. After retirement, he scored a position with ESPN as a college basketball analyst. An excellent color commentator, Brad eventually landed a similar position at Fox Sports. This time, however, he covered his true love, NASCAR.

Watching his career from a teenager to where he currently works has been exciting. It also has impacted my life, providing a definitive example that dreams do come true. In NASCAR, 43 means Richard Petty, The King. The number 43 is now flying high in the rafters of Quicken Loans Arena in Cleveland beside the new king, Lebron James. The number 43 is also proudly displayed in the gymnasium of the new Charles D. Owen High School Gymnasium. Brad wore 43 because of a childhood hero. I find it almost revelatory how our childhood heroes can inspire greatness and that greatness can transcend generations, regardless of the sport.

As Seen Through My Eyes

Brad Johnson, Super Bowl champion, XXXVII

Courtesy of Charles D. Owen High School

As a young boy, I had the great opportunity to grow up in Black Mountain, North Carolina, and graduated from Charles D. Owen High School in 1987. Jon was grades ahead of me. He was also a childhood friend and teammate of mine on the Owen High School basketball team, coached by Bill Burrows. Jon was a very hard worker respected by all his teammates and classmates. Jon was also an avid golfer growing up and absolutely loved to play the game. He was always talking about how challenging each shot was and how each shot had an impact on the next shot and, ultimately, the final score. Back in the early 1980s, not many kids were talking and playing golf like they do now. Jon was ahead of his time with his passion for golf! It is awesome to read his book and for him to share his golf life lessons, but it's more exciting that Jon is sharing his relationship with Jesus Christ.

Yes, it's true I loved to play sports growing up and found anything and everything to find a way to improve as a player and athlete. I played basketball and football, but most would find it surprising that basketball was absolutely my first love. My dad, Rick Johnson, always told me, "It's better to be prepared and not have an opportunity than to have an opportunity and not be prepared." He also said, "If you want to be better than your competition, then you need to work harder and practice when others are not practicing to gain the edge."

An edge for me was to jump rope and shoot basketball before school while others may be sleeping. One of the dreaded punishment drills Coach Burrows would have us do was the "worm crawl," if we turned the ball over in practice. Yes, it's true. I would even practice the worm crawl when no one was watching because I knew if I made a mistake in my workouts that it should be no different than if Coach Burrows was demanding it. I find that in life, people's eyes are not always on us, but God's eyes always are. Hopefully, the analogy of the worm crawl can be used in your life. I encourage all of you, especially in your time alone, to think, pray, and ask, "What would Jesus do?"

1985 Owen Warhorses
Back Row L/R: Michael Decker, Mike Marett, Dan Hensley,
Jon Decker, Donald McAbee, Brad Johnson, Mark Marett.
Front Row L/R: Terrell Dillingham, Kelly Buckner,
Lee Stafford, Jim Davis. Courtesy Charles D. Owen High School

In the spring of 1982, Brad Daugherty graduated from Charles D.
Owen High School, after rewriting the school's record books. The
next fall, a new Brad was roaming the halls of Charles D. Owen High
School. His name was Brad Johnson. I met Brad—two years younger
than I—during youth basketball. His parents, Rick and Ellen Johnson,
were in charge of the youth basketball league in Black Mountain.
Although Brad was two grades behind, he dominated all the games
played whether it was baseball, football or basketball. To this day, Brad
Johnson is the best athlete I've ever known. There is no doubt in my
mind that Brad could have played major league baseball or in the NBA

if he had chosen those paths for his life. He was just that good at the three major sports. However, the lure of football proved stronger than the others. One day while playing golf with Rick Johnson, I asked him which sport Brad would focus on in college. "Jon, at six foot five inches, you are a dime a dozen in the NBA," he said. "But at six foot five inches, you are the perfect size for quarterback in the NFL." Rick's objective scouting report for his son was spot on. In January of 2003, Brad Johnson quarterbacked the Tampa Bay Buccaneers to victory over the Oakland Raiders in Super Bowl XXXVII in San Diego. This story is not about Brad leading his team to the most coveted prize in the NFL. However, it does reveal why Brad Johnson won the Super Bowl and the relevance of his personal journey through my eyes. I could write an entire book as to why Brad Johnson became arguably the most successful athlete in Western North Carolina history, the examples he set as an athlete, as a Christian and as a teammate. But one story captures the essence of Brad's success. It details his dedication to hard work, competitive spirit, and desire to be the best. I often use the story while emphasizing to junior golfers what it takes to be successful. When I think of Brad Johnson and why he reached the pinnacle of his sport, I recall the story of "The Worm."

Brad's summer workout regimen was incredible. He would run in the morning, jump rope, lift weights and shoot basketballs every day. Brad's parents ran a summer camp in Black Mountain, Camp Ridgecrest. During seventh and eighth grade, Rick would call our house and ask if we wanted to come up to Camp Ridgecrest and play the all-star camp basketball team. My brother Michael and I, along with other local kids, would go to Ridgecrest and play organized games. Rick would take our local team and travel to South Carolina and play against church leagues. By high school, our team was going to Appalachian State University basketball camp together; and one summer, our team went undefeated for the entire week during camp. It became obvious why our teams did so well. We had the best player on the floor in Brad Johnson. And we had two of the best coaches in Bill Burrows and Bruce Arrowood.

Coach Burrows and Coach Arrowood instilled discipline into the Owen Warhorse program, and both believed in tough love. The coaches had a rule about the common mistake of dropping the ball. If you dropped a pass anytime during practice you had to do a worm. Instructed to assume the worm position, offenders would go to the baseline underneath the basket, lie on his stomach, lift his torso off the ground with his arms then walk using only his arms as he dragged his feet all the way to half court, a total distance of 45 feet. As soon as anyone dropped a ball, the coaches would yell, "That's a worm!" The worm was a great way of maintaining our team's focus during practice, especially shooting drills.

One morning before school, Brad was in the gym putting in some extra time on shooting drills. We used a toss back for these drills, in which you would throw the ball and the toss back would propel the ball straight back; the faster the pass the faster the ball would be propelled back toward you. As Coach Burrows walked by the gym, he noticed his star player practicing his jump shot—a solo figure working up a sweat in pursuit of perfection. Brad's proficiency was spellbinding as his coach witnessed swoosh after swoosh. Then the unthinkable happened. Brad dropped the return pass from the toss back. Brad immediately walked over to the baseline, got down on his stomach and crawled with his arms 45 feet to half court. He got up and continued shooting. It was as if the coaches had witnessed the faux pas and yelled, "That's a worm!" Keep in mind that Brad was unaware Coach Burrows was looking on. Giving the extra effort, while no one else is watching, is why the great ones succeed. On January 26, 2003, Brad Johnson caressed the Vince Lombardi Trophy symbolizing years of hard work and dedication. From the comfort of my living room in Orlando, I couldn't help but think about his hard work as a child. I thought about his dedication and I thought about the worm.

As Seen Through My Eyes

Bill Burrows, retired high school coach
at Charles D. Owen High School

Owen opens with a win

By Jim Hamer
Times Sports Editor

High school conference basketball tournaments test a coach's mettle more than any one element of the game.

Owen High coach Bill Burrows will testify to that after his Warhorses' 68-50 win over visiting North Buncombe Tuesday night in an opening round game of the Ivy Conference Tournament at Swannanoa.

Burrows stopped en route to the dressing room, looked up at the scoreboard and shook his head.

"It's always good to win this time of the year," he said, "although it was sloppy. An ugly win is better than a pretty loss."

Then Burrows sounded a warning to the Warhorses before he went off to deliver the same message in person.

"We've got to play better if we plan on advancing any farther in this conference tournament."

It was a wire-to-wire good old-fashioned, country-kicking the Warhorses put on the Black Hawks ending a long 2-21 season for North Buncombe.

Owen led 18-8 at the quarter, 36-24 at halftime and 54-38 after three periods.

The final eight minutes was an exercise in frustration by reserve players rusty from lack of playing time. It was compounded by officials who premiered the game whistling numerous personal fouls and a technical on an Owen player who frowned after he was singled out.

In other first round Ivy boys game Tuesday, West Henderson humbled Mitchell 61-49, sending the Mountaineers home with a final 6-15 record.

Hendersonville upset Madison 57-30, ending the Patriots' year at 13-11.

Tonight's semifinal round at the Mountain Heritage High gym in Barnsville will send top-seeded Mountain Heritage, with a 19-3 record, taking on the 10-13 Bearcats at 6 o'clock. Tonight's semifinal girls game will pit top-seeded West Henderson (21-1) against Madison (13-9) at 6:30.

The Cougar boys and Falcon girls both enjoyed byes in the seven-school field.

Thursday's semifinals at Heritage will find the North Buncombe girls (17-7) playing Owen (18-10) at 5:30 followed by the Owen boys vs. West Henderson (17-6) at 6. The championship games will be played Friday at Heritage.

"North Buncombe played a good straight-up man-to-man defense which gave us an opportunity to run our halfcourt offense," Burrows said after his team improved its record to 18-5.

"We executed very poorly against their defense and didn't run our offense at all. We got a lot of transition baskets, but I'm not pleased at all with our halfcourt execution tonight.

"Our defense was very active and did some nice things and created some more baskets."

Again it was a balanced Warhorse scoring attack led by Brad Johnson's 16 points that proved too much for the Hawks.

"Brad and Kelly (Buckner) played well offensively for us, and Jim Davis did an extra good job that allowed other people to get open. If Davis was 6-foot-4 instead of 5-11, he'd be a (college) prospect," Burrows said.

Davis added 13 points for Owen and Jon Decker netted 12.

Johnny Waychester was the only Black Hawk in double figures with 10 points.

Asheville, E. Burke split

ICARD — The Asheville High Cougars concluded their regular Western 4-A Conference season dividing a pair of games with East Burke here Tuesday night. The AHS girls defeated East 47-41, behind Rhonda Magg's 18 points.

Andrew Pitts led the East Burke boys to a 70-66 win over Asheville with 21 points.

The Cavalier girls (4-6, 8-11) grabbed a 19-8 first-period lead, but Asheville (9-5, 16-7) took the lead for good in the second period as Magg scored eight points. Asheville led 27-14 at half and built a 37-35 advantage going into the last quarter. Deretta Morgan added 16 points for Asheville.

In the boys game, East Burke (3-8, 10-13) jumped out to a 17-11 lead in the first eight minutes and never trailed. The Cougars (4-10, 13-10) were paced by Robert Conyers and Curtis Dawkins, each with 22 points.

JIM HAMER/Times
Owen's Bill Burrows enjoys play during Tuesday game.
Warhorses knocked off North Buncombe to advance to semi-finals.

Courtesy of the Asheville Citizin Times

This book by Jon Decker is an outstanding read. It is the completion of a lifelong dream of Jon's whose beginnings can be traced back to his sophomore year at Charles D. Owen High School in Black Mountain, North Carolina. Jon was a member of the Owen Warhorse basketball family. Our program was unique in several ways. Once you were a Warhorse, you were in this family for life.

During a ten- to twelve-year period in the 1980s and 1990s, with kids like Jon, we established a program that was recognized as the best in Western North Carolina. Jon was somewhat of an intro-vert—a shy, easygoing, bashful young man. He came from an outstanding family and was a great representative of his family, community, and our basketball program.

Sports

Tough Defense
Owen's Jim Decker tries to elude Reynolds' Warren Gentry in battle between Warhorses and Rockets in Swannanoa. Owen won 83-76.

Owen's John Decker (23) attempts to move past Rodney Hawkins (10) of Erwin Warriors' Alfred Stubbs (22), Alvino Johnson (31) look on as Warhorses go on to win Tuesday night

Being the smallest center in Western North Carolina,
my game was played under the rim and on the floor.
Courtesy of the Asheville Citizen Times.

He wasn't very big but rather a skinny, laid back, and relaxed individual, who was an outstanding student and exceptional golfer. Not a basketball player per se, but when he stepped onto the court, he became a "beast." He was a great hustler who took charges, boxed out, dove on the floor, and played with heart, integrity, and passion. All these things are uncoachable but are the things very few of us have. Jon's Christian witness is evident in the book and in his daily life. I hope that this book will be read by all who want to enhance their self-awareness and enrich their Christian walk.

Thanks, Jon, for being you and for being a true Warhorse, a thoroughbred, who had a lot to do with making people think I could coach. God bless you for making me a part of your book, with love and respect.

r Favorite Seen In Ivy Conference

GETTING THE WORD — Owen High Coach Bill Burrows, Kelly Buckner, Lee Stafford and Jon Decker. Owen is a contender right, gives instruction to senior players, left to right. Jim Davis for the Ivy Conference title. (Staff Photo)

The 1984-85 Warhorse seniors were small on paper but could
run like the wind. Courtesy of the Asheville Citizen Times

The three most influential men in my life are my father Sam Decker,
my mentor for golf Phil Rodgers, and my high school basketball
coach Bill Burrows. As a teenage boy playing on the junior varsity
team, I marveled at Coach Burrows' varsity basketball team's dominance. Led by prep All-American Brad Daugherty, the varsity rolled
over competition in Western North Carolina. Coach Burrows pushed
his players to the limit. Frankly, his coaching style intimidated me.
My dad was a stern disciplinarian, and the idea of another discipli-

narian in my life began to frighten an insecure teenager. Although I played very well as a sophomore on the junior varsity team, I made the decision not to play my junior year on the varsity team. Coach Burrows and Brad Johnson both talked to me, but I decided to quit. I wasn't going to play—out of fear—for the man they called Wild Bill.

The summer before my junior year of high school, Coach Burrows got the call up. His good friend Bobby Cremins asked him to join the Georgia Tech coaching staff as an assistant. Junior varsity coach Bruce Arrowood became his successor at the helm of the varsity. Several weeks before the season started, I had a change of heart and decided to play, a decision that, in retrospect, helped shape me as a man. Our team won nineteen games that year and advanced to the finals of the Sectional Tournament before getting knocked out by Buncombe County rival Enka. I got a taste of varsity basketball while playing meaningful minutes as the sixth man until breaking my wrist during practice late in the season.

Due to family obligations, Coach Burrows came back to Owen to again coach the varsity team at the start of my senior year. I remember having very frank conversations with Coach Burrows about my true passion—golf—not basketball. I believed Coach Burrows respected my honesty and I wanted to play for his team, to step up to the plate and put my teenage fears aside. It was one of the most important decisions of my young life. Through the leadership of my two coaches, I began growing in manhood.

By my senior year, Brad Johnson was starting to get national attention from college basketball and football programs. Coach Burrows arranged for our team to travel to Atlanta and practice on the Georgia Tech coliseum court before the Georgia Tech/Clemson game. After practice, our team sat and watched Brad shoot under the watchful eye of Coach Cremins and his staff. Brad's performance was nothing short of impressive. We showered in the locker room, went across the freeway to the historic Varsity Restaurant for dinner then returned to the coliseum to watch the game. I will never forget the thrill of meeting Mark Price and John Salley and using Ivan Joseph's locker.

Coach Arrowood was my JV coach as well as my varsity coach my junior year. He pushed me just as much as Coach Burrows and got the most out of all his players. I love his commitment to all his players as well as his commitment to Jesus Christ.

The 1983-84 team was big inside with great shooters outside. L to R Shannon Boling, Rodney Marett and Jon Decker. Courtesy Charles D. Owen High School

Coach Burrows was nicknamed Wild Bill by the Georgia Tech players. Watching him display great passion for the game while pacing the sidelines could be intimidating to the average person. However, it was much deeper than just showing emotion. Coach Burrows loves his players, and in turn, his players love him. The more he ran me, the harder I wanted to play for him. During our suicide runs after practice, Coach Burrows would halt the drills for a moment and look us all in the eyes. "I love you all," he would sincerely proclaim. I always seemed to run faster after hearing those words.

A conversation I had with Coach Burrows years after Brad's Super Bowl victory remains fresh in my memory. "Remember when we had the talk about you quitting basketball?" Coach Burrows asked.

"Coach," I said, "I was certainly not the best player you ever coached, but I learned more from playing for you than any player that you coached." It was not a boastful statement, just an honest assessment of my experience under his leadership. I'm sure many others feel the same way about Coach Burrows' influence on their lives. Coach Burrows' success is anchored in the fact that he makes every one of his players feel special and loved. The man I feared so much as an insecure teenager taught me that hard work, dedication and teamwork, along with love, are what push individuals to greatness, no matter what their passion is in life. Thank you, Wild Bill, I love you, too!

Burrows Back At Owen High

By BOBBY HAYES
Staff Writer

BURROWS

After a year's leave of absence Bill Burrows has returned to Owen High as head varsity basketball coach.

Burrows, who had compiled an 87-41 record during his five-year tenure at Owen and led the Warhorses to the 3-A state championship game in 1982, took a leave of absence last September to work on his master's degree and serve as a graduate assistant basketball coach at Georgia Tech under Bobby Cremins.

Burrows, however, is happy to be back at Owen. "It wasn't that big a decision," he said. "It all boiled down to whether or not to stay another year at Tech without my family. We decided it was best not to return under those circumstances."

Burrows enjoyed his stay at Georgia Tech, however, and said he gained a lot from Cremins. "That's where I want to be if I ever go back into college coaching because of Cremins," Burrows said. "Bobby and I are very close. I learned a lot from Cremins. He allowed me to contribute to the program."

With Burrows returning, Bruce Arrowood, who had served as Burrows' assistant for five years before leading the Warhorses to the finals of the 3-A District 8 Tournament with a 19-6 record last season as the head coach, will again become an assistant coach.

Burrows sees no problem in working with Arrowood again. "We've always had the total program together," Burrows said. "We share equal responsibility."

Courtesy of the Asheville Citizen Times)

ROY

Progress has always been prone to creep into the mountains of Western North Carolina, where folks prefer to walk slow, talk slower, and carry a big stick. So you can imagine my surprise and satisfaction when I recently visited my alma mater, the brand, spanking new Charles D. Owen High School in Swannanoa. The school is perched on the side of a beautiful mountain with breathtaking panorama. The football stadium is state of the art. The gymnasium and classrooms are a significant upgrade from my time there. However, the most impressive thing I saw during my visit was the Hall of Fame. Lining the walls of the hall located near the gym are the names of former NBA All-Star Brad Daugherty, Coach Bill Burrows and Super Bowl champion Brad Johnson. One name stands out, not for all the accomplishments but because of the road he took to the accomplishments. Included in UNC basketball coach Roy Williams' path to a hall-of-fame career is a stint as head basketball coach at Owen High. In fact, it was his first head coaching position. The accomplishments of the man they call Roy would add to the lore of Charles D. Owen High School, making it one of the unique places in the state of North Carolina.

In the fall of 1983, I was paired with Roy Williams in the third and final round of the annual Labor Day Golf Tournament in Black Mountain. Roy grew up in the Asheville area and after coaching at Owen, became an assistant coach under UNC legend Dean Smith. I was so excited when I saw my pairing in the final round. Roy and I had a great battle on the course. The conversations were entertaining and enlightening. Although I was extremely nervous to meet Roy for the first time, he made me feel very comfortable. I started asking him questions about Michael Jordan, Sam Perkins and James Worthy. I'm sure by the end of the round Roy was worn out with all my questions. On the last hole, I calmly made a four-foot putt to shoot 74 and beat him by one stroke. Roy shook my hand and later told my parents how much he enjoyed playing with me. I was on cloud nine!

The next spring, our golf team won the WNC Sectionals for the first time in school history advancing to the state tournament in Chapel Hill. Roy and our coach, the late Ralph Singleton, were close friends. Roy came out and followed our team for two days. His presence inspired us to a fifth-place finish. After first-round 74, I stood on the 36th and final hole one-over-par for the day and was bursting with confidence. In fact, I laced a drive down the middle of the fairway and declared to my dad, "I'm going to get in the top ten." Classic mistake! I fatted my approach shot into the water fronting the 18th green. Roy and Coach Singleton were watching as I approached the lateral hazard. Suddenly, my nerves were so tingly I felt like a pin cushion. I dropped the ball in a sandy area and skulled my next shot over the green under a tree. I was dead! I blindly chipped out from behind the tree and heard a funny thud. Fortunately, my ball had hit the flagstick and was two inches away from the cup. I anxiously walked up and tapped in for six as I looked for somewhere to hide. I learned a very difficult lesson that day about not staying in the moment and felt as though I had let the team down.

Roy calmly walked over and congratulated me on how well I had played for two days. He also took the time to explain the options of a lateral water hazard which revealed that I had made a very poor decision in my drop and could have saved at least one stroke had I properly understood the rules of golf. When I teach the rules of golf to my students, I sometimes remind them of the many mistakes I have made in golf. Roy showed me patience and knowledge, but more importantly, he gave me his time, and for that, I can only say one thing, "Thank you, Roy!"

SEVE

On May 7, 2011, the golfing world lost the great Severiano (Seve) Ballesteros to cancer. In my teaching career, I have observed hundreds of hours of lessons with some of the greatest players to ever play the game. Payne Stewart, Tom Kite, Paul Azinger, Brad Faxon and Raymond Floyd; all come to mind as swings and lessons I will never forget. Having the chance to work and watch as Fred Griffin and Phil Rodgers taught these players helped build my foundation as a teacher. But all of those lessons combined were not as exciting or entertaining as the three days I spent watching Seve.

During the late 90s, Seve Ballesteros came to Orlando to work on his golf game. He had heard of the ModelGolf video system and wanted to see his swing on video and practice his game. He wore penny loafers while hitting off the mats during the video lesson. I watched as balls flew right and left with his driver. I was amazed at how this golfer could win any tournament, much less the British Open and Masters, with such an uncontrollable driver. An up-close-and-personal look at his golf swing revealed its natural beauty. However, the Model revealed its many flaws. After the lesson, we walked over to the short-game practice area, and Seve dazzled us, hitting flop shots with a 3-iron from the greenside bunker. Then I began to understand why this guy won.

After bunkers, it was off to the putting green. We set up cameras to film his stroke. I have never seen a better stroke. Seve told us stories of how he would hustle men as a young boy. He would lay a garden hose down to the hole, put holes in the hose, and turn the water on a slow drip. The water would make a trough to the hole.

Seve said in broken English, "You couldn't miss" as he would hit one-handed putts from 20 feet into the hole. The men never caught on, and he used the money to help feed his family.

Seve's lessons were invaluable. I also appreciated his time, humor and most importantly, what he taught me about the game of golf. Putting makes up for bad drives; creativity in golf should be fun and challenging; and never bet on the golf course with a hungry Spanish boy!

As Seen Through My Eyes

Phil Rodgers, former PGA Tour player/Top 100 Teacher

Photo Courtesy Carl Alexander

Jon Decker has been a friend of mine for over twenty years. We worked together at The Academy of Golf at Grand Cypress in Orlando, Florida. Jon has always had a great thirst for the knowledge of the game of golf. Not only the golf swing but how his students can improve their physical, mental, and course management skills. Jon has the ability to convey this knowledge to his students in an understandable and enjoyable way. He builds a very solid foundation toward the continued improvement of new and seasoned players. Jon's instruction and teaching skills are a great asset to the advancement of the great game of golf.

ZINGER

While the world was watching Paul Azinger captain the United States Ryder Cup team to victory at Valhalla in 2008, I reminisced about a time when the Captain was not leading but being led. In fact, he was relearning the fundamentals of the game. On that day, I learned a valuable lesson myself: How the golf ball should fly through the air. The wedges were hit low and the long irons were hit high. This was the trademark of one of the game's greatest players, a man who had battled cancer and persevered. The man, who won the 1993 PGA Championship, played in four Ryder Cups, and gave a touching eulogy at Payne Stewart's funeral. The man they call Zinger.

On a beautiful spring day at Grand Cypress, I was assisting Phil Rodgers instruct his golf school. The Phil Rodgers Golf School and Short Game School were always popular at Grand Cypress, and this particular school was no exception. This school included five middle handicappers. Paul Azinger happened to be in town that weekend and made a visit to the golf school. On Saturday, Phil worked with Paul one on one, but unfortunately, I was unable to witness the lesson. My fondest memories from Grand Cypress are when I would watch Phil and Fred Griffin teach the greatest players in the world.

The Sunday session of the school was held on the academy's par-4 practice hole, and Paul drove over to thank Phil for the lesson. "Sorry to interrupt your school Phil, I just wanted to come over before I leave and say thank you," Paul said. "You really helped me."

"Let me see you hit some shots before you leave," Phil said. Total silence gripped the students as Paul got out of the golf cart.

Paul looked at the stunned group of men and said to Phil, "I don't want to take your students' lesson time."

One of the students looked up and said, "Are you kidding? We all suck! We want to watch you hit the ball!" The entire group began to laugh. Paul struck every iron with startling, machine-like precision. Paul is known for having a strong golf grip which promotes a very penetrating ball flight. Many teachers would try to change such a strong grip. Phil kept saying to Paul, "Knuckles to the sky," during the release of the golf club. Phil took what Paul did naturally in his grip and swing and made it better, the sign of a great teacher. The grips of tour players are much stronger now than thirty years ago because players are rotating, not sliding, as was taught then. Phil showed me that day how one can work with an accomplished player and make them even better!

NEVER FORGET A NAME

On a beautiful spring afternoon, I was standing behind the counter of the Grand Cypress Academy of Golf pro shop when a gentleman walked through the front door. "Could you please direct me to the restroom?" he asked.

"It's down the hall on your right," I said.

The man looked at my name tag and said, "Jon Decker, where do I know that name? I know that name. I might forget a face, but I never forget a name." I looked at the man who I had never met and thought, "This guy is crazy!" The gentleman left the pro shop and I resumed my work. Several minutes later, he walked back into the pro shop and said, "Did you go to Charles D. Owen High School?" That's when I realized the man was serious. He wasn't making idle conversation. God was intervening and making a point to introduce me to someone I had never met—a man who never forgets a name.

Surely the man noticed the stunned look on my face. How could he know me? I now resided in Orlando, Florida not North Carolina. The man reached out his right hand and said, "Hi, my name is Pete McDaniel. I am the former sports editor for the Hendersonville newspaper and remembered your name. I remember covering you in basketball and golf." I couldn't believe it! I was in total shock! We talked for several minutes during which I learned that Pete was working for *Golf Digest* as a senior writer/editor and was writing all of Tiger Woods' articles for the magazine. Pete and I knew some of the same people from the Western North Carolina area, and we reminisced like two childhood friends catching up on our lives, even though we had just met. As a result of our meeting, I began to give Pete lessons which led to a unique friendship.

On March 31, 2014, I was sitting in the Atlanta airport and decided to give Pete a call. I left a voicemail to which Pete responded a short time later. "Pete, I'm writing a book and I wanted to know if you would edit my book?" I said.

"I would love to, Jon. My advice to you is when you write an instructional book."

I quickly interrupted him. "Pete," I said, "this is not an instructional book." I went on to explain the premise of my book. Pete asked me to send him an outline of my chapters. I e-mailed him the outline and four chapters.

Several weeks later I received an e-mail from Pete. It was very encouraging to me because I respect Pete as a man, writer and Christian. His encouragement gave me a lift and inspired me to push on and continue my writing. God brought Pete McDaniel into my life to help me follow His plan for my life and to edit my book. To God, I say thank you for all the inspirational men and women who have helped shape my life and thank you for giving Pete the God-given ability to never forget a name!

Bob Sowards, Director of Instruction, Kinsale CC/former PGA Tour player

Working with Bob prior to his round at the 2012 PGA Championship at the Ocean Course at Kiawah Island.

Waiting as Bob is interviewed by Michael Collins of ESPN Radio. Photo Courtesy Scott (Skillet) Studenc.

I learned to play the game of golf by taking a paperback book written by Ben Hogan called *Power Golf* over to the side of the last hole on the little 9-hole course I grew up on and tried to copy everything he was doing in the book. Through trial and error, I figured out what would make the ball curve a certain way and how to get it around the golf course. I played this way for the better part of my life until I met

Jon Decker in the spring of 2007 as he was coming to New Albany Country Club to be the director of instruction. I had heard that he had a great résumé and was an up and coming top instructor that I thought maybe could help me in my quest to become a PGA Tour player. I am very bad at asking people for help and most of the time will forge ahead and try to "dig the answers out of the dirt" to answer any questions about the golf swing like my idol, Ben Hogan did.

After qualifying for the PGA Tour for the 2008 season and playing a couple of events, I realized my ball striking was not good enough to compete on a fulltime basis, so I asked Jon for help. Being a "feel" player, I knew nothing about biomechanics and didn't understand at first what he was trying to do. I "tested" him the first few times we worked by making a swing I knew was wrong but getting away with a good result. He would tell me that the result was good but the process wasn't, so from the first week we worked together, I trusted Jon completely. Jon used numerous drills to get his point across about what we were working on and understanding that I needed to be able to "feel" it. I would not have been able to change so quickly if not for the drills he designed for me. To describe what we changed in my golf game would take way too long for this purpose, but suffice it to say, we broke my swing down completely and started from scratch in the middle of the 2008 PGA Tour season.

I can honestly say that since I have met Jon, I have improved every year in some aspect of my golf game, from my ball striking to short game to knowledge of my game to overall knowledge of the golf swing and biomechanics. Before working with Jon, I was always a guy that was right around the cut line in bigger tournaments like the PGA Club Professional Championship, and now I am in contention every year with a consistency that was never present before I started working with Jon. I feel that I am much better now than I was in 2008 when I was a full time PGA Tour member. It takes time to fully integrate changes into a player's game and to fully trust the changes under pressure that are contrary to everything you've done your whole life.

Proud moment when the PGA of America came to the
New Albany Country Club to film a feature on 2014
PGA Professional Player of the Year, Bob Sowards.

During my interview process for the position of director of instruction for the New Albany Country Club, I learned the history of the interim director of instruction at the time, Bob Sowards. As one of the top club pros in the world, Bob is known for his playing abilities. Among his litany of victories are three Ohio Open titles and the 2004 Club Professional Championship. He is the only club professional in the history of the PGA of America to win all three tournaments of the PGA Winter Tour Series in one season. When I arrived at New Albany in the spring of 2007, I knew of Bob's talent and playing record but had never personally met him or seen him play. While Pete McDaniel never forgets a name, my God-given talent is to never forget a swing. I remember walking by as Bob was setting up to hit a shot. I stopped, watched his swing and said to myself, "I can help this guy!" Eventually, Bob and I got to know each other fairly well. "My goal is to make the Ryder Cup team," Bob told me in one of our early conversations. I stood there in awe of the passionate man with big dreams and a homemade swing.

In critiquing a golf swing, the trained eye of a teaching professional can find flaws that are the primary cause of inefficiencies. Bob is a world-class player, but there were fundamental issues with his setup, especially his ball position. Bob tended to play the golf ball too far back in his stance, especially with his wedges, leading to deep divots and distance-control issues. In his overall swing, Bob also tended to drive his legs and pull the club too early in his downswing. This quick transition from backswing to downswing led to erratic ball-striking under pressure. Bob learned his swing as a youth just like many before him influenced by that popular method of teaching. However, through video cameras and research on biomechanics, teaching fundamentals have dramatically improved during the past thirty years. After watching several swings, it was easy to detect his flaws. I knew I could help him, but convincing Bob would take time and patience.

In the fall of 2007, Bob prepared for tour school, the finals of which were being held in Orlando. I was diligently attempting to acclimate myself on my new job while settling into my new residence and navigating my way around a new environment. The week of tour school I had begun my winter schedule at Grand Cypress in Orlando. I went out to watch Bob play and quickly caught up to his group. As I stood behind the tee box, Bob gave me a brief smile and quickly returned his focus to golf. His playing partner was a tall, young, athletic kid from Coastal Carolina University. The young man's mighty swing sent the ball soaring as it disappeared in the distance. "That guy will win a major," I said to Bob after the round. The man I was referring to was Dustin Johnson, who went on to become a multiple winner on the PGA Tour and an eventual major champion (2016 U.S. Open winner). Bob played fantastic during tour school, earning his tour card. I felt extremely fortunate to have been there to witness Bob's great accomplishment.

On his drive back to Ohio, Bob called me and thanked me for coming out to watch him play during the week. I gave him my honest feedback on his game, and the discussions began to revolve around the changes he knew were necessary for his ball-striking to improve. In January, thirty-nine-year-old Bob Sowards began his rookie year on the PGA Tour by flying to Hawaii to play in the Sony Open. Although he made the cut in his initial tournament, Bob was not unlike most rookies in that his game was inconsistent. Traditionally, rookies get late tee times weekly during the morning and afternoon waves and have only a few days to learn the nuances of golf courses, not to mention those of new caddies. Life on tour is not as glamorous as it may appear to the average fan.

In the spring of 2008, I arrived in Ohio ready to start my summer work. Bob was getting his feet wet as a rookie on tour, and once again, we started talking about working on his swing. By May, Bob knew it was time to make some changes and asked me to look at his swing. I was both honored and happy to be his swing consultant. During our first lesson, I talked to Bob about the need to change his ball position and showed him why he slid in his swing. Bob asked a lot of questions, constantly testing me to see if I was paying attention. He often would hit a shot with his old swing to see if I would just say good shot. He would look at me and say, "What do you think?"

"It was a good shot, but you didn't do what we want," I would say. He later told me at that point he knew he could trust me. I saw real progress at the end of the first day of instruction. Bob and I shook hands and agreed to form a partnership which has lasted these many years. The next week Bob was playing in the Memorial Tournament at Muirfield, and I would see Jack's masterpiece as a first-timer inside the ropes of a PGA Tour event. My dream was coming true, not as a player but as a coach.

On Friday afternoon of the 2008 Memorial tournament, Bob calmly walked out onto the practice tee and prepared to warm up for his late tee time. Our time together as player and coach was all of three days and in many ways, I was probably more nervous than Bob. After hitting balls on the range Bob said, "Let's go putt." I eagerly followed Bob up the steps to the gang plank high above the patrons en route to the putting green. My bird's eye view of the golf course confirmed its awesome beauty. As a hero from nearby Dublin, Bob was greeted with a chorus of cheers. "Let's go, Bob!" fans shouted as we walked side by side toward the green. "This is so cool," I said to Bob. "Rock stars have nothing on tour players," I thought.

Unfortunately, Bob's game didn't match his fans' enthusiasm, and he missed the cut. Now it was off to Memphis and the St. Jude's Classic. Before Bob left for Memphis, however, we were able to work on his swing a few days, to no avail though as he again played poorly. As a coach, it was frustrating because Bob was doing very well in our practice sessions on the range. In reality, we both knew the changes would take time. Deep inside for the first time in our player-coach relationship, I feared Bob may drop me as a coach and go back to his old, instinctive swing. Minutes after Bob missed the cut in Memphis he called me. "We got a lot of work to do!" he said, resulting in a big sigh of relief and comfort for I knew Bob was in it for the long haul. He was determined to improve his golf swing!

Perhaps it's my Southern accent or the fact that not all people interpret things the same way, but after the St. Jude Classic, Bob and I had a major breakthrough in his swing development. Bob understood the importance of changing the ball position and was able to do it in time. However, lengthening the backswing was another issue. Bob interpreted my teaching as moving off the ball to turn and lengthen his backswing. By using the term "turn off the ball," I finally communicated the information in a way that he understood. Positive results were immediate. To soften his transition, I had Bob hit golf balls off of exercise disks. These disks are commonly used by trainers to help their clients stabilize their core muscles while lifting weights. I had Bob stand on the disks while hitting balls. At first Bob thought I was crazy, and he really struggled to even stand on the disks. In time, though, he gave in and got use to hitting off the disks. His swing got longer, allowing his weight to cover the ball on the downswing.

That August, Bob's swing really started to click. I knew it was only a matter of time until he started seeing the results on the golf course. Next up for Bob was the Wyndham Classic in my home state of North Carolina. I was excited because my brother, Michael, lived in Greensboro, giving me an opportunity to return home and visit family while working with Bob. It would be an unforgettable week for player and coach. Michael lived several miles from Sedgefield Country Club, which made my stay with him very convenient.

Monday morning I arrived at the golf course and met Bob on the driving range. Bob was hitting the ball so well that all we focused on was his initial turn in the backswing. As we were walking down the fairway on the first hole of the practice round, Bob said, "I played here on the Nike Tour in 1998 and didn't like the course. It's a hooker's golf course." In laymen terms, that meant many of the holes turn from right to left. Bob's assessment provided the perfect opportunity for another breakthrough—this time with his course management. Bob prefers to fade his driver but can draw and fade his three-wood.

"Bob," I said, "this golf course is perfect for you. On every hole that goes from left to right, hit your driver, and every hole that goes right to left, hit your three-wood."

"Even if the hole is 500 yards?" he said.

"Yes," I said, "can you hit the fairway with your three-wood?"

He responded, "Yes."

"Now hit your hybrid or long-iron to the green," I said. "Those clubs are your strength. I want you confident on the tee box and playing to your strengths. You are trying to fit a square peg into a round hole with the driver on dogleg lefts." It was the best advice on course management I ever gave Bob, who resisted at first. In time, though, he saw the results of a strategy that won Jack Nicklaus 18 major championships.

By Wednesday night, it was time for me to fly back to Ohio and return to work at New Albany. I gave Bob a hug, confident that he was ready from a swing standpoint and felt good about his conservative game plan for the dogleg lefts. "Bob, if you are near the top 10 this weekend, I promise I will drive down to watch you play on Sunday," I said.

Bob smiled and said, "You got it!" Bob got off to a great start with a first-round 66, followed by a 67 on Friday. Saturday morning, I laid out my clothes in preparation to drive back to Greensboro that night. Bob made nothing happen through 14 holes of the third round. He was stuck in neutral on *moving day*. I had real doubts as to whether I was going to make the eight-hour drive after work. Bob would need a strong finish! I was checking my computer for updates between lessons. On the par-five 15th hole, CBS cut to Bob and the commentator said, "Here's Bob Sowards for eagle." He made the putt to go two-under for the day. I called the pro shop and could hear everyone cheering. On the par-three 16th Bob made birdie for three-under on the day. That stamped my ticket back to Greensboro! My cell phone rang as I was pulling out of the parking lot. It was Bob. I could hear the excitement in his voice as I congratulated him on his 69. "I'm on my way now!" I said.

"You got it," Bob said. "We'll see you tomorrow."

Adrenaline-driven, I checked into a hotel in Charleston, West Virginia, where I managed a few winks before setting off to Greensboro at 4:00 a.m. I arrived in plenty of time to observe Bob's warm-up session. Michael came out to watch as well. Bob was paired with Tim Clark for the second day in a row. "Wow!" I said to Bob as he wrapped up his warm-up. "The driving range sure is empty." That was one of the many perks of teeing off in the third to last group on Sunday of a tour event. As I walked onto the putting green, I noticed it was empty except for Carl Petterson, Bob and me. I watched as Carl dropped three balls on the green and hit his very first practice putt which was more than 50 feet. Carl took a long stroke and sent his ball tracking toward the practice cup. Amazingly, it dropped into the hole. "No wonder this guy is leading," I thought to myself. Bob's stroke looked great as he hit his warm-up putts. Finally, the time had come for Bob to make the long walk to the first tee. I said, "Bob, you're chopping down a tree today, one swing at a time." We gave each other a hug and a smile. Looking at Bob, I noticed that his face was white as a sheet! "Go have some fun, guys," I said as I shook the hand of Bob's caddie, Ryan (Bean) Bruncak. Bob calmly split the fairway with his opening drive, hit a wedge to within eight feet of the hole, and made the putt for an opening birdie. I was amazed at his poise under pressure that day as he lived his dream, contending on Sunday for a PGA tournament title.

The first week I began working with Bob, I mentioned that he shouldn't break his tee with his driver. I was really stressing rotation instead of knee drive to make his swing more level. After splitting another fairway on the fourth hole, Bob picked up his tee and gave me a big smile. He was loose and having tons of fun. I started laughing, to which my father inquired, "What's so funny?" It was Bob's simple way of saying, under the most intense pressure of his life in front of hundreds of people around the tee box, "Thank you, Jon. I got it." I will never forget that smile or that moment as Bob fully understood what we had been working on day in and day out for months.

Bob bogeyed the 72nd hole to shoot a final-round 68 and finish in ninth place, while Petterson continued his hot putting to capture the Wyndham Championship. It remains Bob's best finish on tour and a day I will never forget as a teaching professional. The 2008 season not only allowed me to fulfill a dream of being inside the ropes but also confirmed that I could help players at all levels. The challenges of teaching a beginner and those of teaching a tour player are different, but they require a similar amount of determination and understanding. Although Bob is no longer on tour, he continues to be my proud student of accomplishment. Currently, he has qualified for the PGA Championship nine times. On four of those occasions, I assisted him as coach. In fact, during a player profile interview with TaylorMade for the 2014 PGA Championship at Valhalla (Kentucky), my stock rose even higher thanks to Bob. "If you could change one thing about your career, what would it be?" Bob was asked. "I wish I had met Jon Decker sooner in my career," he said. I am eternally grateful for Bob's kind words, opportunity to serve as his coach and enduring friendship. Making a swing change is difficult. Just ask Tiger Woods. To do it in mid-season on the PGA Tour is almost impossible. Never stop trying to achieve your goals, Bob. I can attest to the fact that your golf swing has evolved from homemade to one destined to hold up under pressure. Your best playing days are ahead of you on the Champions Tour. Keep those big dreams alive!

Proud moment receiving the 2015 Southern Ohio
Teacher of the Year Award with my student-the
2015 SOPGA Player of the Year, Bob Sowards

As Seen Through My Eyes

Cory Luke, Head Golf Professional,
New Albany Country Club

February 8, 2011, is a day that will always weigh heavy on my heart. On this late winter afternoon, I was told of our loss of Corporal Nathan B. Carse. I can remember my conversation with Chris Miller over the phone was one of disbelief and shock. The only thing from the conversation that I can really remember was asking, "Are you sure it was Nathan?" In the days following his death, several articles about his service were released on the Internet, and that is when it hit me: Nathan was gone.

I grew up a couple miles away from Nathan in a small town near Lima, Ohio. Nathan and I became great friends at an early age as we played little league baseball together, rode to school on the same bus, and shared many of the same passions for the outdoors such as hunting and fishing. I can remember numerous evenings staying at his house where we would talk about anything you could imagine. It was always great having these conversations with Nathan because we both knew anything we would talk about was between us. I will always remember Nathan for doing what he believed in and not what was popular or what everyone else was doing. Doing the right thing, or what he believed in, included taking care of his family, especially his two younger sisters. I have never met anyone as caring and protective of his family as Nathan. Many times I would find Nathan splitting wood, building a deck or fixing something around his parents' house. He would do anything for anyone at any time without hesitation.

Although the days leading up to his funeral were hard for everyone, I am sure Nathan was proud of what he saw looking down. I and several of his friends and classmates all stood alongside of Phillips Road as a small private plane flew above heading to the Allen County Airport. We had all seen planes arrive at Allen County Airport many times, but this time, it was special as this plane was carrying our friend and hero Cpl. Nathan B. Carse. We all waited patiently alongside the road waving our American flags as he was driven past on his way to the church. Many memories of Nathan were shared over the next couple days and evenings as the memorial services took place. We all had our favorite stories, and many of them made us laugh.

There are many things that I will never forget about Nathan and the times we had growing up. His willingness to give his own life for others is something that I will always admire and never forget. I will always think of Nathan as a special friend. His unselfishness and willingness to help others led him to the military, where he was able to serve this great country.

For your friendship, bravery, and service, I say. Thank you.

Love ya, buddy.

SERVICE

Corporal Nathan B. Carse

"When He had finished washing their feet, He put on his clothes and returned to his place. "Do you understand what I have done for you?" He asked them. "You call me 'Teacher' and 'Lord,' and rightly so, for that is what I am. Now that I, your Lord and Teacher, have washed your feet, you also should wash one another's feet. I have set you an example that you should do as I have done for you. Very truly I tell you, no servant is greater than his master, nor is a messenger greater than the one who sent him. Now that you know these things, you will be blessed if you do them." (John 13:12–17)

On February 8, 2011, Corporal Nathan B. Carse died in Kandahar, Afghanistan, during Operation Enduring Freedom. He served with the 2nd Engineer Battalion where he cleared improvised explosive devices (IEDs) to pave the way for safe passage of others. An IED exploded which resulted in his death. Corporal Carse was thirty-two years old. He was survived by his mother Janis and two sisters, Megan and Kristin. I never knew Corporal Carse or for that matter, any of his family members. However, I did know his close friend, Cory Luke. Cory is the head golf professional and my coworker at the New Albany Country Club. Cory and I are also good friends. I didn't attend Nathan's funeral, had never been to his home town of Harrod, Ohio, and knew nothing about his passions for life. Every day someone from a sleepy, small town or a bustling, crowded city in this country is serving and protecting me, and I don't even know their first name. Through God's ultimate plan, his unyielding desire to guide me and teach me lessons through this moment in time called life; God brought a man into my life, who I will never personally know. Through the examples set by this man, I live under an umbrella of freedom, a freedom I sometimes selfishly take for granted. This story is about a man's sacrifice to his country and how it helped me reevaluate my priorities. Ultimately, this story is a brief caption of one man's life and his commitment to service.

Nathan and Cory were childhood friends, who rode the school bus and played sports together, all the while enjoying the simple pleasures of life growing up. Cory described Nathan as "someone who would not give in to peer pressure." Nathan believed in taking a stand and doing what was right and dreamed of serving in the military. On February 17, 2010, Nathan enlisted in the United States Army. He was called to serve not by Uncle Sam but by his own heart. Nathan simply wanted to serve his country.

After basic training, on August 13th to be exact, Nathan was deployed to Afghanistan, where he served for six months until his death. The town of Harrod, Ohio, had lost one of their very own, a brave young man who gave his life while serving his country. During the funeral procession, the fire department's trucks lined both sides of Highway 309, extending their crossed ladders toward the heavens as the funeral procession coursed underneath them. It was a beautiful tribute to a man who bravely served our country. Corp. Nathan B. Carse's service to our country officially concluded as he was called home by God to begin his everlasting life. John 15:13 states it best, *"There is no greater love than to lay down one's life for one's friends."*

After Nathan's death, his close friends sought to form a scholarship in his honor to preserve his name and legacy. The scholarship would assist young men and women in pursuit of higher education. Nathan's close friends, Ria Cole, Chris Miller and Cory Luke established the Nathan B. Carse Memorial Scholarship Fund earmarked for high school students involved in community service, athletics or choir, who maintained a good academic record—all passions of Nathan's. The primary fundraiser for the memorial fund is an annual golf outing at the Colonial Hills Golf Course in Harrod.

In September of 2012, I had the privilege of participating in the Second Annual Corporal Nathan B. Carse Memorial Golf Outing. Every year, I get asked to play in charity golf events. Having a job where you work on the weekends makes it very difficult to take time off of work and in essence lose income, so often I will graciously decline these offers to play. I will admit the first time I went to the golf outing, I primarily went in support of my good friend Cory Luke. I considered it a sacrificial way to help a friend by supporting his charity event.

When I arrived at the golf course, I received a warm welcome and I saw a familiar face—Tom Holtsberry, the course's owner. I knew Tom from my days at Grand Cypress. Tom and I became friends during his trips to work on his game at Grand Cypress in the winter months. Suddenly, God's plan was beginning to unfold before my very eyes, and I knew there was more to this particular charity event than playing in a scramble golf tournament. God was leading me and instructing me in true sacrifice—the kind made by Nathan. It was an important life lesson on service.

The sun shone brightly as we began play on that beautiful autumn day. Suddenly, we stood on the third hole in total reverence as the calm was briefly interrupted by the roar from the engines of two F-16s flying in formation overhead. It was not a planned air show by tournament organizers but a spectacle straight from God's gracious planner. Our group immediately felt the presence of Nathan as we all enjoyed the awesome power of the F-16s. No one in our group hit a shot as we stood mesmerized by the planes. Our team finished in second place that year. The biggest winners, though, were the students as all the winnings were donated back to the scholarship fund. I departed Harrod that day determined to return and participate next year.

Prior to the 2013 tournament, I offered to put on a putting clinic for participants. It was my small way of contributing to a most worthy event. I believe the clinic was a nice addition to another successful event. After playing in the event for two years, I started bonding with Nathan's friends, met his family, and fell in love with the hometown feel of Harrod and Lima, Ohio. I wanted to help even more, so the next year, I added a video golf tip to the memorial fund website. Through the experience, I've learned more about Nathan the man and even more about myself. In particular, I've learned that giving up a weekend to support a worthy cause is not really a sacrifice when the worthy cause involves a man who gave his life for our country.

When Nathan enlisted in the army, he knew there was a possibility that he may pay the ultimate sacrifice for his service, which is part of the risk of those who truly serve. This ultimate sacrifice is part of our nation's history and also part of how Christianity was formed. Jesus Christ gave his life to serve others. He knew of His own impending death when He washed the feet of every disciple. Jesus used that moment to teach the disciples how to serve others, a valuable lesson they all needed. Jesus knew that eventually the Christian message would be spread by the disciples and that many of them would die for the Christian cause. He also knew their treasures would be stored in heaven. The ultimate sacrifice of Jesus Christ, who died for our sins, is what service is truly all about. I am proud to be a Christian and fall short every day. I am proud to have Jesus Christ as my Lord and Savior. I am also proud of the men and women who serve this great country, including firemen, policemen and all who serve others. I am proud to say that every year I will participate in the Corporal Nathan B. Carse Memorial Golf Outing, not because it is a sacrifice on my part but to say thank you, Nathan, for service well done!

Courtesy Paul Rockwell, owner Average Joes

"As Jesus was walking beside the Sea of Galilee, he saw two brothers, Simon called Peter and his brother Andrew. They were casting a net into the lake, for they were fishermen. 'Come, follow me,' Jesus said, 'and I will send you out to fish for people.' At once they left their nets and followed him" (Mathew 4:18–20).

I never imagined that in my early forties, I would be all alone. I never imagined that after being married for more than twelve years, I would be divorced. As I sat in front of the mirror in my condo on a Friday night, a sense of urgency to get on with life overcame me. "I have to get out and meet people," I thought. "I can't sit around here every night and feel sorry for myself." To make things even more difficult, I was in a new city where I only knew my coworkers. All of my friends were in Florida or North Carolina. I was alone. I was not going to church, and I was scared. I made up my mind that evening to venture outside of my comfort zone and start meeting new people. This leap of faith allowed new people to come into my life, people who would lead me to church and support me in the writing of this book. The same people I would one day call friends. It all started when I stepped into the land of Average Joes.

Average Joes is a chain of sports pubs in the Columbus, Ohio, area. I anxiously walked into the unfamiliar surroundings that Friday night and immediately saw some coworkers from the New Albany Country Club. I ordered a drink and some food then began to feel comfortable in my new surroundings. After a fun evening, I returned home and promised myself that I would frequent Average Joes. I would be a familiar face to the bar staff and other steady customers, certain that I would eventually be able to network and develop friendships.

One evening while ordering my dinner at Average Joes, I noticed a promotional flyer for an autism golf tournament. My brother, Brett, was born with autism, so I've always had a desire to help when it comes to autism. I set up a meeting with the owner of Average Joes, Paul Rockwell, and offered to host a clinic for his bar staff and waitresses before the tournament. What better way to reach the masses than through bartenders—the eyes and ears of the community. Golfers love going to Average Joes after a round. Familiarizing the bar staff with my teaching style would surely pay dividends with referral business. The autism clinic was a success and gave me a chance to meet some real quality people in the community. I became a regular at Average Joes, which allowed me to promote my golf clinic with a poster and golf tip. More importantly, it felt good to walk into a place where so many people knew me by name. The bar staff, waitresses and owner made me feel at home, something I so desperately needed at the time. God often uses people, places and circumstances to guide us through life. Christianity was never meant to be experienced alone. It was through Average Joes that my first step in meeting new people outside of work occurred. Then came the critical next step—my introduction to Greg Stone.

Left Donny (Doc) Raines. Right Greg Stone

Greg is a high school teacher at Watkins Memorial High School, instructing special needs students in algebra, geometry and resource math. He also coaches the golf team. Ironically, Greg and I had quite a few things in common. For instance, we were both divorced and love working with kids. In addition, both of us are Dallas Cowboys fans, who grew up in the Methodist Church. Although I wasn't worshipping at the time, I felt God calling me back to regular church worship. It was through Greg Stone that I found the Stonybrook United Methodist Church. Attending Stonybrook would be my second leap of faith.

In the late spring of 2012, I met Greg at church and was immediately impressed with the energy of the contemporary worship service. This church is where I would meet Pastor Mike, the man who would write the foreword for this book. Stonybrook is where I would also meet Pastor Nikki and youth pastor Ben Lilly, be inspired by the music from the band led by Garrett Keener, and eventually meet Pastor Bob. God certainly does work in mysterious ways that can only be received when we believe in Him and take a leap of faith. God's plan for me and my membership at the Stonybrook United Methodist Church two years later began one lonely Friday night.

Thank you to the bartenders, waitresses, and owner Paul Rockwell of Average Joes for always making me feel at home. Thank you to all the locals of Average Joes for taking me in as one of your own. And thank you to the Stonybrook United Methodist Church for changing my spiritual life. Jesus taught the disciples to fish for people because in life we need each other to survive. We are all broken, all lonely at times and face a world of sin and chaos. Greg "fished for people" when he invited me to attend church worship with him, a life-changing moment in my spiritual growth. I pray that through this book, I will also fish for people and help others to find Jesus Christ, a lost soul find their own Stonybrook, and help a hungry and thirsty golfer find their own Average Joes!

CHAPTER 19

Lost and Found

We all fell to the ground, and I heard a voice saying to me in Aramaic, "Saul, Saul, why do you persecute me? It is hard for you to kick against the goads." Then I asked, "Who are you, Lord?" "I am Jesus, whom you are persecuting," the Lord replied. "Now get up and stand on your feet. I have appeared to you to appoint you as a servant and as a witness of what you have seen from me and what I will show. I will rescue you from your own people and from the Gentiles. I am sending you to them to open their eyes and turn them from darkness to light, and from the power of Satan to God, so that they may receive forgiveness of sins and a place among those who are sanctified by faith in me." (Acts 26:14–18)

On a hot summer night in late June of 2012, I pulled my Toyota 4Runner into the single-car garage of my condominium. The sun was falling over the horizon as I peeked through my rearview mirror and watched the garage door slowly close. I wanted to make sure the coast was clear so there would be no witnesses. As the door clanked against the cement floor with a resounding thud, I heard the sound I had been longing for all day—the sound of silence. This was not my first time craving this time alone. I had repeated this same ritual for thirty long days. As the garage door light turned off, I knew it was time—time to let go. I sat in my car and cried my eyes out in total silence and darkness, just like the previous nights. I was at the bottom of a very deep barrel. Sixteen months earlier, I had finalized my divorce, the end of a twelve-year marriage. Nine months after my divorce, I would fall in love all over again to a woman with whom I thought I would be spending the rest of my life. However, the baggage I was carrying, a house that I was upside down with and a condo that was well below value made it impossible for me to relocate to my new love. I was financially handcuffed, not to mention I was unable to find work there. Our relationship ended just as fast as it had begun. Without warning, she called off our brief love affair. The flame of our love was extinguished and stress became my new partner in life. Once the picture of health, I began physically showing the emotional drain in a dramatic weight loss—dropping twenty pounds in six months. As I mustered the strength each day to forge ahead in my career, I got a call from my doctor. "Jon, your PSA is at 4.1," he said in a concerned tone. "Get to a urologist immediately." I had developed a prostrate infection, the likely culprit, stress. I was on the verge of giving up. I asked God to remove me from my pain. Each night I thought of heaven and asked God to take me as I cried myself to sleep. I wasn't worshipping in church or reading the Bible, and the thought of writing a book wasn't even in the recesses of my mind. I started losing faith in God but somehow managed to pray. It was all I knew to do as I looked at my life and asked, "Why?" I was lost.

On the road to Damascus, a defiant Saul of Tarsus was lost. He was consumed with destroying those that supported the Christian movement. He and his men journeyed to Damascus in search of those who worshiped the Messiah. But in an instant, Saul's life and the fate of the Christian movement changed. Saul was blinded by the brilliant light, Jesus Christ. Years later, Saul would become the apostle Paul, a changed man in more ways than by name. Saul was now found in Jesus Christ. He would be used by Almighty God as a vessel to lay the foundation for the church as we know it today, teaching Christianity to thousands of people, healing the sick and spreading the Word of God. Saul's life represents what all human beings experience—a lost life journey. To be a Christian, one must transform from being lost to being found. It is a moment when one openly acknowledges Jesus Christ as their personal Lord and Savior. For me, this happened as a thirteen-year-old when I walked to the front of the Ridgecrest Conference Center in Black Mountain after the pastor asked, "Who wants to receive Jesus Christ as their Lord and Savior?" That night I openly professed my faith in Jesus Christ. The ultimate destination for Christians is heaven, a reward promised in the scriptures to those who accept Christ. It is our desire to some-day live an everlasting life in God's kingdom. However, before this can transpire, the struggles of the world must ultimately test the most faithful of followers. Before we can taste the sweetness of heaven, the lost must often endure the struggles of the human race and endure the stench of a fallen world, that which is brought on by sin. To be found is the prize, but to be lost is the journey.

Lessons in life can be taught through the examples of a third-grade teacher, by witnessing the tragic death of a loved one, or by asking a thought-provoking question to a child, only to get a response that is so pure and innocent that it turns over the life-learning table, allowing the teacher to learn through the eyes of a child. I have learned through all these examples, but one lesson, more than any, changed my life as a novice writer. It was not by a person or event but through a television series that confirmed art as an effective imitator of life.

On September 22, 2004, I began watching the highly publicized television series *Lost*. After several episodes, it became clear that this series was not only going to be successful from a ratings standpoint but the mysteries, storylines and complexity of each episode captivated the audience like no series before it. In effect, *Lost* became an American phenomenon. I remember thinking to myself, "This series could go in a hundred different directions. They must be making this up as they are going along." I could not have been more wrong in my assessment. The writing was brilliant. In fact, all six seasons and all 121 episodes were written before the first scene was ever shot—a fact that still amazes me. The storyline had a clear beginning and the mystery-laden stories were interwoven to guide the viewer to a well-planned dramatic conclusion, even if they didn't know the precise direction. As a matter of fact, the actors were only made aware of the story's direction when the scripts were handed out before the filming of each episode. The series was a mystery to everyone but the writers. And much like life itself, the audience was left waiting to watch the iconic series unfold one episode at a time. The creators of *Lost*, Jeffrey Lieber, J. J. Abrams and Damon Lindelof had a chaotic, science fiction, supernatural, mystery-filled story to share with the world. And share it they did!

The premise of *Lost* was the story of the plane crash of the fictional Oceanic Airlines Flight 815. The flight was from Sydney, Australia to Los Angeles. Somewhere over the Pacific Ocean, the plane crashes on a mysterious, deserted island, one unknown to rescuers. Some survive the crash while others perish. The writers brilliantly used flashbacks and symbolism to develop the storylines of many of the survivors. In addition, during the six seasons, many of the storylines became consistent with biblical themes. The writers explored the age-old questions of faith versus science, good versus evil and light versus dark. The writers also showed the parallels of the characters on the island, their lives before Flight 815 and many of their lives after they are rescued from the island. In the end, the series, with all its complex storylines and action-packed adventure, came down to one simple premise: Lost souls working together to survive on the island while supernatural, unexplained events attempted to stop them.

The opening scene for *Lost* titled, "*Bamboo Forest*," occurred with a close-up camera shot of a closed human eye that suddenly opens. The eye belonged to the character Jack Shephard, a surgeon and survivor of the plane crash. In the opening scene, Jack is lying on his back injured, facing upward in the middle of a bamboo forest. As his right eye opens, you can see the reflection of the bamboo forest high above. As he is lying on his back in a confused state of mind, a yellow Labrador retriever named Vincent comes slowly walking through the bamboo forest approaching Jack. All of a sudden, Vincent races past Jack's head into the forest. It is as if he is trying to lead Jack to the other survivors. Jack staggers to his feet, starts slowly walking forward, and gradually starts sprinting through the forest toward the beach. As Jack runs, he passes a brand new tennis shoe hanging from one of the bamboo trees, presumably debris from the crash. On the beach, the airplane is in huge pieces with the main engine still running. People are yelling frantically for lost loved ones while some survivors are tending to wounded passengers. The island would now be the survivor's new home. The opening scene would catapult more than sixteen million viewers into mystery and suspense weekly. The writers chose this one scene as the series' alpha or its beginning.

Like the Bible, *Lost* is symbolic using light and dark to represent good versus evil. John Locke is one of the main characters. He boarded the flight in a wheelchair but was miraculously able to walk after the crash. Because of this life-altering event, Locke doesn't want to ever leave the island. He teaches the game of backgammon to a teenaged survivor named Walt. Locke explains to Walt, "Backgammon is one the world's oldest games. It is five thousand years old. That's older than Jesus Christ. Two players, two sides, one is light and one is dark." This scene early in the series set the tone for effective use of symbolism throughout the series. The backgammon board, a consistent symbol throughout the six seasons, is believed by many fans to represent the island. Locke begins to relish his role while living on the island and is driven by his faith in the mysterious place. Locke and Jack, the latter being a surgeon relying on scientific disciplines, become bitter rivals. Jack believes the plane crashing on the island was a random act or coincidence. The rivalry stems from the age-old Biblical debate of faith versus science.

During the series, the storylines became very confusing—so much so that a lot of viewers became lost. To help quench viewers' thirst for answers, the producers replayed each episode at the end of each season. Included were subtitles shedding light on a character's past, plus explaining the symbolism, flashbacks or the significance of the scene. The writers and producers began to give valuable clues to provide much-needed insight. At that very moment, I fell in love with the series, realizing the writers' ingenuity and expertise. The writing was well-thought-out and strategically planned. In some ways, *Lost* helped develop my writing style. I loved the way the writers used a flashback moment from the characters past to set up a scene, then jump ahead to engage interest and somewhat entice the viewer, then drop back or move forward to close out the scene with a well-thought-out message. I knew while watching that I wanted to incorporate some of the same literary techniques in my book. I just didn't know how. It wasn't until I read the Bible and watched the series that I began to correlate the two. As I began writing this book and reading scripture on a daily basis, I realized how the greatest author of mankind, Almighty God, and the greatest storyteller of the human race, Jesus Christ, used symbolism, foreshadowing, parables and prophetic messages to write the most-read book in the history of mankind, the Bible.

In human history, there has been no one better at telling a story and delivering His message than Jesus Christ. Jesus used parables to tell profound prophetic messages to relate to the common man. The New Testament is full of these wonderful stories. One of my favorites is from chapter 2 of the Gospel of John when Jesus cleanses the temple. Jesus came into the temple in Jerusalem and found people selling animals. He turned over the tables and ordered everyone to exit, shooing the animals out, as well. "Take these things out of here! Stop making my father's house a marketplace!" He exclaimed. The Jews then asked for a sign, to which Jesus responded, "Destroy this temple and in three days I will raise it up." Jesus masterfully used foreshadowing to announce his crucifixion and resurrection. The first time I heard this story, like the Jews, I thought Jesus meant the temple building itself. The true meaning of Jesus' statement was that his body was metaphorically the temple, and after his crucifixion, He would rise from the dead, walk among His disciples, and expose His disciples to the power of the Holy Spirit. This resurrection would be the birth of Christianity as we know it today. God's masterful plan was laid out and carried out by Jesus. Years later, John documented its powerful use of foreshadowing.

The Gospel of John refers to the Holy Spirit as light and evil as darkness, like the angel in my high school dream referring to Jesus as light and like the symbolism of backgammon in *Lost*. The Gospel John states it beautifully in John 1:1–10.

> *"In the beginning was the Word, and the Word was with God, and the Word was God. He was with God in the beginning. Through him all things were made; without him nothing was made that has been made. In him was life, and that life was the light of all mankind. The light shines in the darkness, and the darkness has not*

overcome it. There was a man sent from God whose name was John. He came as a witness to testify concerning that light, so that through him all might believe. He himself was not the light; he came only as a witness to the light. The true light that gives light to everyone was coming into the world. He was in the world, and though the world was made through him, the world did not recognize him."

God's Word has not only comforted me during my lost moments in life, but His Word has also validated what was said to me by God Himself and what is written in the Bible. God's mighty voice still resounds in my being, *"I am the Alpha and the Omega, the First and the Last, the Beginning and the End" (Revelation 22:13).*

In *Lost,* the alpha for the series was a place (the bamboo forest). On May 23, 2010, millions of viewers watched the TV series finale. In this famous scene, Jack is staggering through the forest after being fatally stabbed in the abdomen. As he staggers through the forest in a blood-stained shirt, he passes the same bamboo tree from the opening scene with the tennis shoe—now molded and dirty—dangling from it. Jack instinctively goes to the exact place where the show began and slowly lowers to the ground. As he lies on his back, he hears a bark, and Vincent comes running through the bamboo forest and settles next to him. Jack looks toward the sky and through a patch of the deep forest, sees the airplane taking off with the other survivors. He smiles as if peacefully acceptant of his impending death. As he takes his last breaths, a close-up shot shows his right eye closing a final time. The writers chose Jack's final resting spot, the bamboo forest, as not only the alpha for the initial opening scene of *Lost* but also the omega for the entire series.

I know that my time on this Earth will one day cease—a fact with which I am at peace. I also know that my time, as Jesus said in my dream, has not yet come. I don't know how, where or when I will die. However, I do know how I want to be remembered. Having felt the presence of Jesus Christ in my dream and in my life as a Christian, I know that my soul will rise and leave my body when God says it is my time. That's something I have briefly experienced. I want my body to be cremated and my ashes spread throughout the grounds of Augusta National. I don't expect a service at this prestigious club that can be held in a church. I don't want my family, friends or any of my students to go to a gravesite or see a tombstone that displays my name, just to remember my life. I don't want to be remembered where my flesh lay. I want to be remembered for what my soul represented in my life. I will not walk the earth in human form after three days, as Jesus Christ did. My seat will be in heaven. I want my family, friends and students to remember my alpha and omega as a place and time. I want the place to be Augusta, Georgia, and I want my time to be every April during the Masters.

My soul will be free, and my loved ones will know that I am in a much better place. I desire to have my students think of me while they view the Masters, knowing that I am watching from above. I want my students to think of me as they enjoy the thrill of sinking a long birdie putt or struggle to get out of a bunker. I believe that golf and life are enjoyed more when they are shared with a friend or family member. God chose Augusta as my alpha for a reason. He knew the game of golf would be an integral part of my life and that one day I would share my stories in the form of a book. He chose arguably the most famous golf venue in the world for my birth. I am choosing Augusta as my final resting place. It is my omega where my ashes will be spread as my everlasting life begins.

God's masterful plan for my life is still unfolding, my journey a work in progress. Like Saul, I often walk down the road of life hellbent on making my own plan come to fruition. Prior to meeting Jesus, Saul was determined to stop the growth of this new religion called Christianity. I'm sure he believed he was doing the work of God. However, one encounter changed Saul's perspective and the course of human history. All Christians have their *Saul moment* when they profess Jesus Christ as their Lord and Savior. I was blessed to have two moments. The first one happened when I professed my faith in Christ during church, while the second one came in a dream when I experienced the Holy Trinity.

I've certainly grown as God has lifted me from the depths of my divorce and heartbreak. Although I am still sometimes lost, I now openly thank God for these difficult growth moments—a process that is often emotionally painful. I have learned through these times one simple lesson: God will never leave me! God uses these lost moments to draw me in, allowing personal reflection to His plan for my life. I now have a better understanding of one of God's greatest gifts—that of grace. *"My grace is sufficient for you, for my power is made perfect in weakness" (2 Corinthians 12:9).*

I no longer dream of winning a PGA tournament or breaking Jack Nicklaus' record of 18 majors. I am now comforted by the scriptures and their promise that my *found* will be heaven. This promise, though comforting, is deferred because of one simple sentence that Jesus Christ spoke to me during my dream, "It is not your time. You have much work to do." I know there is more work to be done in the numbered days God has given me. A portion of my work is now complete in the form of this book. Ultimately, I am now found by the way I have changed my priorities in the life with which I am blessed. My purpose in life is more defined. God is now first in my life above all else, including my family, career, friendships and personal desires. I freely speak to God, through His son Jesus Christ, like a childhood companion and ask for guidance through the Holy Spirit in all life's decisions. I ask the Holy Spirit to lead and protect me. I ask for patience, the lack thereof a shortcoming I deal with daily. I am also found in God's Word, which I read daily along with my devotionals. Prayer is now my security blanket to comfort and keep me close to my Heavenly Father. I pray while driving, often during lessons, while playing a round of golf, or during a quiet moment at work. Prayer has no limits, anytime or anywhere. Like a small child craving the presence of a parent, I reach out and seek. I yearn for intimacy with Him.

This new priority system now drives me to find my true purpose in life, not fame and fortune on the PGA Tour but spreading God's message through the game I love. I dream now of starting a golf ministry, providing a safe haven where underprivileged children from all over the world can learn the game, find Jesus Christ, and discover the joy in serving others. I aim to promote the game of golf as well as spread Christianity to capture more lost souls. I want to help feed the homeless through the game of golf, asking teaching professionals to teach a clinic for food and then delivering that food to shelters and those in need. The journey to write this book, learning the game of golf, my divorce, lost loves, friendships and new perspectives are all part of my journey. I will never truly be found until I experience all that I am meant to one day lose. Ultimately, Christ asks us to lay down our possessions and follow His lead. I will be found through the blood and sacrifice of my personal Lord and Savior, Jesus Christ, to an everlasting home that needs no light, where my treasures are stored and my sorrows have been left behind. Under my original plan for this book, my story has now been told. However, in early 2013, the Holy Spirit stepped into my mind and heart and said otherwise. In April of that year, the Lord gave me one more story to share with the world—a story of God's amazing grace!

"Amazing Grace, how sweet the sound, that saved a wretch like me. I once was lost but now am found, was blind, but now, I see" (John Newton). Those beautiful words caressed the hearts of all those in attendance at Ora Evelyn Hughes Dougherty's funeral, including a heartbroken great-grandson. Ora Dougherty, or Dee Dee as loved ones and friends knew her, was my great-grandmother. She was eighty-nine years old in 1981 when God called her home. Her only child, my grandmother Ora Lee, said to me at the funeral that solemn day, "'Amazing Grace' was always Dee Dee's favorite song." My great-grandmother's life had been far from easy, raising her only child as a widow during the Depression. Dee Dee's husband, Walter Lee Dougherty, had died at the age of thirty-seven after elective surgery to have excess cartilage removed from his nose. The nurse mistakenly laid him on his

Walter Lee Dougherty

Ora Evelyn Hughes Dougherty
Ora Lee Dougherty

back after the surgery instead of his side, and he drowned from his own blood on March 26, 1917. At the time of his death, Dee Dee was pregnant with my grandmother. Eighteen days after Walter's death, my grandmother was born in Black Mountain, North Carolina. Dee Dee would raise her child alone and never remarry. As a teenager, I couldn't comprehend why "Amazing Grace" would have been Dee Dee's favorite song. As an adult,

Ora Lee as a teenager

I now fully understand. In less than three weeks, Dee Dee lost her husband, a man in the prime of his life, and gained a baby girl. Ora Lee would later marry Leroy Sossamon and give birth to four beautiful children, help raise six grandchildren and proudly witness the gift of life through five great-grandchildren. She was ninety-six when she departed this world. Her story was often shared by our family during difficult times and became a spiritual compass for my family. As a child, her story of struggle opened my spiritual senses and became embedded in my mind like a mustard seed.

Leroy Sossamon   Ora Lee Sossamon

On April 13, 2013, my grandmother, Ora Lee Sossamon, died on her ninety-sixth birthday. My family asked me to speak at the funeral. As I reflected on her life, suddenly the seed implanted in my mind as a teenager began to sprout and grow before my eyes. I thought of a woman who never once got to talk to her father. I'm sure during those ninety-six years she often wondered, "What does my father really look like? What does his voice sound like? Is he really six feet four inches tall?" Imagine the conversation in heaven when they finally met for the first time. I was excited to know that my grandmother, who was known as Momlee, would meet God, Jesus and be reunited with her mother Dee Dee. However, I could not help but wonder about her reaction as she met her Heavenly Father and her biological father for the very first time. I also thought about God's plan for my grandmother, in particular, God's timing. God chose April 13, 1917, to be Momlee's birthday, or her alpha, and April 13, 2013 to be her omega. The irony spoke to my heart. When I stood in front of that packed church in Bryson City, I knew the seed that God had planted in my mind had fully grown. The story about my grandmother's alpha and omega would be the final story of this writing journey. God's timing is not a coincidence. I knew that this timing was part of His wonderful, amazing and masterful plan!

"Amazing Grace, how sweet the sound, that saved a wretch like me. I once was lost but now am found, was blind, but now, I see."

One week before Momlee's death, I brought her flowers on my drive from Orlando to Ohio for an early birthday present. It is a day I will never forget because it was our last moment together on Earth

ABOUT THE AUTHOR

Jon is currently the Director of Instruction at The Medallion Club in
Westerville, Ohio and Senior Editor and Top 25 Instructor for Golf
Tips Magazine. He previously served as Director of Instruction for
the New Albany Country Club and began his teaching career at the
Grand Cypress Academy of Golf, where he worked for twenty years
under Top 100 Teachers Fred Griffin and Phil Rodgers. In 2015, Jon
was named the Southern Ohio Teacher of the Year. From 2003 to
2011, he was recognized as one of the Best Teachers in the State of
Florida by *Golf Digest*. Jon has taught players of all levels, including
players on the PGA Tour, LPGA Tour, Champions Tour and various
other mini tours. He has also coached at the PGA Championship
(2011–2014) and the Women's U.S. Open in 2007. He has written
articles for *Golf Digest* and been featured in *Golf* Magazine and on
Golf Channel. Jon's decision to write this book was based on a super-

natural dream he experienced as a teenager and his understanding later as an adult of the power and force of the Holy Spirit in his life. Jon's faith, his life stories, and his many wonderful teaching experiences around some of the best players in the world were the book's inspiration. The purpose of this book is more than just growing the game of golf. Ultimately, it was written to glorify God and His son Jesus Christ! Enjoy Jon's journey in his life, faith, his unforeseen writing journey, and his experiences as both a professional golfer and a teaching professional.

Pete McDaniel is a freelance writer and best-selling author. A native of Arden, North Carolina, and current resident of Conyers, Georgia, McDaniel co-authored the late Earl Woods' best-selling book "Training A Tiger" and Tiger Woods' best-seller "How I Play Golf." He is also the author of the critically acclaimed "Uneven Lies: The Heroic Story of African Americans in Golf'" and the unpublished book of poetry "22: Musings and Misdemeanors." McDaniel earned a Bachelor of Arts Degree in 1974 from the University of North Carolina at Asheville and recently concluded a 16-month stint as interim director of alumni relations at his alma mater. As senior writer for Golf Digest and Golf World magazines from 1993-2009, McDaniel's primary responsibility was to collaborate on golf instruction and feature articles with Tiger Woods. He was under contract with Golf Digest as an instruction editor/writer from 2010-2013.

McDaniel was the Sports Editor of the Hendersonville Times-News for 13 years, where he earned several North Carolina Press Association writing awards. In 2014, lead-writer Pete McDaniel teamed with famed sculptor Mario Chiodo to produce "Honoring the Legacy: A Tribute to African-Americans in Golf," a permanent exhibit at the World Golf Hall of Fame & Museum.

A recipient of the Harlem YMCA's Black Achievers in Industry Award, McDaniel also co- wrote and co-produced the documentary "Uneven Fairways," which aired on the Golf Channel.

A "Publisher of the Year" award-winner, and inducted member of the African American Golfers Hall of Fame and of the National Black Golf Hall of Fame. In October of 2009, he was honored by the Boys & Girls Club of Mount Vernon, New York, with the Denzel Washington Youth Service Award at the Westchester Hills Country Club in White Plains, New York. His blogs are available at petemcdaniel.com and in African-American Golfers' Digest Magazine.

Printed in the USA
CPSIA information can be obtained
at www.ICGtesting.com
LVHW041649121023
760926LV00001B/4